How to Write
While You Sleep

How to Write While You Sleep

And Other Surprising Ways
To Increase Your Writing Power

Elizabeth Irvin Ross

Celestial Arts
Berkeley, California

Celestial Arts
P.O. Box 7123
Berkeley, California 94707

Text design by Victor Ichioka
Cover design by Fifth Street Design
First published by Writer's Digest Books in 1985
Library of Congress Cataloging-in-Publication Data
Ross, Elizabeth Irvin
    How to write while you sleep / Elizabeth Irvin Ross.
    Includes bibliographical references
    ISBN 0-89087-688-6 $12.95
    1. Authorship. I. Title.
PN145.R57 1993 808'.02—dc20   92-31266
                                       CIP

Printed in the United States of America

1   2   3   4   5 - 97 96 95 94 93

The following two pages constitute an extension of this copyright page.

Permissions

For
Maury, Michael, and Scott,
and
my Mother and Father
with love

Contents

Acknowledgments

I have been fortunate to have the love and support of many people, to all of whom I owe a debt of gratitude: my husband, Maury; our sons, Michael and Scott; my mother, Collette; my father, Robert; Maury's parents, Esther and Harry; his brother, Evan; my sisters, Christine Irvin, Patricia Bloom, Jeanne Denney; my brothers, Timothy and Kelly Irvin; my brother-in-law, Paul Denney; Collette and Kevin Plunkert, Jessica, Olivia, and Harold Bloom; Dorothy, Katie, Tom, Robert, and Neil Cocolin; Douglas and Walter Payne; Elizabeth and Sidney Sherrard; Robert McCluer; Maud, Henry, Nellie, and Chester McCluer; Nellie and Chester Parsons; Frances and John Irvin.

I would like to thank my friends who encouraged me while I was working on the book: Barbara, Karl, Barry, and Andy Hertzberg; Michelle Burke Boyd; Walter Birch; Dr. Herbert Greenberg; Ronald Johnson; Sherry, Steve, Randy, and Nikki Tammara; and Manny Stein.

I appreciate the assistance and support of Bernadine Clark, Carol Cartaino, Howard Wells, and Richard Rosenthal at Writer's Digest Books.

A very special thanks to Philip Wood for publishing my book; David Hinds, Editor-in-Chief who offered significant suggestions, Veronica Randall, Managing Editor for her expertise and enthusiasm; and to Alexis Brunner for proofreading the manuscript.

I am grateful to Celestial Arts and Writer's Digest Books for making my dream of sharing the Write-Now method with other writers a reality, and to all my students and fellow writers in the Write-Now workshops.

My everlasting gratitude to The Creator, who makes all things possible.

PREFACE

Poor writing is . . . a symptom
of inhibition and nervousness.
Better English is the language
spoken and written by someone
who feels at ease.

Rudolf Flesch

W HEN I READ THESE words a dozen years ago, I started to laugh. There I was battling the flu, trying to ignore the two dogs barking outside, and worrying about finishing my article.

"How could anyone be relaxed and write under these conditions?" I thought. I resigned myself to the fact that noise, fatigue, and procrastination were occupational hazards, and as a writer, I'd have to learn to live with them. When I told my writing class about my reactions to Rudolf Flesch's comment, the students said they experienced similar frustrations which made them tense whenever they began writing. They admitted they didn't know how to handle the tension.

I decided to try to find a way to deal with these writing obstacles that seemed to restrict and inhibit even the most dedicated writers. I read about the effects of stress on the body and mind and studied stress management and behavioral modification techniques. I was fascinated by the way the subconscious mind works and how it can be conditioned to change mental attitudes. After taking graduate courses in psychology and delving deeper into the subject of stress, I decided to become a therapist.

In my practice, I noticed that stress was a primary factor in whatever problems my clients had: overeating, excessive smoking, marital difficulties, etc. I taught them relaxation exercises to calm them and help them deal with the element of stress. They learned visualization techniques to build up their confidence so they could attain their goals. The exercises helped me as well; I did them to unwind before my writing sessions. Afterward, I would imagine myself without a particular writing problem—namely fatigue while writing. Instead of saying, "Just thinking about working on my article makes me tired," I said to myself, "When I'm working on my article, I feel as energetic as I do when I'm swimming." I would then see myself doing a lap in the pool.

I practiced this exercise—combining the elements of relaxation, visualization, and suggestion—every day for two weeks. Not long afterward, I started to notice a change. When I sat down at my typewriter, I *did* feel more energetic, more ready to write. Later, I designed specific exercises aimed at alleviating other types of writer's stress: lack of ideas, discipline and writing time, disorganization, and rejection. Pilot programs to test the effectiveness of the exercises were conducted during my graduate studies. The Write-Now method, the subject of my master's thesis, was enthusiastically endorsed both by the writers in these programs and by Norwich University. I've since taught the Write-Now method to all of my writing classes.

It gives me deep satisfaction to know that I can offer my students a total writing program—one that deals both with controlling stress and with developing writing skills. I feel that same elation in being able to share the Write-Now method with you in this book. By applying it, you will experience a new level of satisfaction with your own work. And if you practice the exercises and write regularly, you will become a relaxed and effective author—one who writes with ease.

CHAPTER ONE

The Write-Now Method: What It Is, Why You Need It

The greatest discovery of my generation
is that human beings can alter their
lives by altering their attitudes of mind.

William James

CHAPTER OVERVIEW

1. How do mind and body work together in the writing process?

2. How was the Write-Now method developed?

3. How can you condition your mind and eliminate obstacles to writing?

DAVID IS A PHOTOJOURNALIST who liked taking pictures to accompany his articles; until recently, writing them was a different story. Even when his deadline loomed near, he procrastinated.

"I used to have to stay up all night, working like crazy to finish an article on time," he told me. "What a hassle. Now when I get the go-ahead on an assignment, I start on it right away. The Write-Now exercise I've been doing for a month just before I sit down to write has made writing as much fun as taking pictures."

Joan, a real estate salesperson and mother of twin boys, had a different writing obstacle. "I was always too tired at night to write," she recalls. Her evenings were spent either showing houses, catching up on laundry, or shopping for groceries.

Joan recently solved her problem by learning to write while she sleeps. A Write-Now exercise done at bedtime recharges her energy and her creativity. Now she wakes up an hour earlier than usual to work on her novel.

Both David and Joan have discovered something valuable: the writing process involves the mind and body working together as partners. If your mind tells your body that you're tired, you'll feel like sleeping instead of writing. But if your mind is "geared up" for a writing session, your body will do its part to help get the words down on paper (or up on a computer screen). The relationship between mind and body is like the joint effort of a husband and wife working together to make a solid marriage.

Joan and David have learned something else, too: they can change their attitudes, prevent fatigue and procrastination, and thus become more productive. By taking appropriate steps to remove the attitudinal obstacles to their writing, they increase their writing potential. (You'll see how they did it later in this chapter.)

These two ideas—that mind and body share a working relationship and that it's possible to alter attitudes and outlooks—are integral elements of the Write-Now method—a method that can make you a better, more effective writer.

How The Method Was Born

The Write-Now method of writing evolved about twenty years ago from my experience as a writer, writing teacher, and stress therapist.

As a writer, I wanted to eliminate my own bad writing habits. I was like David; I put off my writing assignments until the last minute—a practice that resulted in much stress, and often writer's block.

In the classroom, I heard my students complain about the anxieties they faced when they sat down to write: they were interrupted by outside distractions, stymied by their own disorganization, and stifled by rejection slips. I could identify with their distress; I was experiencing my own frustrations as deadlines drew closer and I couldn't get projects completed. I recall one particularly awful episode: I had two articles due, a workshop to conduct, and my sons' Boy Scout meeting to attend—all in one day.

There had to be a way to overcome these obstacles that made writing a stressful, often frustrating, and sometimes dreaded undertaking. Drawing from my work in helping people deal with their anxieties, I began introducing in my writing classes some of the relaxation exercises I used with clients to reduce their stress. I added visualization techniques and suggestions, thus forming a complete writing program—one that reduced stress and improved writing skills.

Over the years, I've questioned hundreds of students about the effect the Write-Now exercises had on their writing lives. Their responses convinced me that the relaxation-visualization-suggestion exercises had a positive influence. In further developing the Write-Now method, I listened to my students' comments about what worked and didn't work for them and have refined the various exercises in my classes (and in this book) to meet their needs.

In my own life, the Write-Now exercises have helped me plan writing time, stick to a writing schedule, and set realistic deadlines. I also regularly do a Write-Now exercise that boosts my energy levels so I can more effectively handle my family and career responsibilities.

Today I conduct fiction and nonfiction workshops for full-time, part-time, and beginning writers on college campuses in and around Philadelphia. I also teach the Write-Now method to employees of corporations like IBM and other businesses, including insurance companies and banks, whose personnel regularly write business letters, reports, memos, and proposals.

The students in my Write-Now workshops represent a diverse cross-section of the writing population. These doctors, salespeople, homemakers, teachers, executives, engineers, accountants and others have generously given me their reactions to the Write-Now exercises in this book. In fact, it was the successes my students found as a result of the Write-Now workshops that convinced me to write the book and share with you this approach to writing.

Why This Book

How to Write While You Sleep will show you how to use the most important resource you have as a writer—your subconscious mind. The subconscious is like a gigantic filing system in which myriad precious facts, ideas, emotions, and feelings are neatly tucked away. The valuables in this storehouse eventually mesh to become the stuff of poems, articles, and stories. Indeed, your inner mind can filter down to your awareness the characters, climax, and conclusion for a story—*if* you are prepared to accept them.

The Write-Now method helps you reach a relaxed state in which your subconscious mind can work for you. This approach to writing also helps you bypass the barriers that can prevent you from processing the information your subconscious delivers. In other words, with Write-Now, you'll no longer be thrown off the writing track by a lack of time, energy, or ideas. You'll learn how to picture yourself without these problems—and eventually eliminate them.

What's Inside

The first three chapters of *How to Write While You Sleep* introduce you to the Write-Now method and explain how it works to enhance your writing. You'll discover how to increase your creativity during your waking hours *and* while you sleep. You'll also learn how to decrease the stress associated with writer's block.

The second part of the book (Chapters 4 and 5) focuses on how to schedule quality writing time and eradicate hindrances that waste it. You'll learn the Write-Now 3-T method of instant organization—Time, Table, Together—that helps you make optimum use of whatever time you have for writing. In this section, you'll discover how to deal with interruptions, rejections, and other writing restrictions. To help nurture attitudes and environments conducive to writing, I'll give you effective Write-Now exercises designed to help you meet your writing goals.

Part Three (Chapters 6, 7, 8) centers on the specifics of fiction and non-fiction writing and how to get it published. Here you will learn Write-Now exercises that can improve your concentration and comprehension, and ultimately save you time when you're researching the facts, statistics, anecdotes, and case histories you need to make a salable book or article. The Write-Now fiction exercises will spark ideas for plots and characters that add realism and excitement to your stories. You'll learn a new way to develop a plot with the 4 C's of plotting. You'll find out how to analyze a movie by identifying its conflict, complications, climax, and conclusion; then you can analyze your own writing to see if it contains those elements of a believable plot. Chapter 8 covers the realities of selling your work; it will teach you how to do business with editors and publishers looking for quality writing.

In Chapter 9, I'll share with you the questions (and my answers) most frequently asked by students in the Write-Now workshops and by other writers interested in the method. With that as a send-off, you'll be well prepared to apply the Write-Now method to your own writing. But be sure to check the annotated bibliography for references you may want to study further—either to increase your understanding of various elements of the Write-Now method or to learn more about writing as a process, a craft, and an experience.

Though *How to Write While You Sleep* offers you many ways to improve your writing practices and increase your writing potential, it does *not* cover the mechanics of writing. For example, it will not teach you how to punctuate sentences, spell five-syllable words, eliminate errors in subject-verb agreement, or use a thesaurus to find a synonym. There are many books that cover grammar, punctuation, spelling, and the other basics of good writing; I'll recommend some excellent ones along the way.

What this book does is give you a method to help you take control of your writing life. With it, you'll learn how to break bad habits and reduce the stress that might be keeping you from getting published.

Your Subconscious Is The Key

The Write-Now method is a total program for writers. It combines three common principles—visualization, suggestion, and relaxation—with practical, concrete exercises to improve your creative abilities and build constructive writing habits. How the program works has a lot to do with the features of its key ingredient: the subconscious mind.

Your subconscious controls the autonomic functions of the body—your heart rate, breathing, etc. It also records everything that has ever happened to you. But, for our purposes, the subconscious possesses one especially relevant feature: when the mind and body are relaxed, the subconscious accepts as absolute fact exactly what you tell it. When you are totally relaxed, your conscious mind—which regularly censors your thoughts and makes critical evaluations—is bypassed. It is in a somewhat lulled state and makes no judgments on your suggestions.

If, for instance, you want to wake up at 7 A.M., you could condition yourself to do so by saying before bedtime, "I'll wake up at seven in the morning." If you make this suggestion while you're relaxed, your conscious mind won't challenge you by saying, "But you need your alarm clock to wake up." After several nights of making the suggestion while you're totally relaxed, your subconscious mind will accept your suggestion as true. And you will wake up at 7 A.M.

The way you feel about yourself is also based on how you've conditioned your subconscious. If you think you're overweight, your mind gives you that thought based on what it's been told. You begin to accept as true such comments as "You're too fat," or "Why can't you be thin like your sister?" And you interpret them accordingly: "Because I'm fat, I'm unacceptable." If you don't offer a counterthought such as "I like myself the way I am" to cancel out the negative suggestions, you can develop a poor self-image.

Conditioning Your Mind

In my work with people who want to break bad habits, I frequently meet clients who have for years conditioned themselves to believe things that are not necessarily true. I know, for example, that many heavy smokers believe that smoking keeps them calm. By smoking, they reinforce their belief. Until they identify the source of their stress (job, spouse, unreasonable expectations) and learn how to reduce the related tension, they continue the habit. Once the stress is alleviated, their minds can be reconditioned to accept the fact that when tension builds, they can substitute a constructive practice for their destructive smoking habit.

Mental pictures and suggestions condition our minds either positively or negatively and cause us to act in a certain way. In his book *The Magic of Believing*, Claude Bristol discusses the important role of the subconscious mind in our lives. He notes that we are conditioned to do or think many things.

> *This subtle force of the repeated suggestion overcomes our reason, acting directly on our emotions and our feelings and finally penetrates to the very depths of our subconscious minds. It is the basic principle of all successful advertising—the continued and repeated suggestion that first makes you believe, after which you are eager to buy.*[1]

Advertising agencies spend more than $20 billion a year trying to catch the attention of the average consumer—who watches television for more than six hours a day and digests nearly 100,000 words from magazines, signs, newspapers, and other printed matter. The advertiser must create the perfect image and appropriate suggestions to convince people to use a particular product. Repetitious slogans, jingles, and phrases such as "Coke is it" and "Where's the beef?" are eventually absorbed by our subconscious minds.

Athletes, as well as advertisers, religious leaders, politicians, and other people persuaders, know the dynamic power of mental pictures and suggestions.

Jack Nicklaus claims that imagery and suggestion are the two things that make him a success on the golf course. In his book *Golf My Way,* he describes the visualizations that work for him.

> First I "see" the ball where I want it to finish, nice and white sitting up high on the bright, green grass. Then the scene quickly changes and I "see" the ball going there: its path, trajectory, and shape, even its behavior on landing. Then there's a sort of fade-out, and the next scene shows me making the kind of swing that will turn the previous images into reality.... I never hit a shot, even in practice, without having a very sharp, in-focus picture of it in my head.[2]

Writers and inventors have long recognized that the subconscious stimulates creativity and can be conditioned to eliminate stress and improve performance. Phyllis Whitney, author of over sixty books, knows the importance of the subconscious. After thinking about her story characters, she relaxes for a few minutes, visualizes a scene, and hears her characters speak. Later, she records her "observations" and tells her story.

Thomas Edison's inner mind worked for him in a similar way: it would often reveal the missing ingredient for one of his inventions. He was known to analyze in detail the components of a potential discovery—and then to lie down. "Within minutes," he once said, "the solution would flash to me out of thin air."

Mark Twain, Albert Einstein, and William Blake were others who trained their subconscious minds to work for them.

Seeing Yourself As A Writer

The Write-Now method uses the same familiar principles of mental pictures and suggestions to condition your mind and correct and improve your writing habits. It's the way you "see" yourself as a writer that can either stimulate or inhibit your creativity.

Remember how tired Joan felt whenever she tried to write at night? Because she associated the idea of writing with fatigue, she couldn't muster the energy to work on her novel.

Having ruled out poor health or insufficient sleep as possible causes of her tiredness, Joan set out to recondition her mind to accept the fact that fatigue didn't have to interfere with her writing. She used an image suggested by other writers in the Write-Now workshop who had already eradicated their fatigue problem: it was an image of themselves in a relaxed state participating in their favorite sport. Every night before she went to sleep, Joan pictured herself jogging to boost her energy levels.

If lack of energy prevents *you* from writing, you might try a similar visualization—you could picture yourself playing tennis, football, baseball, or swimming. As the physical activity in your mind's eye ends, "see" yourself walking briskly to your desk. You are as excited about the prospects of working out your creative muscles as you were your biceps or quadriceps during the physical workout. You silently repeat the following suggestion ten times to reinforce the picture: "I am as energetic and enthusiastic about my writing as I am when I'm (mention the sport or activity)." Within a short time, the mental picture you had of yourself feeling chronically tired before and during writing will be erased.

For Joan it took two months of doing the exercise every night—i.e., using the suggestion while picturing herself jogging. Slowly, her subconscious mind began to accept the suggestion as true; she was then able to approach her writing with enthusiasm.

It may seem strange or contrived to you to have to repeat the suggestion several times, but it's necessary so your mind will absorb it. Television and radio commercials are a prime example of just how effective repetitive suggestions can be. After you've heard relief spelled R-O-L-A-I-D-S a dozen times, you just might buy a pack the next time you overindulge in a gourmet meal.

Remember, too, that you're not saying the suggestions aloud. Once you've done the mental imaging exercises a few times, they won't seem unnatural. You may, in fact, already have the habit of suggesting things to your subconscious mind. It's like repeating to yourself several times the items you want to pick up at the grocery store—milk, cheese, coffee, cookies—so you won't forget them.

The Element Of Relaxation

Neither the most appropriate suggestion nor the most vivid imagery can be truly effective in conditioning yourself as a writer unless the third component of the Write-Now method is present: you must be relaxed.

Several years ago, I conducted a series of workshops designed to sharpen both fiction and nonfiction writing skills. Follow-up sessions to determine if the participants had actually used the writing techniques we covered yielded a surprising conclusion: only a few writers—those who felt confident and relaxed while writing—profited from the instruction. The others revealed anxiety about their abilities. Their underlying doubts about themselves produced stress, which prevented them from using the new information or improving their writing. (The same thing can happen to a tennis player who works daily to perfect his game. If during the match he's worried about losing, he's probably not relaxed. He may even play poorly as a result of not seeing himself as relaxed and confident. With tennis, as with writing, both the proper mental attitude *and* diligent practice are essential.)

To build their confidence and reduce tension, I introduced various Write-Now exercises to the anxious group of writers. After several classes, the students began to relax; the new writing skills soon became an integral part of their work. Since then, all my writing classes have included the Write-Now relaxation exercises.

In my work as a consultant to industry, I've found that the classroom isn't the only place where anxiety and tension can impede performance. The stress that business managers and supervisors experience when they have to write monthly reports is just as great as that of professional writers on a deadline. Learning to relax is an important step in reconditioning their attitudes about writing.

Relaxation And Conditioning

Equally important is knowing when that reconditioning effort is most likely to take root. As mentioned earlier, visualizations and suggestions are most readily accepted by the subconscious mind when a person is totally relaxed. To understand when such relaxation occurs, you should know something about how your brain functions.

During a twenty-four-hour period, your brain experiences four basic wave patterns: beta, alpha, theta, and delta. Beta waves precede alpha waves and occur while you're going about your daily activities. The alpha period takes place naturally twice a day—just before you fall asleep and again as you're waking up. Theta brain waves follow alpha waves and are marked by extreme drowsiness. Delta waves are present during deep sleep.

During the alpha state, your mind and body are completely relaxed, and oxygen to your brain cells is increased with deep breathing. Brainwave rhythms, which can be measured on an electroencephalogram (EEG), drop from thirteen to eight cycles per second. What does that mean for you as a writer? It means that although you're awake and alert during the alpha stage, you feel an inner consciousness. At this time, your mind is ready to accept the suggestions you give it. Through brain wave training in both the alpha and theta stages, you can increase your creative abilities. (More on creativity in Chapter 2.)

Scientists contend that brain waves can reveal some of the secrets of creativity. In a Menninger Foundation research project they conducted in 1975 on the relationship between creativity and brain wave activity, Drs. Elmer and Alyce Green concluded:

> *Many artists and scientists who have been unusually creative in their fields have written about their experiences. Many described a kind of reverie or near-dream state in which intuitive ideas and solutions come to consciousness in the form of hypnagogic images.... A person can learn to be creative. Creativity does not have to be something you are born with, but might be something that you can learn.*[3]

Whether you're giving yourself suggestions to spark your creativity or working on changing your attitude about writing, your mind is primed for conditioning during the alpha and theta states. (Conditioning your mind during the theta stage prior to the dream state is discussed in Chapter 3.) The alpha state is an ideal time to begin the Write-Now relaxation exercises because your body is beginning to unwind as you get ready for sleep.*

Progressive Relaxation

Deep breathing has a very soothing effect on the entire body; it helps you relax. To reach that state, lie down in a quiet room, close your eyes, and take several deep breaths. (If you're trying to relax during the day and you can't lie down, do the exercises while seated in a comfortable chair.) Take the air down to your diaphragm, hold it, and count slowly to three. Exhale through your mouth.

After several deep breaths, you're ready to do progressive relaxation exercises similar to those developed by Dr. Edmund Jacobson in the 1930s to relax voluntary skeletal muscles. I've modified them for the Write-Now exercises.

Start with your toes. Tighten and relax them. Do the same thing with your calves, thighs, buttocks, stomach, back, shoulders, arms, hands, neck, and

---

* *The alpha state you experience as you're waking up is also an excellent time to give your subconscious mind a suggestion. And since your body is already relaxed, you may be able to omit the progressive relaxation steps of the Write-Now exercises.*

facial muscles. Feel the tension as you tighten the muscles and relax them. As you do the relaxation exercises, blood lactate, a substance produced by the metabolic activity of skeletal muscles, is reduced and muscle tension decreases. Anxiety is caused by skeletal muscle contraction; relaxation reverses this state. During this time, your body cells need less oxygen and your metabolism slows down— deep relaxation is the result.

Painting a mental picture of some carefree place will contribute to your overall state of relaxation. Some of the favorite places writers in my Write-Now workshops focus on include: a quiet beach, a rose garden, and an apple orchard. "The important thing is to pick a peaceful and pleasant scene," a sportswriter named Joe cautioned in one of our workshops. "I used to picture myself sailing on the lake. But after my boating accident last month, I switched to a different scene. Now I see myself hiking through the Maine woods in late spring. Anything associated with water makes me tense."

Several years ago I visited Walden Pond in Concord, Massachusetts during the height of the brilliant foliage season. Even today, when my schedule is especially hectic, I recall the serenity of those surroundings. It relaxes my mind.

More Than Positive Thinking

At this point, you might be tempted to assume that the Write-Now method is little more than an exercise in positive thinking. On the contrary: Write-Now is much more than positive *thinking*. It is positive *action* taken in the alpha state. The difference between the two approaches is that positive thinking is done during the day when positive thoughts are often negated by outside thoughts and distractions. But Write-Now is practiced when the mind is free from concerns and open to suggestions—i.e., when you're relaxed.

Practicing a Write-Now exercise is like sitting down to an eight-course dinner when you haven't eaten all day. Your stomach is anxious for the food; you're ready for a feast. But if you've just devoured (i.e., been "distracted" by) a hamburger, French fries, and a milk shake, the most delectable array of food won't tempt your palate, and you won't feel much like eating.

In his book *Total Mind Power*, Donald Wilson touches on the importance of giving yourself suggestions when you're most likely to accept them. "There is a vast difference between suggesting to yourself that you do something," he writes, "and directing yourself to do it from the position of a focused awareness [alpha state]. The difference is the use of 10 percent versus 90 percent of your mind."[4]

When your body is totally relaxed and your mind is free to accept your suggestions unconditionally, you're ready to practice the Write-Now exercises.

Preparing For A Write-Now Exercise

Before beginning any exercise, identify your writing problem and establish a goal. Perhaps your writing roadblock is the same as David's—procrastination. Your goal, then, would be something like this: "During the time I set aside for writing, I will write. I won't delay or put off my writing."

If you can't put your finger on your exact writing problem, read through the list of Write-Now exercises in the Table of Contents. Some of the exercises might suggest a problem area you've been wrestling with. Or, as you read the book, make note of anything that presents a writing problem for you.

When you've identified your writing obstacle and written a goal specifically related to it, select a Write-Now exercise designed to correct it. Formulate a suggestion appropriate for overcoming the problem similar to the one given in the exercise you've chosen or you can use the goal, suggestion, and visualization given in each Write-Now exercise.

The suggestion for conquering your tendency to put things off might be the following: "Because writing is important to me, I'll approach it with the same interest I have when I'm involved in (name your favorite activity). Other things will be done after I finish my writing."

Whatever suggestion you write, make it concise and positive. The above suggestion is the one David used in his Write-Now exercise. In conjunction with the suggestion, he visualized "taking pictures." It took him about four weeks to beat his procrastination.

Once you've targeted your writing problem and written a specific goal and related suggestion, think of a scene (the beach, a wooded area, or a scene mentioned in one of the exercises) that will allow you to mentally relax. All of these prerequisites are necessary to benefit from a Write-Now exercise.

The following Write-Now exercise is the one David practiced to overcome his tendency to procrastinate. The first three steps are basically the same as for any Write-Now exercise; Steps 4 and 5 reflect whatever writing problem you're working on.

David did the exercise just before he sat down at his desk. When you practice the Write-Now method during the day, you can do the exercises either several hours before or just prior to your writing session. When you do the exercises at bedtime, plan a writing session any time the next day.

Write-Now Exercise
Avoiding Procrastination

1. Get comfortable in bed (or an easy chair if you're doing the exercises during the day). Noise should be at a minimum. Close your eyes. Take three or four deep breaths. Inhale through the nose. Take the air down to the diaphragm. Count to three. Exhale through the mouth.

2. Imagine that you are lying on a lounge chair near a pond. It is a pleasantly warm fall day. The surrounding trees reflect the reds, greens, and golds of their leaves in the water. All of nature is in harmony. You, too, feel that your mind and body are in harmony. (You can substitute another scene especially pleasing for you.)

3. Push your heels down on the chair/bed/floor. Feel the tension. Now relax them. Do the same thing with your hips, back, shoulders, neck, head, arms, and hands. Push down against whatever surface they're touching. Relax. Tighten and relax the muscles while taking three deep breaths. Repeat silently ten times: "I'm becoming more and more relaxed." (The main objective is to relax your mind and body so that the subconscious mind will accept your suggestion.)

4. "See" your suggestion becoming a reality. If, as mentioned earlier, procrastination is the problem, visualize yourself doing something you enjoy—gardening, reading, taking pictures, listening to music, etc. Immerse yourself in the activity and feel the pleasure that you derive from it. Next, "see" yourself going to your typewriter. Silently repeat the following suggestion ten times: "Because writing is important to me, I'll approach it with the same interest I have in (name activity). Other things will be done after I finish my writing."

   Drop off to sleep. If you're doing the exercise during the day, complete the exercise and say, "When I open my eyes, I'll feel great."

Documenting Your Progress

Use a notebook to keep track of your progress. A chart like the one below will help you record the specifics of each Write-Now exercise you practice. Regularly checking your progress reinforces your commitment to reaching your goal.

A completed chart for Joan's Write-Now exercise dealing with overcoming tired-ness may have looked like the one below.

 Write-Now Exercise
Overcoming Fatigue

Writing Obstacle: Fatigue

Column 1: The date you begin working on your goal

Column 2: Your writing-related goal

Column 3: A brief description of how you picture your goal

Column 4: A suggestion for reaching your goal

Column 5: The date you achieved your goal

(1) Sept. 4

(2) I won't let my tiredness and lack of energy keep me from writing.

(3) I see myself jogging; I feel exhilarated during the workout.

(4) I am as enthusiastic about my writing as I am when I'm jogging.

(5) Nov. 3

Notes on My Progress:

September 11—I don't think I'm progressing fast enough with this exercise. It's hard for me to picture myself jogging and then visualize myself writing.

September 21—I think I'm getting into the flow of the exercise. I can go through the relaxation steps almost without thinking about them.

October 9—I feel good. The exercise is really helping me feel more energetic about writing.

Between Columns 4 and 5 in the chart, you may want to insert another column for the date you begin to notice an improvement in whatever area you're working on. If after a week or so you don't see any change (either in dealing with the problem or feeling comfortable with the exercise), reword your particu-lar suggestion and pick a different mental picture to visualize. Remember to work on just one goal at a time. Be careful not to incorporate several suggestions for improvement into one. Focus on one suggestion specifically designed to achieve one goal. Make notes to yourself on your progress; such documentation helps you keep focused on your goal.

Many writers get results when they do the exercises every night for four to six weeks. Once you learn the five-step sequence, the whole procedure takes less than five minutes. The advantage of doing the exercises before sleep is that your body is to some degree already relaxed.

Don't be discouraged if you don't get results right away. If procrastination, for example, has been a habit you've had for a long time, it might take several months to recondition your mind to accept a new attitude about it. Set realistic goals for yourself based on how deep-seated a habit/writing problem is and how it affects other areas of your life. Remember, someone who has smoked cigarettes for thirty years will need more time to break the habit than someone who has smoked only three months.

Write-Now will keep you moving toward your objective. It's a method for full-time writers who must surmount new types of stresses in their writing lives. It's also for part-time and beginning writers who want to improve skills, build confidence, and realize their writing potential.

Psychologist William James believed that if you act as though you have achieved your goal, you *will* achieve it. With the Write-Now method, you'll learn how to act like a published writer. Combine that behavior with perseverance, hard work, and faith in yourself, and you *will* be one.

Notes / Chapter One

1. Claude M. Bristol, *The Magic of Believing* (Englewood Cliffs, N.J.: Prentice Hall, 1948), p. 71.

2. Jack Nicklaus, *Golf My Way* (New York: Simon and Schuster, 1974), p. 79.

3. Elmer and Alyce Green, *Beyond Biofeedback* (New York: Dell Publishing, 1977), p. 124.

4. Donald L. Wilson, *Total Mind Power* (New York: Berkley Publishing, 1978), p. 219.

 Chapter Two

The Write-Now Method and Your Creativity

A poem begins in delight
and ends in wisdom.

Robert Frost

CHAPTER OVERVIEW

1. What is the creative process?

2. How can you influence your creative potential at every stage of the process?

3. How does the Write-Now method do away with roadblocks that inhibit creativity?

YOU HAVE THE POTENTIAL to be creative. When that potential matures and you fashion an article, theory, solution, sculpture, melody, or dance, we can use Robert Frost's words to describe the process.

The creative process consists of four stages: preparation, gestation, illumination, and verification. Identified in 1926 by British political scientist Graham Wallas in his book *The Art of Thought,* these four stages play a part in any creative venture.[1] Psychologists agree that their application is universal in both scientific and artistic endeavors.

Let's look first at how the process works in the realm of science. During the preparation stage, a scientist gathers and analyzes data related to an idea he has, and performs experiments to find a solution to some problem. The next stage—the gestation period—is a time of inactivity, a time to let ideas incubate in the scientist's subconscious.

During this stage, he may decide to take a vacation from his work. While swimming in the ocean—far from the laboratory—the scientist is suddenly struck with a solution to the problem he's been working on in the lab. He experiences a flash of insight during this illumination stage. After returning to the laboratory, he tests the validity of the solution. Does it "fit" with all the other data? During this last stage—verification—he performs the necessary experiments to check the appropriateness of the answer he got during illumination.

Every step of the creative process builds on the one before it; the order of the steps is always the same.

The Writer And The Creative Process

For a writer, the process might begin (preparation) when an idea delights your imagination and you begin to analyze its potential—you might think about creating a new character for your story. In the gestation stage, you incubate your idea, saturating your mind with the information you've given it during preparation. The idea evolves and takes shape—the character's appearance, voice, behavior, and personality are forming in your subconscious. Time passes, and one day your idea emerges, perhaps suddenly (illumination) as a finished product—you finally know what role the character will play in the outcome of the story, or you know what you must do to make him more believable. Then you test the idea (verification) in conjunction with other elements of the story— you analyze the character in relation to other characters, the story theme, etc.

The verification stage may *verify* that what you discovered during the illumination stage does strengthen your story. Or you may determine while testing the idea that the character doesn't blend with the story or produce quite the effect you intended. Perhaps the character's presence presents a new conflict that you don't want to introduce; maybe he draws attention away from the protagonist in your story.

In any case, if the "answer" you got during the verification stage doesn't blend with the rest of your story, you may decide to abandon the idea—e.g., drop the character. Or you may decide to go back to the preparation stage and gather more information—why you need the character; what his purpose will be; what he adds to the story, etc. After gathering sufficient new information about your idea, you go through all the stages of the process again.

The part that creativity plays in a successful writing project may be easy to understand from the above examples. But it's also important to notice that the process doesn't just happen on its own. And comments from my students reflect that there are potential hazards to creativity at every step.

"It's hard for me to come up with an idea each month for my column," Nancy told us in class. "I don't see how some authors write a couple of books a year. Where do they get so many ideas?"

Arnold had a different problem; he had difficulty concentrating on his subject during the preparation stage, then had trouble distancing himself from it during the gestation period. "When I get an article idea for the company newsletter, I start looking up information. But it seems I'm distracted a lot and digress from the subject. It takes forever to get background material. And when I *do* start typing, I don't stop until I'm finished."

Nancy and Arnold are not alone; many writers have difficulty following through with the four stages of the creative process. They haven't yet learned how to make their creativity work for them.

In this chapter you'll learn how to use the Write-Now method as a catalyst that enables you not only to nurture your creativity, but also to make the most of every stage of the creative process. Since each step builds on the one before it, it's important to work through each stage completely in order to get the maximum benefit from the process as a whole. By practicing specific Write-Now exercises, you'll be better prepared to capitalize on your creative potential. In turn, your writing will be easier because your mind will be relaxed and open to accept those creative moments when they occur.

Preparation Stage

Getting an idea for a writing project and gathering information about it signals the start of the creative process. But without the proper conditions, the preparation stage of the process may never get off the ground. If your powers of observation are impaired, ideas may escape your notice. Worry, work, and real-world responsibilities can cloud your vision and underexpose your senses to the stimuli that trigger ideas for books, articles, poems, essays, etc.

In their book *Stop, Look, and Write,* authors Hart Day Leavitt and David Sohn recognize the importance of developing one's powers of observation. It's from the world around us that we gather nuggets of information.

> *The way you select words and organize them into whole composi-*
> *tions depends on the way you see human experience. If you literally*
> *do not see anything, you will of course have nothing to say.... To*
> *"see" in the best possible way, one needs to practice looking for such*
> *things as similarities, differences, emotions, gestures, colors, details,*
> *and conflicts.*[2]

The bits of information we retrieve, store, and eventually ponder generate ideas. Ideas, fleeting as they are, *can* be harnessed. And, like a good carriage horse, they can pull you through the creative process to your goal of becoming a published writer. But, instead of harnessing a carriage horse, many writers find themselves corralling a mule that refuses to budge.

Some writers, too, look at life only from *their* point of view and *their* prejudices; they entertain—and harness—ideas that pertain solely to their own interests and opinions. With blinders firmly secured, they look neither to the left nor right. They plod along like the mule, rarely stretching their legs or minds. Alternative lifestyles, interesting people, divergent philosophies, and fresh experiences that *could* stimulate the flow of ideas and add new perspectives to their lives—and subsequently, their writing—go unrecognized.

"It wasn't until I started to do some volunteer work with the Big Brothers' Organization that I began to realize that not every child had someone who really cared about him," Jed told one of my classes. "I was naive enough to think that all kids had parents like mine who cared about how I turned out. Being a Big Brother not only opened my eyes to the needs of others—it gave me the opportunity to write a couple of articles about the program."

A Writer's Curiosity

When you tune your senses to the attitudes, thoughts, and actions of people around you, you pique your curiosity. As Samuel Johnson said, "Curiosity is one of the permanent and certain characteristics of a vigorous mind." A writer who lacks curiosity is at a distinct disadvantage. He lacks the momentum to activate his imagination—and it's the imagination that shifts the creative gears into motion.

If a novelist sets his story in China and isn't curious enough about the country to research its people, customs, and terrain, the book will lack both color and credibility. Barbara Cartland and James Michener, popular fiction writers, regularly read scores of history books to add authenticity and flavor to their novels. They give their powers of observation a workout in recreating scenes and moments that will, in turn, stimulate their readers' curiosity.

Successful scientists and researchers, like all creative individuals, rarely give their curiosity much of a rest. Thomas Edison, for example, asked himself questions—and wouldn't be satisfied until he found the right answers. In one instance, he tested over 6,000 varieties of bamboo fiber in an attempt to find a workable lamp filament.

A similar searching quality is found in successful writers' curiosity. With their minds open and inquisitive, they are ready to seize an idea for a character, theme, article, or book whenever it unveils itself—often in something they have seen or heard.

The novelist Henry James experienced his world with his finely tuned senses. He described the germ of a story as "the precious particle...the stray suggestion, the wandering word, the vague echo, at touch of which the novelist's imagination winces as at the prick of some sharp point: its virtue is all in its needle-like quality, the power to penetrate as finely as possible."[3]

For novelist Joyce Cary, one "precious particle" was a woman with wrinkles on her forehead; he saw the woman on a boat. "A girl of about thirty," he told a friend, "wearing a shabby skirt. She was enjoying herself. A nice expression, with a wrinkled forehead, a good many wrinkles. I could write about that girl...."

Cary subsequently forgot about the incident and the girl. Several weeks later he woke up with an English story and an English heroine. Later, while revising the story, he wondered about all the wrinkles on his heroine's forehead. "And I suddenly realized that my English heroine was the girl on the boat. Somehow she had gone down into my subconscious and came up again with a full-sized story."[4]

Because Joyce Cary was able to "see feelingly," as the poet Archibald MacLeish referred to it, he could build an entire story based on a casual observation.[5]

For Lori, a nurse in a suburban Philadelphia hospital, the "precious particles" and casual observations often come from her patients. "The ideas for my poems are sparked by a remark or an emotion from the people I take care of," she told us during one class discussion. "They like to talk about their families, jobs, and sometimes problems they can't cope with. I think writers have to be good listeners; otherwise, you can't convey genuine feelings on paper."

Generating Ideas

Writers who have become desensitized to their environment (at home, at work, at play) may find it hard to write about the things they probably know best. Their potential to recognize story or article ideas—in their own backyard, so to speak—is stifled.

If you've been known to complain, "There's nothing to write about in my life," you could be setting up a roadblock in your own creative journey. You may be dulled to the very things that could spark your creativity. By doing the Write-Now exercise below, you can reawaken your senses to the sights, sounds, events, and people around you. You can solve the problem of being out of touch with your surroundings.

Write-Now Exercise
Enhancing Sensory Awareness

Goal: To become more aware of and more in tune with your surroundings.

1. Get comfortable in bed (or an easy chair if you're doing the exercises during the day). Noise should be at a minimum. Close your eyes. Take three or four deep breaths. Inhale through the nose. Take the air down to the diaphragm. Count to three. Exhale through the mouth.

2. Imagine that you're lying on a lounge chair near a pond. It is a pleasantly warm fall day. The surrounding trees reflect the reds, greens,

and golds of their leaves in the water. All of nature is in harmony. You, too, feel that your mind and body are in harmony. (You can substitute another scene especially pleasing for you.)

3. Push your heels down on the chair/bed/floor. Feel the tension; now relax them. Do the same thing with your hips, back, shoulders, neck, head, arms, and hands: push down against whatever surface they're touching, then relax. Tighten and relax the muscles while taking three deep breaths. Repeat silently ten times: "I'm becoming more and more relaxed." (The main objective is to relax your mind and body so that the subconscious will accept your suggestion.)

4. Picture yourself either at home, at work, or just relaxing. You see the people around you as individuals. Like the flowers in a garden, they have unique characteristics and traits; they are not just people fulfilling certain roles. Your once-dulled senses are alive now enjoying the wonders of nature and anticipating new experiences with each new day.

5. Silently repeat the following suggestion ten times: "I am becoming more aware of the scenes, people, and happenings in my daily life."

Drop off to sleep.

Practice this Write-Now exercise at bedtime exactly as given for fourteen days. During each writing session the following day, write down at least one idea that you could later develop into a story, poem, article—whatever form you write in.

One way to see the many sides and environments of your life and to pull ideas from all of them is to categorize your existence. Divide it into seven different areas. Depending on your own situation, these might be the following: work, family, hobbies, friends, problems, books, TV/movies. (Several areas might be different for you.)

During the first two days after doing the above Write-Now exercise, analyze your first category—in this case, your job. During your writing session, make up a list of questions to stimulate work-related ideas. For example: What do I like/hate about my job? What do I really think of my boss? Do I feel intimidated by the boss? Is my personal life suffering because of my career? If I had my choice of jobs, what would I do?

On the third and fourth days, focus on your second category: namely, your family. This topic suggests infinite possibilities for story or article ideas.

Will the family survive in the twenty-first century? How much do I know about my family history? Was my childhood happy? If I could be a member of any family, whose family would I choose? What kind of relationship do I have with my father? Mother? Brother?

Use this same method (a list of questions) to analyze each category for two days. Record your ideas daily. Keep a notebook handy to expand on any idea that you think could be developed in a future writing project.

Carol, a legal secretary in one of the Write-Now workshops. claimed that after doing this exercise, she began to look at her job differently. In doing that, she got an idea.

> *I wrote an article about how to win an argument with your boss without losing your job. It occurred to me after working for a very "bossy" boss for a year that there were probably a lot of people like me who were afraid to speak up to a supervisor for fear of being fired. After talking to several people, my opinion was confirmed so I wrote the article. In it, I suggested a way to talk tactfully and unemotionally with a boss. I even tried it with my own to get a promotion—and it worked!*

Gathering Information

Once you have something (an idea) to write about, the next step in the preparation stage of the creative process is to get information about it. Your research will likely take you to many kinds of resources—libraries, museums, government publications, books and magazines, organizations and associations, data bases and research centers, to name a few. No matter what you're writing, you'll probably have to research *something*—maybe the botanical name of a flower, the characteristics of an Amish community, or the geography of a South American river basin. You may find the information you need on your own bookshelf in an almanac, dictionary, or book of quotations. On the other hand, you may find that your research task takes you to faraway places and unfamiliar resources. There are scores of reference books and guides to make your fact-finding easier. (See Chapter 7, page 157, for some general research tips; consult the bibliography for some basic reference and how-to research books for writers.)

About four years ago, after designing the Write-Now exercise for getting in touch with your surroundings, I practiced the exercise and focused on the "family" category in my own writing sessions. As a result, I decided to find out more about my ancestors.

I remembered having read my great-grandmother's diary several years earlier. I was touched by her description of homesickness during her first year at Mount Holyoke College in 1861. How she longed to be aboard the stagecoach that passed by the college every day on its way to Virginia, her home! I remembered reading the love letters she exchanged later with my great-grandfather, a colonel in the Union army. Many of his letters, written at night near the battlefield, reflected the sorrow of the times.

I became intrigued with my family history and read all the love letters and diaries that had been passed down through my mother's family. I was fascinated with the customs and lifestyles of the 1800s. How did women dress then? What would they have thought of the women's movement? What was marriage like in those days?

My research on this project began about a year ago, and I continue to snatch free moments for finding out more about my family roots. I'm keeping all the information on file for future use.

Concentration Is A Must

No matter how good your intentions for gathering information and developing your idea, the research part of any creative process is subject to snags and pitfalls of its own. Writers who spend a lot of time digging for facts often find their attention diverted to other topics. Like Arnold, they lose their concentration and their focus. As a result, they waste time and lose momentum during the research part of the preparation stage.

I've experienced this problem firsthand. When I began researching the creative process about five years ago, I became fascinated with Thomas Edison's perseverance and curiosity. I read his biography and books about his inventions. I digressed from the subject for several days and read about how to apply for a patent after doing a patent search. (Being an amateur inventor, I found this information useful.) However, I did get sidetracked and that threw me off my schedule. I should have waited until I completed my research—and then have gone back to read the other material.

The next Write-Now exercise is one I now use when I'm gathering information on an idea. The exercise helps me improve my concentration. If you do it every night for a week, or right before going to the library, you'll learn to glean only the facts you need from your reading. If your research involves visiting places and interviewing experts on the subject, rephrase the suggestion in Step 5 to help you concentrate on your topic no matter how or where you research it.

 Write-Now Exercise Concentrating on Research

Goal: To gather relevant information by concentrating on material related only to the research topic.

1.
2. Do steps 1-3 of the Write-Now exercise as outlined on pages 22-23.
3.

4. See yourself totally absorbed in a movie. You're enjoying the movie. You're concentrating completely on its plot, characters, theme, setting, music, etc.

5. Next, see yourself reading research material with the same intensity, concentration, and enjoyment you had while watching the movie. Silently repeat the following suggestion ten times: "When I'm reading, I'll concentrate completely on the information that pertains to my article/book/story and is of interest to my reader. Nothing will disturb my concentration."

   If it's bedtime, drop off to sleep.

   If you're doing the exercise during the day, complete the exercise and say, "When I open my eyes, I'll feel great."

After you've gathered all the facts, anecdotes, statistics, and references you need for developing your idea, carefully re-read and analyze the information you have. Do you have enough material to make the piece interesting? What have you learned from your own experience in the area you're writing about that you could share with your readers? What insights on the topic did you get from experts you interviewed? Do you have enough facts to make your short story or novel believable or your article/book credible?

Saturate your mind with the information you've collected so that the next step—the gestation period—of the creative process will produce results. Without sufficient data (the information you have gathered), your subconscious mind has nothing to collate.

Organizing Your Information

Organizing your research notes and making sense of the information you have is often no small task. Unlike the picture on a puzzle box that shows you exactly what the puzzle will look like when it's assembled, your story or article has no predetermined shape. *You* decide what it will look like. *You* determine how to put the facts together to produce a coherent piece of writing.

One way to keep your writing organized is to use an outline. Though there are many outline styles, their purpose is the same: to arrange your information in a logical order. I have developed the S-O-S outline (State the subject; Outline the points; Summarize your thoughts) and teach it to my students as a quick and efficient way to organize their information. (The outline is described in detail in Chapter 7, page 166.) Putting your research material in order is a must before you attempt to write a rough draft—the last part of the preparation stage of the creative process.

▼ Write-Now Exercise ▼
Rough Draft

Goal: To write a free-flowing rough draft that presents relevant information in a logical order.

1.
2. Do steps 1-3 of Write-Now exercise as outlined on pages 22-23.
3.

4. Think about some of the points in your outline that will be included in your article. Picture yourself writing in a journal. Your only concern is to get your ideas down in some logical order. No one censors your information, so you write uninhibitedly. Then see yourself beginning to write your rough draft.

5. Silently repeat this suggestion ten times: "When I'm writing a rough draft, my objective is to get down all the information and thoughts that relate to my subject. No one will criticize my work, so I can write freely. Editing and revisions will come later."

If it's bedtime, drop off to sleep.

If you're doing the exercise during the day, complete the exercise and say, "When I open my eyes, I'll feel great."

Use the suggestion in Step 5 of the exercise before writing any rough draft. After using the exercise with three future stories or articles, you'll automatically write all your drafts this way—quickly and with purpose.

When you begin your rough draft, write as fast as you can. Let the ideas flow from one major point on your outline to the next. Don't stop to check a rule of grammar, look up a word, or rewrite paragraphs. If you can't think of a word you want, draw a line indicating that you'll fill it in later. The draft doesn't even have to contain complete sentences; a phrase or word that captures your thought is enough.

Patrick, a lawyer in the Write-Now workshop, admitted during one session, "The rough draft was the roughest thing for me to do. Looking up the information was easy. However, when I started the draft, I found myself trying to make every sentence perfect as I went along. I checked spelling, punctuation—everything. I scrapped many projects because it was so annoying. After using the Write-Now exercise, I learned to get my ideas down in the draft quickly. I know I can go back later and clean it up."

Before proceeding to the gestation stage of the creative process, read your rough draft several times. If you feel you don't have sufficient information presenting a clear, complete picture of your topic, you may have to do more research. If you can't answer a question that you yourself have about the subject, chances are you haven't researched it enough. Whether or not you use all the information you collect in your research isn't important. What *is* essential is that you have enough background information to write about the subject with interest and accuracy.

The Gestation Period

The gestation stage of any creative process is a time for incubation. You have generated and developed an idea; you've researched it; you've written a rough draft. Now you put the rough draft on a back burner; the simmering process begins.

Like a good spaghetti sauce, your writing needs time on its own. You've added all the necessary ingredients (facts and analysis). Everything slowly blends together. The object is to get as far away from your writing as possible. Most writers enjoy this legitimate "goofing off" time. Just as the chef wouldn't be overly concerned about the simmering spaghetti sauce, you shouldn't be preoccupied with your writing during this period. Besides, getting away from it all for awhile will likely help you look at your work objectively when you return to it.

You can jog, play golf or tennis, go to a movie, watch television, or read a book. Do something you enjoy. An activity that lets you relax both physically and mentally is best. By not dwelling on your rough draft with your conscious mind (and becoming physically tense as a result), your subconscious has a chance to work. Your inner mind takes time to blend, sift, and consider all the data it received during the preparation stage.

How long does the gestation period last? That depends on the complexity of the problem you're trying to solve. Edna Ferber once observed, "A story must simmer in its own juice for months or even years before it is ready to serve." In fact, the gestation period might last only a few minutes, or it might take several years.

Thomas Edison got the idea for the phonograph in 1864 but didn't construct one until 1877. It took thirteen years for him to put all the information together; he experienced illumination several times as he worked to perfect his equipment. The gestation period for Sir Isaac Newton's theory of gravity was also lengthy. The apple fell on his head when he was eleven years old, yet he didn't formulate his theory for twelve more years.

Carla, a fiction writer in one of my classes, found that her conscious efforts to name a character in her gothic novel proved fruitless for two months. It wasn't until she stopped dwelling consciously on the problem and let her subconscious take over that she found an answer.

"I read over lists of names from books on naming a baby and telephone directories, and I couldn't decide on one. Then, about a week later, I was taking a walk and I saw two blue jays in a birdbath. The name suddenly came to me— I named my character 'Jay.'"

What Happens During Incubation

How does your subconscious mind come up with answers, insights, and solutions for improving your writing? Psychologists and experts in the field of creativity cannot explain what actually occurs in the mind to induce illumination after a period of gestation. But they do have some theories to explain the phenomenon and the importance of this incubation time.

Alex Osborn, a leader in the use of creative problem-solving, suggests some of these possibilities in his book *Applied Imagination.*[6] He says that during the gestation period, an unconscious effort in the form of inner tension exists. Although you might not be aware of what's happening in your brain, the problem is being analyzed. Your realization of what's going on is similar to your awareness of what happens in digestion: even though you're not paying attention to your body breaking down the food you ate for dinner, the process occurs.

A second theory is that by taking a break (the gestation period) from a creative project, you can recharge your enthusiasm, which may have waned because of your intense involvement with the project. Your revitalization during this leave of absence from your writing may trigger new insight.

Finally, Osborn discusses the idea that the power of free association is strongest when left on its own during the gestation stage; during this time, your subconscious is free to mix and match various alternatives and solutions from the material it absorbed during the preparation phase. Osborn suggests that sleep is one of the best ways to spark illumination, because it rests your mind—which increases your powers of association.[7]

You will probably find that pulling away from your work requires conscious effort. It's natural to want to finish or "tidy up" a writing project. "One of the hardest things for me," volunteered John, a salesman in a recent Write-Now workshop, "is to get away from my article. When I've finished the first rough draft, I keep writing until the piece is completed."

How well I know that compulsion to keep going! When I was working on a series of articles on adoption agencies in Philadelphia, I felt that I had to keep writing until I had all three pieces finished. I left no time for them to gestate. If I watched TV or went out with friends over a weekend, I felt guilty. I thought I should be working on the articles.

Distancing Yourself From Your Writing

Many writers experience this feeling of being absorbed in their work. It takes discipline to train yourself to engage in mind-diverting activity when you reach the gestation period of the creative process. The following Write-Now exercise will help you let go of your work for a time. The exercise has worked for me and other writers who want to make the most of the incubation stage.

Write-Now Exercise
Pointers for Gestation

Goal: To enjoy time away from a writing project so that the subconscious will work and produce a finished product.

1.
2. Do steps 1-3 of the Write-Now exercise as outlined on pages 22-23.
3.

4. See yourself making coffee. You fill the pot with water, measure the amount of coffee you need, put it in the filter lining the top container, and put the pot on the stove or hot plate of the coffee maker. The contents combine to make coffee.

5. Now, imagine that you're engaged in a mind-diverting activity. Silently repeat the following suggestion ten times: "My article/story/book is like the coffee. All the necessary ingredients are simmering in my sub-conscious mind; my mind will take the time it needs during the gesta-tion period to blend everything together."

If you do the exercise at bedtime, drop off to sleep.

If it's daytime, complete the exercise and say, "When I open my eyes, I'll feel great."

Do the above exercise prior to each gestation period for future writing projects until it becomes natural for you to let your subconscious do its work without interruption.

The Illumination Stage

The insight about a new character or an appropriate opening for your article might strike you like a bolt of lightning—as it did Carla. At that moment, you've passed into the illumination stage of the creative process. It's sometimes de-scribed as the Eureka! moment—out of the blue, you get the answer you've been waiting for. It's like finding a valuable ring after you've searched every-where for days and have finally stopped looking. To your surprise, you find it in some unsuspected place.

"Look sharply after your thoughts," said Ralph Waldo Emerson. "They come unlooked for, like a new bird seen on your trees, and if you turn to your usual task, disappear."[8] The answer/solution/insight to a writing question or problem can come at any time following the gestation period. This illumination stage might occur when you're driving to work, mowing the lawn, or playing baseball. You might hear, see, or smell something that causes the insight to flash into your awareness.

Henry Wadsworth Longfellow got the inspiration for his poem "Wreck of the Hesperus" as he sat by the fire one evening. Charles Darwin's idea about natural selection came when he was riding in his carriage; yet Darwin had spent years thinking about the idea during the preparation stage of the creative process. Albert Einstein, too, experienced illumination at seemingly unlikely moments—both while shaving and taking his children for walks.

W. I. B. Beveridge in his book *The Art of Scientific Investigation* reported:

> *Probably the majority of discoveries in biology and medicine have happened unexpectedly, or at least had an element of chance in them, especially the most important and revolutionary ones: chemotherapy, insulin, and penicillin.... It's the interpretation of the chance observation and the scientist has to recognize it and grasp it. Insight will often occur by chance following the gestation period.*[9]

But, as Louis Pasteur observed, "Chance favors the mind that is prepared." Your prepared mind has been busy going through your rough draft. Your subconscious has been working during the gestation period, and now it's time for you to seize the moment when your writing clicks into focus.

In a report on creativity appearing in *Success!* magazine, writer William Hoffer discusses a widely-held premise: "Creativity doesn't merely happen; one must prepare for and cultivate it."[10] During the first two stages of the creative process, you prepare to bring forth the insight you need. Thus you are more ready to capture it when it *does* come.

Hoffer tells the story of Art Fry, a scientist at 3M. While singing in his church choir, Fry became annoyed with the scraps of paper he used to mark pages of his hymnal. The pieces of paper kept falling out and landing on the floor. Then an idea struck him: he took some adhesive (considered to be a failure because it didn't stick very well) invented by a fellow worker and smeared it on small sheets of paper. "I found that it was not only a good bookmark, it was great for writing notes. It will stay in place as long as you want it to and then you can remove it without damage." The popular product, Post-It Notes, is the result of Art Fry's encounter with the illumination stage of the creative process.

Hoffer shares the story of another creative person, Paul MacCready, the chairman of AeroVironment, Inc., who had spent a lot of time experimenting with and attempting to build the first man-powered aircraft.

While on vacation, MacCready decided to get away from his preoccupation and do some studies of birds—their turning radii, flight speeds, etc.

"Suddenly," MacCready said, "I realized that the way to build the man-powered airplane was to make it more like a soaring bird—not tiny, but extremely large and lightweight." His invention is the Gossamer Albatross, the first man-powered aircraft to fly across the English Channel. As a result of his creation, the American Association of Engineers has named MacCready "Engineer of the Century."[11]

Ted, a salesman and former student of mine, experienced illumination about the emphasis of an article he had been writing. The inspiration came while he was fishing. "I threw my line into the water," he explained, "and suddenly it hit me why my article was all wrong. Instead of stressing how to meet the needs of the customer, I had been focusing on making the sale. Before going to the lake, I had read the article a dozen times and couldn't figure it out."

Planning For The Spontaneous

Though the moments of insight/illumination that writers and other creative people experience seem totally spontaneous, they don't happen by themselves. "There is such a thing as inspiration [illumination]," writer Phyllis McGinley believes, "but it is no miracle. It is the reward handed to a writer for hard work and good conduct. It is the felicitous words sliding, after hours of evasion, obediently into place. It is a sudden comprehension of how to manufacture an effect, finish off a line or a stanza. At the triumphant moment this gift may seem like magic, but actually it is the result of effort, [and] practice."[12]

As Alex Osborn suggests, getting a good night's sleep is probably the best way to prompt illumination. The next Write-Now exercise, done at bedtime, will prime your subconscious to enter the illumination stage. Before doing the exercise, write down on a 3x5-inch index card what you want your inner mind to reveal to you—what insight you hope to get. Maybe you want to change your main character to make him more solid; maybe you're not satisfied with your plot—it doesn't seem believable. You might be struggling with the theme for a poem or a suitable ending for an article. Write down whatever you'd like to discover. Read over all your notes and your rough draft before doing the exercise.

Write-Now Exercise
How to Prompt Illumination

Goal: To get the answers/insights you need from your subconscious mind.

1.
2. Do steps 1-3 of the Write-Now exercise as outlined on pages 22-23.
3.

4. See yourself reading your finished story/article/poem/essay/chapter/book. You're pleased with your writing because it contains what you've written on the index card.

5. Silently repeat this suggestion ten times: "I want a (mention what you wrote on the index card) for my story/article/poem/essay/chapter/book. I'll get my answer either in a dream or when I wake up."

Drop off to sleep.

Practice this exercise every night for a week. You should soon experience illumination. If you don't, try the same exercise for another week. If no illumination occurs, it could mean that your mind needs more information; your mind may be telling you that it can't give you an answer or some insight because you haven't asked it the right questions—you haven't given it enough material to work with. Go back to the preparation stage, get more information, and allow for a period of incubation before doing the exercise again.

The Verification Stage

After you experience illumination, you're ready to verify the new information you've received. The verification stage is a time for testing the validity of the insight/answer you acquired in the previous stage. Just as Darwin, Einstein, and Edison checked their new theories by experimenting in the laboratory, writers must test their insights in relation to their writing project as a whole. During this stage, you begin to see clearly how your writing should be developed. You blend into your rough draft the information you gleaned during the illumination stage; you verify the new material to see if it fits with the old. Is the new point of view in your article appropriate for your intended readers? Does the summary paragraph seem too serious when compared with the rest of the article? Is the last major point you added fully explained and tied in with the theme of your essay?

Now is the time to be analytical about and critical of your work. Whether you've used the S-O-S outline (discussed in Chapter 7) or some other guide for writing your rough draft, incorporate the new information into it. Ask yourself: "Is this the way I wanted this piece of writing to develop?" The answer to that question could mean writing one more rough draft—or ten more. If you continue to have difficulty getting your ideas down, repeat the Write-Now exercise for rough drafts detailed earlier in this chapter.

Many writers, scientists, and others need time for their ideas to become reality. The verification stage is a time of hard work. Genius rarely happens overnight. It is the uncommon artist who gets it right the first time around. Beethoven's notebooks indicate his compositions preceding the gestation stage were mediocre at best. After the gestation, illumination, and verification stages of the creative process, he was able to reshape the compositions into masterpieces.

A Time For Rewriting

The verification stage is a busy time for writers. The rough drafts of F. Scott Fitzgerald, Robert Penn Warren, Philip Roth, and other writers reveal that much of their talent came from conscious, painstaking labor and an understanding of how the gestation period worked to their advantage. Many of them rewrote their manuscripts dozens of times during the verification stage—changing, shaping, polishing, and perfecting—until they were satisfied with the final version.

Carla, Ted, and Lori, writers mentioned earlier in this chapter, used the following Write-Now exercise to help them rewrite their rough drafts to reflect the new insights and information they got during the illumination stage and to verify that it was what their writing needed. As a result of practicing the exercise, Carla changed her character's name; Ted refocused his article, writing it from the customer's perspective; and Lori included more of her own work experience in her writing.

Write-Now Exercise
Obtaining Verification

Goal: To test the new information received during the illumination stage and determine whether it fits in and adds to the entire piece of writing.

1.
2. Do steps 1-3 of the Write-Now exercise as outlined on pages 22-23.
3.
4. See yourself reading the final copy of your work. Answer the following questions: Does the insight I received add to this piece of writing?

Is the subject developed completely and accurately? Is the writing well organized?

5. Silently repeat the following suggestion ten times: "If the information I received during the illumination stage doesn't 'work' in my writing, I will know it. If there is anything that should be changed in this piece of writing to make it better developed or more organized, it will become apparent to me."

If it's bedtime, drop off to sleep.

If you do the exercise during the day, complete the exercise and say, "When I open my eyes, I'll feel great."

Do the exercise for five days during the verification stage; if you get any ideas about changes you should make, record them immediately. Then incorporate the changes into your writing. If the answer you received during the illumination stage proves inappropriate when you test it against everything else in your work, you may want to return to the preparation stage in search of more information about your original idea. Then proceed again through all the steps of the creative process.

Before sending your manuscript to an editor, go over the fiction checklist on pages 152 to 153, or the nonfiction checklist on pages 198-199.

In this chapter, you've seen how the Write-Now exercises can influence your creativity and enhance each stage of the creative process. The Write-Now method helps you improve your powers of observation and concentration and your ability to organize information during the preparation stage; shows you how to distance yourself and relax without guilt during the gestation period when your subconscious goes to work; prepares you to capture the moment of insight at the illumination stage; and finally, enables you to look objectively at your work during the verification stage to see if the new insight you received is truly appropriate for whatever you're writing.

In the next chapter, you'll learn how to further stimulate your creativity by using Write-Now exercises to plan your dreams.

You *can* learn to be more creative. You can condition yourself to accept and use the creative spark when it occurs. Psychologists have found that inventive, original ideas—the result of creativity—often come when you least expect them; but it's the prepared person who capitalizes on them. By practicing the Write-Now exercises regularly, your creative journey may be appropriately described using Robert Frost's words—it will, indeed, begin in delight and end in wisdom.

Notes/Chapter Two

1. Graham Wallas, *The Art of Thought* (New York: Harcourt Brace, 1926), p. 42.

2. Hart Day Leavitt and David Sohn, *Stop, Look, and Write!* (New York: Bantam Books, 1964), pp. 7-8.

3. Brewster Ghiselin, ed., *The Creative Process* (New York: New American Library, 1952), p. 147. (Current publisher, University of California Press: Berkeley, Calif.)

4. Malcolm Cowley, ed., *Writers at Work* (New York: The Viking Press, 1958), pp. 63-74.

5. Hart Day Leavitt and David Sohn, *Stop, Look, and Write!*, p. 8.

6. Alex Osborn, *Applied Imagination* (New York: Charles Scribner's Sons, 1963), p. 318.

7. Ibid., p. 325.

8. Ralph Waldo Emerson, *Essays First and Second Series,* ed. by Ernest Rhys (New York: E.P. Dutton & Co., 1906), p. 48. (Current publisher, J. M. Dent and Sons, Ltd.: London)

9. William I. Beveridge, *The Art of Scientific Investigation* (New York: Norton, 1957), p. 47.

10. William Hoffer, "Creativity, A Special Report: Innovators at Work," *Success!,* Vol. 32 (March, 1985), p. 56.

11. Ibid., p. 57.

12. Olivia Bertagnolli and Jeff Rackham, ed., *Creativity and the Writing Process* (New York: John Wiley & Sons, 1982), p. 72.

CHAPTER THREE

Your Dreams Can Make You More Creative

*Inventions, great musical compositions,
poetry, fiction and all other ideas for
original accomplishment come from
the subconscious. Give it the thought or
the material and keep it going with
a deep-rooted desire for performance
and you will get results.*

Dana Sleeth

CHAPTER OVERVIEW

1. How can you write twenty-four hours a day?

2. Why is it important for writers to plan their dreams?

3. How does the Write-Now method stimulate the kinds of dreams that can make you a better writer?

THE SUBCONSCIOUS MIND never sleeps; the creative process never stops. The gestation stage (discussed in the previous chapter) continues during sleep if you prepare for it. With the proper stimuli and regular practice, you can learn to use your sleeping hours to produce illumination through your dreams.

If you're a writer, that means you can "write" while you sleep. The key to achieving this seemingly unbelievable feat lies in knowing how to make the most of a very natural sleep phenomenon—dreaming.

Dreaming is a universal experience. People who say they don't dream, dream too; they simply have no recollection of it when they wake up. Researchers in dream laboratories around the country routinely monitor people during sleep. They know dreaming occurs during the R.E.M. (Rapid Eye Movement) or dream stage, when the eyelids flicker because of increased brain wave activity as measured by an EEG (electroencephalogram). People who are awakened during the R.E.M. stage can discuss their dreams in detail. Through such dream study, researchers are unlocking the mysteries of sleep and making dreams practical tools to promote growth and learning.

Almost all schools of psychotherapy recognize the importance of dreams in self-discovery and self-improvement.

Psychoanalyst Carl Jung recorded his dreams, images, and symbols in his diaries. His major psychological works evolved from them, including his theory of the Collective Unconscious. Jungian therapists ask their patients to keep dream logs.

Sigmund Freud believed that dreams were an essential activity that opened the door to the inner mind and served as an invaluable source of information to the person.

Though many mysteries about sleep and dreams remain, researchers have identified a number of dream characteristics. They have learned, for example, that dreams are like movies flashing in the mind. Dream events are imaginary, but they do relate to real experiences and needs in the dreamer's life. Let's say you have a tight deadline for an article. During the time that you're working on the article, you might have a dream in which you're driving a car to an important meeting. On the way, you get lost. The anxiety that you feel about being late for your appointment might reflect your fear that you won't finish the article on time.

Another interesting feature researchers have discovered is that you can hear, smell, touch, and taste in your dreams; often, you dream in color. We spend one-third of our lives sleeping; 20 percent is dream time. An adult has up to five dreams during an eight-hour period.[1] That means last night you may have been dreaming for nearly one and one-half hours!

In this chapter, you'll learn how to use that dream time to your advantage as a writer. By conditioning your mind with appropriate suggestions in the Write-Now exercises and planning the kinds of dreams you want, you will learn to use your subconscious to its potential.

Two Kinds Of Dreams

According to clinical psychologists Joseph Hart and Richard Corriere, there are two types of dreams: normal and breakthrough. Most dreams are normal dreams in which the dreamer is a passive observer who neither reacts to nor participates in the action. Watching a building burn and having no feeling about it would be a typical occurrence in a normal dream. One of my students told a Write-Now workshop about a normal dream in which she watched a truck hit a telephone pole. "It seemed as though I was watching a TV movie," she said matter-of-factly. "I had no reaction to it at all."

Normal dreams have a place in your writing life. They can help you make your writing more descriptive. If you want to vividly describe a beach scene in your story, you can plan a dream in which you'll see a beach. As an observer in the dream, you would notice all the details of the beach and later record them in your dream notebook. As a result of the dream, you'd be able to add interest and color to the word picture in your story; you could help your readers "see" the beach, "hear" the waves, "feel" the sand, maybe even "smell" the salty breeze.

During a breakthrough dream, however, you are aware of the dream. You feel anxious, joyful, or afraid; you may realize insights or come up with solutions to problems. You experience a direct breakthrough between your subconscious and conscious mind.[2]

You can learn to use breakthrough dreams as creative input for your writing. Such dreams can provide you with the mood or idea for a poem, article, or story. They can suggest missing links or identify misdirected conclusions in an analytical report or business proposal. In some cases, breakthrough dreams can even give you the elements of an entire piece of writing.

If you plan your dreams, the subconscious mind will draw from your memory bank the reactions to people, places, events, and experiences you've deposited there throughout your lifetime. A collage of your past can produce just the right character, plot setting, or theme for a current writing project. If you don't plan and record your dreams, you might miss this kind of breakthrough.

After thinking for several nights about a poem that could convey her feelings about depression, Anne, a beginning writer, had a breakthrough dream. "I dreamed I was alone in a large Victorian house," she said. "A foot of snow had fallen during the day; the wind drifted it against the door. As I looked out the window, I felt an overwhelming sense of isolation and depression. The blizzard served as the metaphor for depression in my poem."

Researchers in dream labs would agree that Anne had created the right conditions for planning (and having) a dream. They have learned that whatever thoughts you have right before sleep greatly influence the content of your dreams—as was the case with Anne's breakthrough dream.

When To Plan Your Dreams

Another important factor in dream planning is that a person be physically and mentally relaxed. The Write-Now dream exercises, therefore, are always started during the relaxed—or alpha—state when your subconscious is alert and ready to accept your suggestions. Writers interested in planning their dreams should be aware of the various stages of sleep so they can know when their suggestions are likely to be absorbed by the subconscious mind.

The optimum times to plan your dreams are in the alpha and early theta stages. Alpha brain wave patterns measured on an EEG range from 8–13 Hz (cycles per second). (For comparison, brain waves during the beta [wide-awake, active] stage that precedes the alpha period measure from 13–26 Hz.) As you become more relaxed, brain waves slow down to 4–8 Hz. Theta waves (which follow alpha waves) are associated with the near-conscious state and occur when a person becomes very drowsy. Theta waves decrease gradually as you become sleepier and more relaxed. If you can sustain the theta state for several minutes without moving into the delta state (where in deep sleep or unconsciousness the brain wave patterns range from 0.5-4 Hz), you increase your chances of having your planned dream.[3]

The only problem is that if you're exhausted at bedtime and you do the first three steps of the Write-Now exercise, you may be too tired to say the suggestions and finish the exercise. You may pass through the theta state quickly and fall asleep. In order to sustain the theta state long enough to say the suggestions, students in my Write-Now workshops record their suggestions (Step 5 of the Write-Now exercise) on a tape recorder. They repeat the desired suggestion into the tape at least twenty-five times.

When they are planning their dreams at bedtime, they do Steps 1-4 of the Write-Now exercises while in the alpha state. Afterward, they turn on the tape recorder and listen to the repeated suggestion while they become more and more relaxed and then go through the theta state.

A student in one of the workshops summed up the benefit she found in taping her suggestion. "I'm always so tired at the end of the day," said Val, a computer programmer. "It really has helped to listen to my taped suggestion. l used to drop off to sleep after I pictured my goal and never did complete the suggestions. Now I'm starting to have the dreams I plan."

A History Of Dream Planning

Contemporary dream researchers aren't pioneering the effort to plan or understand dreams. Ancient civilizations, too, were intrigued by dreams and knew the importance of planning them. Curative, prophetic, and inspirational dreams were an integral part of religious ceremonies and daily activities of the Greeks, Assyrians, and Egyptians—who all built majestic dream incubation temples in the faith that their dreams would cure them of illnesses.

They fasted, prayed, and pictured their dream goals for days before they planned to have their dreams. The Greek god Asclepius was said to communicate messages of health to the sick as they slept in the temples: researchers report that there were between three and four hundred dream temples in the ancient world for people wishing to be healed by Asclepius—who appeared in curative dreams sometimes in the form of a statue, a boy, or an animal.[4] The majority of people had a curative dream because they prepared for and fully expected to have one.

Dream incubation, or planning dreams for ideas to develop, has long been associated with creativity. Synesius, a bishop in North Africa in the fifth century, left records showing how dreams aided him with his writing and problem-solving. Authors, scientists, and artists throughout history have looked to dreams for ideas and insights. It has been said that Voltaire composed an entire canto of "La Henriade" in a dream. Similarly, Dante, Goethe, Milton, Blake, and Tolstoy were said to have been influenced by their dreams.

The three opening stanzas of "A Vision of Spring in Winter" were given to Swinburne in a dream.

J.B. Priestly dreamed his three essays—"The Berkshire Beast," "The Strange Outfitter," and "The Dream" in detail.

Rene Descartes, the famous mathematician and philosopher, had a dream one night that revealed his life's work would be in the fields of physics, metaphysics, and algebra.

"Let us learn to dream, gentlemen, and then we may perhaps find the truth," commented the German chemist Friedrich Kekulé after having a dream which helped him develop the benzene ring theory in 1865.[5] Indeed, a dream provided truth for the physicist Niels Bohr: as a student at Cambridge University in 1913, he had a dream from which he later proposed the system of quantum mechanics.

In his dream, he stood on a sun, his body enveloped by burning gas. Planets, attached to the sun by thin filaments, whizzed by him on a revolving course. Suddenly, the gas cooled, the sun solidified, and the planets drifted away. At that moment he woke up, realizing that he had just visualized a model of an atom. The sun in his dream was a fixed center and the planets were electrons, held in place by an energy field.[6]

Alan Huang, the head of AT&T Bell Laboratories Optical Computing Research had a dream which gave him the idea for the world's fastest computer. His recurring dream was of two opposing armies of sorcerer's apprentices carrying pails filled with data. Every night they marched toward each other. Sometimes they fought which resulted in tying themselves into a big red knot.

Then one night something different happened. The armies marched into each other but with no collision; they passed through one another—like light passing through light. Huang had been trying for years to develop an optical computer which would transmit data by means of tiny laser beams passing through prisms, mirrors, and fiber optic threads. Theoretically, it could work faster than a cray supercomputer, since light travels faster than electricity. The designs, however, were too cumbersome to construct.

Huang began to make sense of the dream. He saw the solution. Unlike electric currents, laser beams could pass through one another unchanged—like the opposing armies in the last dream. It wasn't necessary to give each laser its own direct pathway. Huang created the first optical computer. He showed the skeptics that lasers in a computer can process information. He encourages his staff to listen to the messages found in dreams.[7]

Writers, too, have long recorded (often in great detail) the influence of dreams on their writing. Robert Louis Stevenson revealed in his journal how the plot for *The Strange Case of Dr. Jekyll and Mr. Hyde* evolved. He had written an earlier manuscript on his theme but, dissatisfied with it, destroyed it. Because he needed money and wanted to sell his story, he began thinking about it again.

> *I had long been trying to write a story on this subject, to find a body, a vehicle, for that strong sense of man's double being, which must at times come in upon and overwhelm the mind of every thinking creature.... For two days I went about racking my brains for a plot of any sort; and on the second night I dreamed the scene at the window, and a scene afterwards split in two, in which Hyde, pursued for some crime, took the powder and underwent the change in the presence of his pursuers. All the rest was made awake, and consciously.*[8]

Bohr and Stevenson, along with other creative individuals, have used their dreams to solve problems they struggled with during their waking hours. To use dreams to their advantage, they realized the importance of dwelling on the subject or problem for days in advance of the dream that would help them. They also recognized the need to describe in detail what they saw in their dreams.

They performed what was a nightly ritual for ancient peoples who incubated or planned their dreams: they prepared themselves to have the dreams they wanted. First, they had to believe that dreams were important enough to assist them in their creative projects. Believing that, they opened their minds to all types of learning—travel, reading, the arts—and they saturated their minds with material related to their special interests.

How To Plan The Dream You Want

If you plan your dreams carefully, they will direct you to the writer's life that you want for yourself. You'll go beyond seeing the subject of your writing in your mind's eye while you're awake; you will also dream about it and thus gain insight that you can use in your writing.

To effectively plan your dreams, have a notebook and pen right next to your bed. Some writers use an 8½ x 11-inch loose-leaf notebook. (I use this type of notebook because the sheets can be easily added or removed and dividers can be inserted—for separate sections labeled characterizations, plots, fiction ideas, nonfiction ideas, themes, etc.) You can also use a tape recorder to record your dreams. But be sure to write them down in your notebook later, so you can analyze them.

In order for the Write-Now dream exercises to be effective, prepare to do them keeping in mind the following points:

1. Immerse yourself in your subject for at least four days before you plan to have the dream. (Saturate your mind with thoughts about your plot, character, poem, article idea, etc.)

2. Have a positive feeling that you will have a dream pertinent to your subject. Silently repeat ten times: "I'll dream about my main character, (name), tonight" or "I'll dream about my article on (topic) tonight."

3. Put your dream notebook by your bed. If you generally have trouble remembering dreams, begin the exercises when you've had a few days to unwind, to relax. Studies show that your dream time (R.E.M.) increases when your day has been free of tension and distractions.[9] People who relax, read, or engage in little physical exertion during the day have better dream recall and more dreams than those who spend tension-filled, hectic days.

4. Pick a time when you can wake up naturally from the R.E.M. state. Alarm clocks can cause you to forget a dream.

As soon as you wake up, keep your eyes closed. Try to recall as much of the dream as possible. If any words, recurring images, or sounds pop into your mind, try to link them to the dream. They often help you associate and remember other things in the dream. Don't think about work, taking a shower, or the coming events of the day. Cluttering your mind with these thoughts tends to make you forget the dream.

One of my students, a policeman, had a recurring scene in his dreams of being chased by trucks, bicycles, cars—even a train—while he was riding his motorcycle. He wasn't afraid, just bored. When he later tried to connect the dream to his writing, he recalled a chase scene in a story he had written a while earlier. "After writing down my dream the next morning," John told the class, "I re-read the story. I then realized how boring the chase scene was, so I took it out."

Describing Your Dream

Write down the description of your dream as though you were writing a rough draft that only you will see. (See the Write-Now exercise for rough drafts, pages

27-28.) Don't worry about spelling, punctuation, complete sentences, grammar, or neatness. The key is to record whatever you remember. Don't try to analyze the dream right after you have it. However, if some very clear message immediately comes to you, record it in your notebook.

Study the page from Lee's dream notebook on page 50. Notice the phrases, her reactions to the dream, and the stream-of-consciousness technique she used to record the dream. Her analysis of the dream as it related to her story is also included on the same page. (Lee actually wrote both the analysis and how she planned to change her character because of the dream later in the day, after she had time to reflect on the dream.)

It's very important to describe a dream *exactly* as you remember it. Calvin Hall, a dream researcher and the coauthor of *The Individual and His Dreams,* offers these suggestions:

> *When writing the description of a dream be as accurate and objective as possible. The description should portray exactly in words what one has dreamed in pictures, no more and no less. The manner used to describe a dream is similar to describing a play or movie.... Record the emotion associated with the dream.... If a person becomes sufficiently interested in dreams and pays attention to them, his recall will improve automatically.... Dreams reveal things about us that cannot be readily found from other sources.*[10]

"I used to think it was a waste of time to write down my dreams," admitted Jerry in one of the Write-Now workshops. "But when I didn't do it, I found out that I couldn't remember many of the details. It took me awhile to get used to writing before having a cup of coffee, but writing really improved my recall. The little bit of effort pays off."

Nathaniel Hawthorne similarly realized the importance of seizing the moment when your subconscious is ready to share its creative output with your consciousness. He described the state of mind that produces creative insight in this way:

> *[The] singular moment . . . when you have hardly begun to recollect yourself, after starting from midnight slumber . . . you find yourself, for a single instant, wide awake in the realm of illusions, whither sleep has been the passport. [In an hour like this the mind has a] passive sensibility, but no active strength, [and] the imagination is a mirror, imparting vividness to all ideas without the power of selecting or controlling them.*[11]

Plan A Dream About A Character

Let's say you want to plan a dream about the main character in your story because she doesn't yet seem like a real person to you. To prepare for the dream, write a description in your notebook of the character's personality, physical traits, tastes in music and art—whatever unique characteristics you intend to give her. (The Write-Now exercise on pages 126-127 in Chapter 6 can help you get a well-rounded picture of your character.) Read over the description of your character on five consecutive nights before doing the next Write-Now dream exercise, which will help you make your main character more true to life.

▼ Write-Now Exercise ▼
Characterization

Goal: To create a main character who is realistic and true to life.

1. Get comfortable in bed or wherever you plan to sleep. Noise should be at a minimum. Close your eyes. Take three or four deep breaths. Inhale through the nose. Take the air down to the diaphragm. Count to three. Exhale through the mouth.

2. Imagine that you're lying on a lounge chair near a pond. It is a pleasantly warm fall day. The surrounding trees reflect the reds, greens, and golds of their leaves in the water. All of nature is in harmony. You, too, feel that your mind and body are in harmony. (You can substitute another scene especially pleasing for you.)

3. Push your heels down on the bed/floor. Feel the tension; now relax them. Do the same thing with your hips, back, shoulders, neck, head, arms, and hands; push down against whatever surface they're touching, then relax. Tighten and relax the muscles while taking three deep breaths. Silently repeat ten times: "I'm becoming more and more relaxed." (The main objective is to relax your mind and body so that the subconscious will accept your suggestion.)

4. As you're dropping off to sleep, think about your main character and five of her physical and personality traits. How does she look? What color are her eyes and hair? Is she tall, chubby, feminine, pretty? (Try to picture her as you would your mother or sister.) Is she witty, charming, sarcastic, aggressive, bright, sympathetic?

5. Give yourself the following suggestion ten times: "In my dream, I'll see____, the main character in my story. I'll picture her face, see her in action, and remember all the details of the dream."

Drop off to sleep.

As you wake up the next morning, keep your eyes closed. Let the images that filled your mind during the dream return before you get out of bed. Then write down everything you can remember.

The first few nights after practicing the exercise, you may have a vague dream about your character; but each night after that, the dream will become more vivid. Subsequent dreams will give your character new dimensions. After reviewing the dream notes you've taken after several dreams about your character, incorporate these dream pictures into the character description you wrote earlier.

If you have a dream that doesn't pertain to your character, record it in your notebook anyway. You might be able to use it in a future writing project.

Don't be discouraged if you don't have your desired dream after doing the exercise several times. Be as confident as a master baker with a cake in the oven. He has mixed the proper ingredients; he knows that within a certain amount of time, the cake will be done. Checking the cake every five minutes doesn't help the baking process, nor does it cut down on the length of time required.

Likewise, if you've immersed yourself in your subject for a sufficient length of time, reviewed at bedtime your notes related to the dream you'd like to have, really believe that you will have the dream, and practice the Write-Now dream exercise, it will happen. Doubts and anxieties about when and whether you will have the dream don't speed the process along or improve your chances of having the dream tonight: they may instead interfere with your concentration on your goal and can even block the dream. Assume that you'll eventually have it, and you will.

Lee, a principal in an elementary school, couldn't figure out how to make her main character (Amanda) seem real. She listed all of Amanda's qualities (idealistic, intelligent, compassionate, pretty, petite, competent), but something was missing from her description of the character, a teacher in an inner-city school. Every night for a week, Lee did the Write-Now dream exercise for creating believable characters. Finally, she recalled this dream: Amanda is talking to her mother. The tone of her voice is disrespectful and sarcastic. In the next scene, she steals a pair of gloves from a department store.

Lee recorded the dream just as she had "seen" it. She later analyzed it. Below is a page from her dream notebook:

> *Amanda, mother, talking. Arguing in nasty tone. Why was she, Amanda, so disrespectful. Walking through department store, sees white gloves, steals. Puts in pocketbook.*
> *(remembers key words, images from the dream)*
> *What else did she do—gloves, nasty.*
> *(puts the images together; recalls the dream)*
> *Dream: Amanda talking to mother. Disrespectful tone and sarcastic. Next, Amanda in department store. Steals gloves. (puts the images together; recalls the dream)*
> *Message: Amanda, too good, not real, not human, no reader I.D.*
> *(realizes the message in the dream)*
> *New Amanda: now short-tempered, disorganized, buxom.*
> *(makes notes on how to change the character as a result of the dream message)*

After recording her dream, Lee re-read the character sketch of Amanda. Soon after, the dream message came into focus. She realized that Amanda had no flaws; she was too good to be true. Lee thought about her character and decided that a few negative traits would make Amanda more human.

The dream message and how it relates to your writing probably won't come to you immediately. More often, the realization hits you after you've had time to reflect on the dream. How you decide to change your character (or theme or plot) may or may not come directly from the dream itself. For instance, one of the changes Lee decided to make in Amanda was to portray her as disorganized. This specific negative trait wasn't suggested in the dream; rather, the message was simply to give her some negative characteristics.

Plan A Dream About Plot

Your dreams can do more than just help you round out your characters. They can also help you with the plot. When you're working on a story trying to think of enough conflicts to build to an exciting climax and a satisfying conclusion, sometimes you reach an impasse: Where should you go from here? Your dreams can provide you with realistic options, spicy subplots, and believable complications for your story.

To prepare for a dream that will shed light on your plot, make a list of the problems your main character must overcome. This will help determine if you've introduced too many or too few challenges for the character, and whether they're realistic or too farfetched to be believable.

Let's imagine that you're writing a rags-to-riches story about a man (Henry) who rises from an impoverished childhood to head his own corporation. You make a list of the obstacles you plan to give him along the way: Henry was an orphan; he had polio; he had no love in his life, or any confidence in himself; he tried to get a patent for a tool he invented, but an uncle who befriended him stole Henry's idea and applied for a patent in his own name.

If this were developed into a story, it might well tax rather than thrill your reader. Could one person have so many problems (and no positive strengths) and still become a success?

To help you see how you might change your plot to make it more believable, do the next dream exercise. You've already prepared for the exercise by listing in your dream notebook all the opposition your main character must overcome before the climax of the story. Read over the list of obstacles before going to sleep.

 Write-Now Exercise Plot

Goal: To create a believable and interesting plot with challenging obstacles.

1.
2. Do steps 1-3 of the Write-Now dream exercise outlined on page 48.
3.

4. You want to have a dream to complete the story you've started. Picture your main character. Read over the list of obstacles you've written in your notebook. Picture your character going through the motions of trying to solve the problem(s). See the climax and conclusion of your story.

5. Give yourself the following suggestion ten times: "The story will be completed in my dream. It will be like watching a movie."

As you fall asleep, concentrate your attention on having the desired dream.

Let's continue our rags-to-riches scenario. After practicing the dream exercise for a week or more, you may have a dream about a man (someone other than Henry) who is plagued with enough bad luck, social and psychological conflicts, and personal problems to try the patience (and sanity) of Job. The person in your dream has nothing to be happy or optimistic about. All his problems seem to be exaggerated. You feel exhausted from having watched this draining movie in your dream.

In your dream notebook, you list all the obstacles you recall from your dream; you write down everything that happened to the man. Later, you compare these complications with the list of obstacles you reviewed before doing the exercise. Suddenly, you realize the message in your dream and how it relates to your story: the dream message is that you've hampered Henry with more obstacles than are humanly possible to conquer. With that message in mind, you study your list of obstacles and see how you might plot your story differently—more realistically.

You decide that Henry could still be an orphan and have polio. But his main problem (and the pivot of your story) might be suing his uncle to retrieve patent rights to his invention. The obstacles (complications) would evolve from that main problem. Because of Henry's self-confidence and keen mind, you decide he's able to build a strong case against his uncle. He is awarded his patent rights; he goes on to manufacture the tool and make a sizable fortune.

Andy, a full-time writer and former student of mine, plotted an adventure novel that lacked suspense. The pace slowed after several pages; even *he* was unenthusiastic about it. In the story, Andy's main character, Don, was an experienced pilot heading a rescue team searching for survivors of a jet crash in the Adirondacks. After three drafts, and three attempts to pick up the pace of the novel, Andy decided to plan a dream to find out how to improve it. To prepare for the dream, he made a list of the complications he had included in the story to keep the plot moving. He practiced the Write-Now dream exercise for plot for ten days.

On the tenth night, Andy had a dream in which he saw Don running a race in which the task was to leap hurdles. After clearing three of them, Don didn't know whether he had the stamina to finish. Andy watched as his dream character kept him in suspense. Would Don continue, or drop out of the race?

The next day, as Andy was describing his dream, he realized why his own story wasn't exciting: Don didn't have enough obstacles to overcome; the story's climax was too predictable. As a result of his dream, Andy gave Don some additional challenges—new "hurdles" to jump. He also changed some of the story's circumstances to add suspense.

In the dream, Don questioned whether he had the stamina to finish the race. This element of self-doubt made the story interesting. Andy decided to give this same obstacle to his character. Instead of portraying Don as a seasoned pilot, Andy recast him as a pilot who had just gotten his license. In the original version, the rescue came on the second day of the search. In rewriting the story, Andy decided the rescue wouldn't come until the sixth day.

On that day, Don spotted the survivors; he knew that if he didn't land the plane before the blizzard struck, they would all freeze to death. He tried to radio for help, but his radio was dead. There was only one thing to do—land the plane. Self-doubt overwhelmed him. He was sure his inexperience would prevent him from bringing down the plane in the narrow clearing. The major conflict Don had was to overcome his fear and self-doubt in order to save the crash victims.

The changes Andy made turned his story around; the new plot left the reader guessing what would happen next. Andy had used his character's dream experience to help him improve his novel. (Incidentally, Don mustered the courage to do his job—he landed the plane and rescued the survivors.)

Plan A Dream About A Setting

The pictures you see in your dreams may themselves be useful in your writing. You may find that some of the descriptions you record in your notebook may have a legitimate place—just as they are—in your writing. This might be the case if you're having trouble picturing the setting for your story.

The following Write-Now dream exercise shows you how to plan a dream that will help you visualize a setting. As preparation for the exercise, visit a place similar to the one you imagine for your story. If you want the action to take place in the city, spend the day walking around one. Take notes on 3x5-inch cards; observe the people, traffic, noise, buildings, activities around you, the weather. If you don't live near a city, clip pictures from magazines and study them. Attend a movie with a big-city background.

In preparing for the exercise, you're trying to feed your subconscious enough information that it can rearrange it and release it to you in a dream.

Ernest Hemingway's imagination was so captivated by the sights and sounds of Paris that he was able to capture its beauty and uniqueness in his book *The Moveable Feast*. He describes the impact the city had on him.

> *If you are lucky enough to have lived in Paris as a young man, then wherever you go for the rest of your life, it stays with you, for Paris is a moveable feast.*[12]

Before you try the next exercise, you may want to read the parts of Hemingway's book that describe Paris. You'll see how his keen observations of the city enhance your ability to visualize it.

✒ Write-Now Exercise ✒
Setting

Goal: To create believable settings.

1.
2. Do steps 1-3 of the Write-Now dream exercise outlined on page 48.
3.

4. As you're drifting off to sleep see yourself standing on a busy street corner in a large city. You watch the cars pass. See people running to catch the bus. Kids eating lollipops. What kind of day is it? Is the city dirty? Overcrowded? Are the people friendly? Is it a European city filled with atmosphere and charm?

5. Give yourself the following suggestion ten times: "I'll have a dream about being in the big city that will be the setting for my story. I'll see the skyscrapers, the people, hear the sounds of traffic and other noises. I'll experience the feeling of being in a big city in my dream, remember it clearly when I wake up, and write a detailed description in my notebook."

Drop off to sleep.

The Write-Now dream exercise for creating believable settings can be adapted to your specific writing project. Steps 4 and 5 of the exercise will reflect the kind of setting you want to dream about. As with all Write-Now dream exercises, preparation for the dream is important.

Let's suppose you're writing a gothic novel. To prepare for a dream with a gothic setting, re-read some of your favorite gothic stories. Type or write out in your dream notebook five or six passages from them describing the interior/exterior of the house in the story, the surroundings, mood, and overall atmosphere relevant to the setting; record any other striking scenes that visually stimulate your mind. Circle all the words that create a mood or feeling. What did you like about a particular scene? How did the author make it effective?

Before going to sleep, re-read the gothic scenes you've selected. Prepare your mind and body for the relaxed state by doing the first three steps of the Write-Now dream exercise (page 48). Instead of seeing yourself on a busy street corner as you did in Step 4 of the previous exercise, imagine yourself in one of the gothic settings you read before bedtime.

Give yourself the following suggestion ten times: "The scenes that I dream about will have a gothic setting. The buildings, surroundings, and atmosphere will be unique, not like those I've read. When I wake up, I'll remember the dream and describe it in detail." Then drop off to sleep.

When you wake up, record your dream scenes in your notebook. Write down your sense impressions: strange noises, bright colors, evocative smells. What kind of mood did the dream scene elicit? What did the buildings look like? Was the atmosphere mysterious? Where was the setting—in the country, near the ocean? What time of year was it?

Julie, a part-time writer and homemaker, had a difficult time creating an aura of menace for her gothic novel. She wanted to suggest a kind of evil passed down through the generations who had lived in her eerie mansion. After practicing the dream exercise for settings, she had the following dream:

> *I was visiting the gravesites of my great-grandparents. I noticed a strong, unidentifiable fragrance coming from a row of shrubs near the tombstones. The scent was getting stronger. I began feeling sick, so I left the cemetery quickly. I walked for about two blocks and began noticing the same fragrance as I passed a dilapidated house. It was frightening, mysterious—like death was following me.*

Julie told our class that when she woke up she was still a little bit afraid. But she wrote down everything she could remember from the dream. She said she was surprised she could smell something in a dream.

> *When I used my dream notes to describe the front yard of the mansion, I included the shrubs with the sickening and foreboding scent. I had one of the minor characters experience the same reaction I had to it in my dream. She tried to warn the house's new occupants of the imminent danger that might befall them. I was satisfied with the sinister mood that my dream helped create for my story.*

As with other Write-Now dream exercises, it's important to have confidence that you will eventually have the dream you've planned. If you do the dream "setting" exercise for a minimum of two weeks, you'll begin to "see" different scenes for your story. Take notes every day. Make a special notation of any sounds, smells, or images in your dreams.

Dreams That Generate Article Ideas

The Write-Now dream exercises are effective tools for nonfiction as well as fiction. All writing requires you to draw on your creative abilities to make the material interesting and relevant for your readers. Your dreams can suggest article ideas and even help you see how to improve the essay, report, or magazine article on which you're already working.

You can get an idea for an article in a dream by reviewing the seven categories you identified for yourself in Chapter 2, pages 22-24. (The idea-generating exercise in this chapter is different from the one in Chapter 2 because you're getting information in a dream that you've planned, rather than receiving the information when you're wide awake.) Concentrate on one of the life categories as preparation for this dream exercise. If you want to discover an article idea in your dream, prepare for it by thinking about the general category (job, family, hobbies, etc.) you think you'd like to write about. Ask yourself questions that pertain to the category.

If you already have an idea in mind as a result of the Write-Now exercise in Chapter 2, use this information as part of the preparation for the dream exercise. In this case, you want your dream to give you insight on how to develop the idea you already have. Review any information you have recorded/collected on the subject in your notebook. (You may have done some preliminary research or talked to people about your idea.)

Saturate your mind with information related to the life category or specific idea you would like to dream about.

Write-Now Exercise
Dream About Article Ideas

Goal: To discover or gain insight on how to develop an article idea.

1.
2. Do steps 1-3 of the Write-Now dream exercise outlined on page 48.
3.

4. See your finished article as though it were a television documentary. Personalize it as much as possible by visualizing how your topic will affect people who read your writing. (If your article is about pollution, taxes, radiation, illness, etc., what impact does the subject have on your readers?) Is the article convincing? Well-documented? Interesting?

5. Give yourself the following suggestion ten times: "I'll have a dream about how to develop (mention your topic or general 'life' category). I'll be able to recall the dream when I wake up."

Drop off to sleep.

The next morning, write in your dream notebook any ideas, images, or words that appeared in your dream. Combine this new material garnered from your dream with information you already have on your subject.

A few years ago, while teaching high school, I was assigned two college prep classes and two classes of students with low academic ability. Almost immediately, I noticed how students labeled themselves and others according to whatever group they were in. I heard students in the low academic ability group categorizing themselves (and being categorized) as "stupid," "dumb"—even "retarded"—simply because they were in the "slow" group, as they called it. Kids in the "fast" group, on the other hand, saw themselves as "smart, gifted, confident" and far brighter than their classmates assigned to what they labeled the "dummy" group.

The custom of ability grouping had set up a caste system in the school. I felt it was a demoralizing and unnecessary consequence, and I wanted to write an article about the situation and its detrimental psychological effects on young people.

I practiced the above Write-Now dream exercise, selecting my "job" as the subject. I planned a dream that would give me an idea of how to convey to readers the lasting negative effect that ability grouping had on a child's self-image. Every night for a week, I reviewed all the information I had collected through research on the subject. Then I had this revealing dream:

> *I was standing in front of the school waiting for the nine o'clock bell to ring that would signal students to go to their classrooms. The kids couldn't see me so they spoke freely. I watched the students in the "fast" group talking and laughing. The ones in the "slow" group were quiet and didn't seem happy to be there. When the bell rang, students from the "slow" group went over to the "fast" group and took their books and lunches and carried them to their lockers. The college prep students showed no appreciation for the gesture, since it was expected behavior.*

When I woke up I wrote the scene quickly in my dream notebook. I listed key words that popped into my mind as I recalled the dream: separation, slaves, expected behavior, no self-worth, inferior, unhappy, dummy. Contrast same-age kids, same school, but the "fast" group: confident, cocky, unsympathetic, haughty, master, intolerant, unfair.

I combined these elements with the statistics, case histories, facts, and anecdotes I'd already gathered and subsequently wrote the article, "Is School Ruining Your Child?"

Dreams That Sharpen Your Objectivity

What if you've already landed an article idea, have developed and written the piece, and have tried to sell it to a magazine—with no success? Maybe you find it hard to look at your work objectively? Maybe you can't see the defects in your writing, but you sense something is wrong with the piece. If you can't recognize flaws, you can't correct them. A dream may be able to give you some clues.

As preparation for the next dream exercise, select a short article (minimum five hundred words) from a magazine or newspaper every day for one week. Read each article carefully. Ask yourself the following questions: Did I understand the article? Was it well documented? Did it hold my attention? Why? As a reader, you become an objective critic of someone else's work. You want to have this same type of objectivity toward your own writing. The following Write-Now dream exercise will help you develop and sharpen your objectivity toward your work.

Before doing the dream exercise, read over your completed article every night for ten days just before going to sleep, and again at some point during the day. The purpose here is to fill your mind with the material so your subconscious can go to work sifting through it.

Write-Now Exercise
Objectivity

Goal: To be more objective when reading your work.

1.
2. Do steps 1-3 of the Write-Now dream exercise outlined on page 48.
3.

4. You are the reader instead of the writer of your article. Just as you objectively read someone else's work when you read the magazine or newspaper article, you are able to read yours in the same way. As

you're studying the article, ask yourself: Do I understand this? Is it well documented? Organized? Does it hold my attention?

5. Give yourself the following suggestion ten times: "I'll read my article as though I am the reader instead of the writer. I'll be totally objective and delete anything that is inappropriate. In my dream, I'll discover my writing problem."

Drop off to sleep.

The next morning make a note of any hints you received in your dream about weak areas in your writing. Maybe you looked bored in your dream; that might suggest that the article isn't interesting enough and might not hold the reader's attention. If you've tried different techniques to improve your writing prior to doing this dream exercise, your dream may even reveal how you might correct your writing problem. In other words, if your mind has already been tuned in to thinking about how to improve your writing, the information you've given it may be rearranged and filtered back to you in the form of a solution.

Read your article again. Take some action on the weaknesses in your writing that became apparent in the dream. The message in your dream may not surface immediately. It might take several weeks of doing the exercise to have a breakthrough dream that focuses on the trouble spots. Keep in mind that an ingrained habit—such as presenting technical material without the "human element"—may take a while to break.

You can also plan a dream to help you incorporate certain creative traits into your personality.

In his book *Your Key to Creative Thinking,* Samm Baker claimed that at least ten mental elements are essential in continual creative thinking and resultant ideas: desire, alertness, interest, curiosity, thoughtfulness, concentration, application, patience, optimism, and cooperation. These findings are based on studies and research done by psychiatrists, writers, editors, and others.[13]

I'll suggest possible dreams for some of these traits or you can make up your own to prepare yourself to have a specific dream review the four points on page 46. At bedtime do Steps 1-3 of the Write-Now method (see p. 22-23).

Desire, a factor in stimulating the creative process, might wane as you are working on your story. After you're completely relaxed, say that you will have a dream in which you see yourself looking through a magazine. Your byline and story catch your eye. Feel the sense of accomplishment that comes with being a published author. Say to yourself ten times: "I have a strong desire to be a writer. I enjoy working on my short stories."

Alertness, the second quality of a creative person, refers to being completely aware of what is going on around you. Many people sleepwalk through life missing the essential things. Henry David Thoreau said the reason he went to Walden Pond was "to front only the essential facts of life, and see if I could not learn what it had to teach, and not, when I came to die, discover that I had not lived. I did not wish to live what was not life, living is so dear; nor did I wish to practice resignation, unless it was quite necessary."

Prepare to have a dream where you are in a situation that increases your alertness. You could be walking down a narrow street in a small village in Europe. Notice the buildings. How old do they look? Are the people friendly? What characteristics stand out most in the village?

Repeat ten times: "I am alert to the essential things happening around me."

Being interested in learning more about your topic is imperative. That requires reading a sufficient amount of resources for an in-depth understanding of the subject. Some writers don't like to do research. The result is an article lacking credibility because of poor substantiation.

Plan a dream in which you see yourself answering questions about your article. Your knowledge impresses your audience.

Say ten times, "I am genuinely interested in the topics I write about and I'll take sufficient time to research them."

Curiosity is another trait common to creative people. As Heraclitus, the philosopher said, "If you do not expect the unexpected, you will not find it, for it is not reached by search or trail." Sometimes what we're looking for in our writing leads us to something else. Trying to find the right anecdote for an article might spark an idea for a short story: Keep your mind open to a variety of creative possibilities.

If you're not as curious about life as you'd like to be, design a dream in which you look at it not through your eyes but through the eyes of a five-year-old child. How do you think he would react to playing with a kitten or puppy; running under a sprinkler on a hot summer day; or riding on a merry-go-round? Can you sense his excitement? The experiences delight him. Your life's experiences can also excite you when you're inquisitive and open-minded.

Repeat the following ten times before going to sleep: "I'm curious about life and this reflects in my writing."

Make it a point to look at one unfamiliar thing a day as a child would see it, i.e., a flower, a new word, an unusual recipe. Find out more about it. Get off the road of the routine and travel an unchartered path for a creative change in your thinking.

In his book *Strategies of Genius*, psychologist Robert Dilts explains how some of the world's geniuses developed their creativity. Leonardo DaVinci's amazing ability to bring his paintings and inventions to life occurred because he was able to see things more deeply and with greater understanding than other people. He called this ability "Saper Vedere" or knowing how to see. The purpose of "Saper Vedere" is to work with the deepest essence of an idea and to create something new.

DaVinci would review before going to sleep the main outlines of the forms he was developing or other projects he was working on to fix them in his mind and understand them better.[14]

Thoughtfulness, another creative quality, deals with considering all the parts of the whole in a deliberate, thoughtful way. When solving a problem, it's looking at every aspect of it as well as possible solutions.

In a writing situation, the inability to begin and end a story might pose a dilemma. Getting readers involved at the start and tying things together at the finish can be a major challenge.

Before doing your dream exercise, read someone else's short story you enjoy. After you finish ask yourself: What was it about the beginning that got me interested? What did I like about the conclusion? After doing steps 1-3 of the Write-Now method, read your entire story. Re-read the beginning and the ending. Tell yourself you'll dream about your story and when you wake up you'll have new insights about how to change it.

Say ten times, "My stories hold the interest of my readers—especially the openings and closings."

Make a note of any information in your dream journal that you get in a dream.

Concentration plays an important role in creativity. If you can't keep your attention on your writing, completing it becomes impossible. Daydreaming and getting side-tracked with distractions can be reduced by doing the Write-Now exercise designed to heighten concentration on page 79 in Chapter 4.

Application, another element in creativity, means literally applying time and energy to the writing activity.

Writers who procrastinate keep their careers from moving forward. By letting rough drafts for stories, nonfiction books, novels, or poems accumulate without refining them or trying to get them published (if you choose) is like letting flowers die because you couldn't be bothered to water them.

Patience in creative thinking implies returning many times to the problem until you arrive at a workable solution; this applies to writing as well. How easy it is to give up when an article doesn't turn out the way you planned. That's when you need to be a critic and look objectively at your work and edit it.

If impatience is one of your shortcomings, identify the area(s) where it's most evident, e.g., getting your manuscripts rejected, not improving your writing skills quickly enough.

Arrange to have a dream in which you're learning how to do something which requires patience and practice. Maybe you're being taught how to play the guitar or use a computer. Feel the satisfaction in knowing you have the patience to continue until you've mastered the skill. Repeat to yourself ten times: "I show patience in all areas of my life including my writing. (Mention the area where you tend to be impatient.)

Optimism fuels creativity. Calvin Coolidge said "Cynics do not create." Isaac Singer believed that "If you keep on saying things are going to be bad, you have a good chance of being a prophet." Being too critical of your writing in the early stages and telling yourself that you can't express your ideas as well as some- one else, will very likely make your prediction come true. Self-confidence and enthusiasm boost your optimism even during the difficult times. An editor once told Louisa May Alcott that she would "never be able to write anything for public consumption." She had a positive attitude and proved him wrong.

If you have a negative attitude about some part of your writing, construct a dream which shows you involved in that aspect, e.g., outlining a book, devel- oping a character. Before going to sleep, picture yourself completely absorbed in the activity and very positive about the outcome. Say ten times, "I'm optimistic about my writing."

The final trait, cooperation, is the desire to share ideas with others. Cooperative people, secure in their abilities to express themselves, welcome input and constructive comments about their writing.

If you are overly concerned about what your readers' reactions will be, have a dream where you are in a comfortable setting, e.g., your living room, kitchen, and you're reading your story/poem/article aloud. The group responds with helpful, constructive criticism and praise. Say ten times, "I appreciate com- ments about my writing. It will help me improve so I can share it with others."

Use your imagination to compose a dream to capture the characteristic you want. Phrase a suggestion that embodies the picture and repeat it ten times after doing the first three steps of the Write-Now method.

Work with one trait at a time and prepare to have a dream several nights a week for three weeks. Record in your dream journal what you recall as you wake up. Later in the day, make the changes in your writing project which your dream revealed.

Psychologists involved in the field of dream research claim you can get answers to your questions in dreams.

Dr. Gayle DeLaney said in her book *Living Your Dreams,* "It is possible to direct your dreams by conscious intent. You can ask yourself a question before you go to sleep and awake in the morning with an answer to your question."[15]

Have you had the experience of going to bed worrying about a particular problem? The next morning the solution popped into your mind.

The answer escaped you during the day because your mind was too tense. But when you went to sleep, it relaxed and released information based on a lifetime of stored experiences, events, and feelings. Like a computer, it collates various probabilities and arrives at a conclusion.

The same thing happens when you pose a question about a writing problem. First access the problem and decide what insight you need to solve it. Before bedtime, write the problem down in detail in your dream journal. If, for instance, you're having trouble creating dialogue, explain why it's an obstacle.

Write down the question that you want answered in your dream, e.g., "How can I write believable dialogue for my novel?" Re-read the description of the problem. Do steps 1-3 of the Write-Now method. Say, "How can I write believable dialogue for my novel?" ten times. Return to the question if your thoughts wander. Have it be the last thing on your mind as you fall asleep.

The final step before getting out of bed in the morning is to recreate the dream. Be aware of an answer you received and record it in your journal.

If you want to discover why you lack certain creative qualities, e.g., the ten discussed previously, you could make up a question to be answered in a dream—"Why don't I have the desire to finish my short stories?" Follow the same procedure as outlined above to get a response.

To find out how to be more curious ask, "How can I become more conscious about what's going on around me?"

To understand why it's difficult for you to concentrate while you're writing pose the question, "Why can't I concentrate when I'm writing my novel/ short story/poem?"

Disciplining yourself to sit down and write on a regular basis often causes an inner struggle that's sometimes hard to resolve.

John Steinbeck wrote in his journal about the importance of disciplining yourself. "There is no possibility. . . of saying, 'I'll do it if I feel like it. I must get my words down everyday whether they are any good or not.'"

If sticking to a writing schedule presents a problem and you're not sure of the reason, ask, "Why do I lack the self-discipline to write regularly?"

Having trouble marketing your work? Scrutinize the latest edition of Writer's Market. Match your article, book, short story, etc. with the appropriate magazine or publisher. Ask yourself before sleep, "Where should I send my article/book/(other)?" or "What would be the best market for my short story/ (other)?"

Keeping your desk and writing materials organized makes you a more efficient writer.

If you're not sure why you tend to be disorderly say ten times, "Why am I disorganized with my notes?" or "Why do I let junk pile up on my desk and accumulate in my files?" Maybe too much emphasis was placed on neatness when you were growing up and it's an unconscious rebellion on your part. By correcting the problem, you simplify the mechanics associated with writing.

The questions listed below ask for answers in dreams to specific writing problems. Reword them to fit your own needs:

1. How can I get more story/book/article ideas?

2. Why are my articles so dry?

3. How should I organize my nonfiction book?

4. What type of subplot can I add to my novel to make it more interesting?

5. How can I make my characters in my short story more real?

6. Is there a way to overcome my nervousness when I interview people for my articles?

7. Why am I so judgmental with my writing?

8. How can I proofread my material more carefully?

Therese, a nonfiction writer picked the first question. She modified it slightly. "What is a good idea for an article?" After the third night she had a rather unusual dream: A friendly monster pushing a baby carriage said to Therese, "Why are you afraid of me?" Therese replied, "I'm not." "Yes, you are. Everyone is," the monster insisted. Then the monster took her to the edge of a cliff and told her to look down at the valley. The beauty overwhelmed her.

Therese recorded the dream in her journal. The monster was a mystery at first until she thought about what had happened during the previous week. She had an appointment with her doctor. He recommended a change in her medication because of the side effects and prescribed a new one for her arthritis. She was leery about taking an experimental drug and interpreted the monster to be a symbol for the medicine. The monster's question, "Why are you afraid of me?" showed Therese's anxiety about the drug. The promise of relief was reflected in the peaceful valley.

Therese realized all of the ideas for articles provided by the dream: 1) What are the latest experimental drugs for arthritis, cancer, aids, diabetes, the flu, and other illnesses? 2) How do certain medications affect the unborn child? 3) What kinds of testing procedures and approvals are required for experimental drugs? 4) Are acupuncture and acupressure effective treatments for back pain and other health problems? 5) What are the current holistic approaches to healing common illnesses without using prescribed drugs? 6) What are some of the serious side effects of the new drugs?

The dream gave Therese many ideas to develop into articles.

Carrie got an unusual answer to the question she asked before sleep. Concerned about not making the deadline for her story, her nervousness made it difficult to focus on her writing.

She posed the question, "How can I finish my story on time?" The next day, instead of being tense when she woke up, she felt relaxed. The answer did not come in a dream but rather in a kind of message—"stay calm." Throughout the day she repeated the message along with the phrase "I'll get the story finished on time," and she did.

Whether you use your dreams to help you get published or to help get you going toward that end, you will find they have much to offer. Dr. Patricia Garfield, a leading researcher in the dream field, has studied extensively how ancient civilizations used dreams to solve problems. She recommends that modern civilizations do the same.

> *You can discover creative products within your own dreams. In a manner roughly similar to the way ancients incubated dreams, you can deliberately induce dreams of artistic creations or dreams that solve your problems. You can use a technique in which you plan the general content of your dreams, but in this case you are seeking a creative product rather than advice or healing. Your dreams can become your own muse, your own source of inspiration.*[16]

In this chapter you've seen how writers and other creative people not only plan their dreams but use the stuff of their dreams to enhance their creative product. The Write-Now dream exercises provide you with a technique that lets you tap your creativity twenty-four hours a day.

Many successful fiction and nonfiction writers recognize that sleep can be a productive activity. Ideas for articles and ways to develop them can be revealed in dreams. Plots can be acted out by your characters on the movie screen of your mind. Messages that provide insights into your creativity and ways to enhance it await you in your dreams—*if* you condition yourself to accept messages from your subconscious mind.

By planning your dreams, your subconscious will continue to work while you sleep. "Give it the thought or material and keep it going with a deep-rooted desire for performance," Dana Sleeth, a successful journalist and believer in the power of the subconscious, advises. You, too, will get results.

Notes/Chapter Three

1. Harry J. Kyler, "The Dream Process: Current Insights," *Intellect*, Vol. 103 (January, 1975), pp. 259-262.

2. Richard Corriere and Joseph Hart, *The Dream Makers: Discovering Your Breakthrough Dreams* (New York: Funk & Wagnalls, 1977), p. 24.

3. Elmer and Alyce Green, *Beyond Biofeedback* (New York: Dell Publishing, 1977), pp. 120-121.

4. Lawrence Cherry, "Sleep's Biggest Riddle," *Science Digest*, Vol. 89 (July, 1981), p. 62.

5. Carl Glassman, "Sleep on It: Using Dreams," *Science Digest*, Vol. 89 (July, 1981), p. 65.

6. Ibid., p. 67.

7. Jason Forsythe, "Breakthrough Ideas: The Dream Machine," *Success!*, Vol. 37 (October, 1990), p. 36.

8. Robert Louis Stevenson, "A Chapter on Dreams," *Memories and Portraits, Random Memories, Memories of Myself* (New York: Scribner's, 1925), p. 172.

9. L. C. Johnson, "Are Stages of Sleep Related to Waking Behavior?" *American Scientist*, Vol. 61 (May/June, 1973), pp. 326-338.

10. Calvin S. Hall and Vernon J. Nordby, *The Individual and His Dreams* (New York: New American Library, 1972), pp. 160-161, 163.

11. Richard J. Jacobson, *Hawthorne's Conception of the Creative Process* (Cambridge, MA: Harvard University Press, 1965), p. 121.

12. Ernest Hemingway, *The Moveable Feast* (New York: Charles Scribner's Sons, 1964), p. ii.

13. Samm S. Baker, *Your Key to Creative Thinking* (New York: Bantam Books, 1970), pp. 27-29.

14. Bryan W, Mattimore, "Strategies of Genius," *Success!*, Vol. 39 (October, 1992), p. 26.

15. Gayle Delaney, Ph.D., *Living Your Dreams* (New York: Harper Collins, 1988), p. 8.

16. Patricia L. Garfield, *Creative Dreaming* (New York: Ballantine Books, 1974), p. 37. (Latest edition: Simon and Schuster: New York)

CHAPTER FOUR

Organizing Time and Tools for Writing

If time be of all things the most precious,
wasting time must be the greatest prodigality,
since lost time is never found again;
and what we call time enough always proves
little enough. Let us then up and be doing,
and doing to the purpose; so by diligence
shall we do more with less perplexity.

Benjamin Franklin

CHAPTER OVERVIEW

1. Why is it necessary to have a specific time and place to write?

2. How can you develop the self-discipline to stick to your writing schedule?

3. How can the Write-Now method help you organize your writing life?

WHEN I GET HOME from the office, the evening flies by. There never seems to be enough time to write. Finding a quiet spot and getting my writing supplies together is almost impossible with three kids running around," explained Jim, during a discussion of time awareness.

Life circumstances such as these can encroach on your writing time. And it's easy to blame people and situations for *your* unfinished projects. How often have you said to yourself: "If only I had a place to write away from the roar of the crowd," or "I'd get so much writing done with just an extra hour and a decent typewriter."

Many of my students in the workshop admitted having these thoughts as they identified with Jim's situation. How could they put some order into their writing lives? To help them find potential writing time, I asked them to write down one thing they enjoyed doing once a week for at least an hour. Golf, aerobics, tennis, and gardening topped the lists of leisure activities. Then we looked at how the students made time for these pursuits.

Jim played golf on Sunday afternoons. How did he manage to practice his game every week? He said that he always set aside at least an hour for golf; he knew just where to go to play; he knew right where his clubs were; and he looked forward to the weekly golf excursion.

These same factors that made golf something Jim looked forward to can help *you* make time for writing. Even if you're managing a household, working two jobs, and trying to keep ahead of repairs on your house, you still have time to write poetry, essays, or romance novels. But first, you must create an atmosphere conducive to writing—just as Jim created a weekly opportunity to play golf.

A Writing Environment

This atmosphere for writing includes having a specific time and place set aside for writing. It means having your writing materials organized and readily accessible. If you're frustrated with your lack of writing time, space, and equipment, you're likely to be too absorbed in these preoccupations to write productively. You may be as thwarted in your writing as Jim was before he learned to apply the Write-Now 3-T method of organization.

This three-part plan consists of the following elements: an awareness of *Time,* a *Table* or desk on which to write, and writing supplies and reference books kept *Together.* With this approach you'll see that a little organization goes a long way in a writer's life. Sometimes it can even encourage creativity to flourish. Let's see how.

For the creative process to work, your imagination must be stimulated. Part of that stimulation comes from creating an optimal writing environment— one where your subconscious mind can find inspiration. For that to happen, you must write on a regular basis. "Unconscious (subconscious) work is not possible, or in any case not fruitful unless it is first preceded and then followed by a period of conscious work," believed Henri Poincaré, the mathematician who developed the Fuchsian Functions.[1] In other words, before and during your writing sessions, you must fill your mind with information about your subject.

In this chapter, you'll learn various warm-up exercises that help release your creative juices. You'll learn how the Write-Now 3-T method of organization and the related Write-Now exercises can help you create a productive atmosphere. And you'll discover how if you *want* to write, you can find time to do it. No matter how busy or overextended you are, if writing is important to you, then you can make it an integral and satisfying part of your daily (or weekly) routine. Moreover, you'll look forward to your writing sessions.

Developing Time Awareness

Time management expert Dennis Hensley, author of *Staying Ahead of Time,* recognizes the importance time plays in a writer's life.

> *Every successful writer must have a way of using and controlling his time and know how to use it. First, realize that there is enough time in which to develop a writing career. A work day consists of eight hours. That means there are three full eight-hour workdays in each twenty-four hour clock day. If you work one eight-hour workday at a regular job (housewife or executive) and sleep away another eight-hour workday, you still have one bonus workday to use as you wish.[2]*

To help you develop time awareness—the first "T" in the organization— plan think about how you spend an average day. What do you do between

7:00 A.M. and 6:00 P.M.? If you work outside your home, the day is probably well-structured. Where could you possibly carve out even fifteen minutes of free time—time enough to write? During a lunch break? Between meetings? Let's say you take a bus or train to work. Your round-trip travel time is forty-five minutes. How could you transform thirty of those minutes into writing time?

As you take your seat, you begin watching people. They get on and off at their stops; you try to imagine what kinds of jobs they have. Can you tell from their appearance how they feel about their work? Such casual observations could be kernels of story ideas. If you're a prepared writer, you keep a small 5x7-inch notebook in your pocket, briefcase, or purse. In it, you make notes and record thoughts about your writing, about life, about people on the bus. You realize that writing time isn't limited to the minutes or hours you actually spend at your desk. You know that using whatever time, whenever and wherever you have it, is the key to making time work for you.

Dan, a bookkeeper in one of my workshops, used his travel time to think through and write a story. He was developing a plot about a man just out of prison after ten years. Dan planned to work on his story for twenty minutes while riding the bus to the office each day. He listed in his small notebook all the problems the former inmate might have trying to explain his lack of work experience and references. Every day that Dan boarded the bus, he focused on his story and concentrated on his character. He didn't waste ten or fifteen minutes trying to figure out what to write about; he simply took notes on the thoughts he had about his story. After a few months, the plot line began falling into place; Dan's character became more and more believable. In fact, most of the story was written on the bus—using twenty minutes every day.

If you're a homemaker, your day probably isn't as structured as that of a person who punches a time clock or takes clients to lunch. If you have young children, you do certain things while they nap. You might read a newspaper, pay bills, or talk to friends on the phone. When can you set aside thirty minutes for writing? And when you can't write, are you still open to *thinking* about writing? Maybe an idea pops into your head while talking on the phone; don't let it escape. Jot it down; describe briefly how you might develop it. (This is material for the subconscious, which can later mold the idea into a piece of writing.)

Don't forget to consider evening or after-work hours when you're looking for potential writing time. What's your schedule from 6:00 to 11:00? What daily and weekly responsibilities do you have? What leisure activities do you manage to take part in?

To get a complete picture of your "average" day, keep track of your activities for a week. Note everything—doing dishes, taking a walk, going out for the evening, putting children to bed, listening to music, repairing the lawn mower, playing tennis, etc. Set up a chart in your writing notebook. (This is a separate notebook—different both from the dream notebook discussed in Chapter 3 and your pocket notebook mentioned earlier in this chapter.)

On the left side of the page, list all your waking hours. For each hour or significant number of minutes record on the right side of the page exactly what you did. At the end of the week, look back on each daily log and circle the times (each day) that you consider leisure time. Then go through the individual logs again and draw a line under those leisure times when you're absolutely free from distractions and interruptions. (Perhaps after 9:00 P.M. when the children are asleep, or before 7:00 A.M. when just you and the dog are up and about.)

Time For Writing

Where is the potential writing time in your daily and weekly regimen? Cheryl, a student in the Write-Now workshop, identified her writing time by using a chart to record her daily activities. Cheryl works full time, writes nonfiction part time, and has two children. She put the word "must" before activities that had to be done during designated hours.

Cheryl's "Typical" Day

(must)	7:30-9:00 A.M. -	Get up, dress, get kids and husband up, have breakfast, drive kids to school, drive to work.
	9:00 A.M.-12 P.M. -	Work.
	12:00-1:00 P.M. -	Lunch.
	1:00-5:00 P.M. -	Work.
	5:00-6:00 P.M. -	Leave work, go to grocery store 3 times a week.
(must)	6:00-7:00 P.M. -	Cook dinner, eat, wash dishes.
(must)	7:00-7:30 P.M. -	Help kids with homework.
	7:30-8:00 P.M. -	Do laundry 5 times a week.
	8:00-9:00 P.M. -	Watch TV or read, talk to friends on phone, spend time with husband.
(must)	9:00-9:15 P.M. -	Put kids to bed.
	9:15-10:00 P.M. -	Tidy up house, take shower, make kids' lunches (9:40-10:00).
	10:00-11:00 P.M. -	Watch TV, listen to music, read.
	11:00-11:30 P.M. -	Watch news on TV, get ready for bed.
(must)	11:30 P.M. -	Bedtime.

To help you analyze your own schedule carefully, let's take a closer look at Cheryl's. Most of it is fairly structured because she works from 9:00 to 5:00. Her leisure time between 8:00 and 9:00 in the evening is circled. This is time for relaxation, but because it's early in the evening, it's still possible Cheryl may be interrupted by her children, guests, or the telephone. Between 9:15 and 10:00 Cheryl may do any number of things around the house. Her uninterrupted leisure time is between 10:00 and 11:00 at night. During this hour, her time is generally her own. (Of course, no one's schedule is so fixed that interruptions don't *ever* occur during that time.)

To see how she might find some writing time in her day, Cheryl studied her log of evening activities and wondered how she might juggle things around. She finally decided that instead of fixing her children's school lunches from about 9:40 to 10:00 every weekday evening, she would do it before washing the dinner dishes when she was already in the kitchen between 6:00 and 7:00. Since the food and lunch supplies were readily available, she wouldn't have to muster momentum (as she did later in the evening) to think about counting out cookies and carrot sticks for her children's lunches. Everything was right there, and she found that both lunches could be packed in less than ten minutes while her husband and children cleared the table and put dishes in the sink. Doing the chore earlier in the evening gave her an extra twenty minutes of free time later.

To conserve her energy for writing, Cheryl decided to do the grocery shopping only once a week. She kept a grocery list on her kitchen bulletin board so she wouldn't have to make an unplanned stop to pick up some item after work. She also decided to do her laundry twice a week instead of five times. This gave her an additional one and one-half hours.

By rearranging and regrouping some of her evening activities, Cheryl found this much leisure time in her work week:

	Daily Tally	*Weekly Tally*
Uninterrupted leisure time	Monday-Friday 9:40 P.M. - 10:00 P.M.	1 hour 40 minutes
	Monday-Friday 10:00 P.M. - 11:00 P.M.	5 hours
Leisure time (subject to interruptions)	Monday-Friday 8:00 P.M. - 9:00 P.M.	5 hours
	Tuesday, Wednesday, Thursday 7:30 P.M. - 8:00 P.M.	1 hour 30 minutes
Total (possible) leisure time		13 hours 10 minutes

Cheryl was surprised to discover how much potential writing time she had in a schedule that earlier had seemed to offer little time for creative pursuits. By combining activities and identifying times when distractions were at a minimum, she was able to free up more than thirteen hours a week! How much of that time could be used for writing?

Cheryl chose not to consider the daily 8:00 to 9:00 P.M. time slot as writing time; she left that as personal time to use as she wished. In planning her writing schedule, she decided to spend at least five hours a week writing and knew she could stretch that to six hours and forty minutes by using the twenty minutes gained by making the kids' lunches earlier in the evening. She scheduled thirty minutes, three times a week, for prewriting activities. Her writing schedule looked like this:

Writing time. 10:00-11:00 P.M. Monday-Friday

(When she was working on an article or had a deadline, she worked from 9:45 to 11:00 P.M. If she was especially pressed, she could skip the news at 11:00 and write until 11:15.)

Prewriting time. 7:30-8:00 P.M. Tuesday, Wednesday, Thursday

(She used this time—when she could possibly be interrupted by children, husband, or phone—to check her writing supplies so that when she sat down to write, she wouldn't have to jump up for a pencil or run downstairs for a dictionary.)

Cheryl was pleased with her writing program and found that having a designated writing time helped make her sessions more productive.

Study your daily schedule carefully. Take particular notice of the circled leisure activities. Are there some that could be grouped together to give you either more writing time or a few minutes for prewriting activities? Unlike Cheryl's daily routine, your underlined activities may not occur at the same time every day. You might have thirty minutes of uninterrupted leisure time every Tuesday and Friday, an hour on Monday, and no uninterrupted time on Wednesday and Thursday.

Make the most of the time you *do* have. Isolate the hours you can designate as uninterrupted leisure time. Even if you start with just thirty minutes, three times a week, it's a start. Once the writing habit becomes part of your routine, look for ways to increase your writing time whenever possible so that you can eventually spend an hour or more every day developing your talent.

Morning And Night Writers

How often, how long, and when you write every day depends on you and your lifestyle. Mike, a former student of mine, mapped out his activities for a week. (He works from 9:00 to 4:00 each day and from 7:00 to 10:00 two nights a week.) By studying his log, he realized the best time for him to work on his science fiction novel was after midnight. "I like to relax after work—watch TV—when I'm not working at night. I'm basically a night person," he explained. "I get my second wind late at night and write for an hour or more."

You probably already have an idea of when your energy is at its peak. This is important to know so you can arrange your writing sessions to coincide with your energy levels. Are you a "morning" or a "night" person? Your biological rhythm cycles might give you a clue. A morning person's energy levels are high in the early hours of the day and drop in the late afternoon. Morning people experience an energy upswing after dinner and maintain a steady level of energy until about 10:00 P.M.

A night person, on the other hand, starts off the day tired, perks up around noon, and stays alert until after dinner. Night people feel their energy wane until about 10:00 P.M., when it picks up again and may continue into the wee hours of the morning.

You can determine which type you are by doing a mental and physical exercise at two different times of day. At 10:00 A.M., ride a bicycle, do some sit-ups, or jog for four minutes. Next, write something for the same amount of time (work on the rough draft of your article, story, or poem for four minutes). If you feel tired after the workout, chances are you're a night person. To find out whether you're a morning person do the exercises at 4:00 P.M. If you feel sleepy afterwards, it's likely the early hours of the day are your best time.

Sometimes, however, you can't arrange your writing sessions around your high energy times. Sometimes, circumstances dictate that a "morning" person must become a "night" person. Flexibility is important; you can't get locked into thinking you can only write at a certain time of day—because if your lifestyle changes, you might not be able to adjust to a new writing time.

When our children were babies, both of them would wake up around 8:00 A.M. Being a morning person, I got up at 6:00 and had breakfast with my husband before he left for work. I began writing at 7:00 and ended my session when the boys got up. That worked well until our sons decided they'd wake up at 6:30 and join us for breakfast.

This early rising schedule lasted for about a year. During that time, I rearranged my evening activities so that I could write from 8:00 to 9:00 P.M. on Monday, Wednesday, and Friday and from 9:30 to 11:00 P.M. on Tuesday and

Thursday. It took me a few weeks to adjust to functioning as a night person, but in time, the new schedule became natural and worked well for years—until our boys decided to wake up at 9:00 A.M. Then I became a morning person again.

Marilyn Durham, author of *The Man Who Loved Cat Dancing* and *Dutch Uncle,* is also a morning person. She has a schedule that makes optimum use of her most productive hours.

In contrast to Marilyn Durham, authors John O'Hara and Taylor Caldwell wrote mostly late at night and into the early morning hours. Norah Lofts splits her writing day—she works from 9:00 A.M. to 1:00 P.M. and again from 4:30 to 7:00 in the evening.

Barbara Cartland, author of over two hundred romance novels, begins her writing day at 1:00 in the afternoon. When her session ends two and one-half hours later, she's written 7,000 words! She says she orders her subconscious mind to come up with a plot and then she "sees" her characters in her mind's eye.[3]

Making A Commitment

If writing in the early morning or late evening doesn't appeal to you, look again at your daily schedule. The time you have for writing already exists somewhere in that schedule. There are no "extra" hours, and no writing project is accomplished by wishing there were: truth is, when you track your time for a week, you discover lots of wasted minutes—even hours. Much of this wasted time is really the *free* time you can translate into writing time. What are you willing to sacrifice? If you watch TV regularly for two hours every night after dinner, which three nights of the week could you forgo a sitcom and write for thirty minutes instead?

Make a commitment that some days, at designated times, *you will write.* The important thing is to set a regular time and *stick to it.* This "appointment" to write gets your mind used to the idea that at a certain hour on a certain day you will be at your desk.

Unfortunately, just scheduling writing sessions doesn't guarantee they'll be productive. Let's say you decide to write on Tuesday, Wednesday, and Thursday from 8:00 to 8:30 P.M. It is now 8:00 on Tuesday evening. Put yourself in the following scenario:

8:00   "Let's see," you begin to think aloud, "maybe I should do something with that idea I had yesterday." You write: *Smoking. Why you shouldn't . . . reasons . . . reasons.* Long pause during which you think, "Coffee—that's what I need to get my brain clicking."

8:10   You go to the kitchen and make a cup of coffee.

8:20   You return to your desk, pick up a pencil and write. *Smoking . . . a crummy habit.* "I can't write that—too general," you think. "Where's my felt-tip pen? Probably on the kitchen counter." You go to the kitchen, get the pen, and look for your cigarette lighter.

8:25   You're back at your desk. You begin to write. *Five reasons why you shouldn't smoke . . . I should talk . . . I'll write about when people get hooked on cigarettes . . . high school . . . and why.*

8:30   You notice the clock on the wall and think, "Enough for tonight. I'll write about something else tomorrow."

Total writing time: About 15 minutes
Total output: 32 words

The other fifteen minutes were wasted on rambling thoughts and self-imposed interruptions. There were no warm-up exercises to stimulate writing. What *could* you have done to create the proper conditions for a productive session? You might have checked to see that you had your cigarettes, lighter, coffee, and writing supplies on your desk *before* you sat down to write. Maybe you could have tried to concentrate more on your subject.

Concentrating On Writing

Now put yourself in this scene. It's 8:00 on Friday night. You're watching your favorite television program.

8:00   You think for a minute about making a cup of coffee as the opening credits of the show appear on the screen. "I'll make it later." You look for your cigarette lighter. It's probably in the kitchen. You don't bother to get up. You are quickly getting absorbed in the plot.

8:30   The show is over. You sat for thirty minutes without being distracted. Nothing interfered with your concentration.

Just as you avoided interruptions during your favorite television show, you can learn to avoid them while you write. You can transfer your ability to concentrate from one activity to another. Writing sessions, like leisure time, can give you a mental and physical lift. When you get caught up in the excitement of creating a poem or article, you will *want* to avoid interruptions. As a result, your writing sessions will be productive.

The Write-Now exercise below will help you focus on your writing. By practicing the exercise, you'll learn to value your writing time and use it wisely. Try it before each writing session for three weeks.

 # Write Now Exercise Concentrating on Writing

Goal: To set up a specific time for writing and to use the time only for writing.

1. Get comfortable in bed or an easy chair. Noise should be at a minimum. Close your eyes. Take three or four deep breaths. Inhale through your nose. Take the air down to the diaphragm. Count to three. Exhale through the mouth.

2. Imagine that you're lying on a lounge chair near a pond. It's a pleasantly warm fall day. The surrounding trees reflect the reds, greens, and golds of their leaves in the water. All of nature is in harmony. You, too, feel that your mind and body are in harmony. (You can substitute another scene especially pleasing for you.)

3. Push your heels down on the bed/chair/floor. Feel the tension; now relax them. Do the same thing with your hips, back, shoulders, neck, head, arms, and hands: push down against whatever surface they're touching, then relax. Tighten and relax the muscles while taking three deep breaths. Silently repeat ten times: "I'm becoming more and more relaxed." (The main objective is to relax your mind and body so that the subconscious will accept your suggestion.)

4. See a clock in your mind's eye. The time on the clock is the same as the hour you've designated for writing. If it's 8:00, you see the hour hand moving from 8:00 to 8:30.

5. Repeat to yourself ten times: "From 8:00 to 8:30, I will concentrate on my writing. Writing is important to me. When I open my eyes I'll be ready and eager to write."

After three or more weeks of doing the exercise, you'll look forward to your writing sessions and be better able to concentrate during them.

Journals, Diaries, And Letters

"Creative people in many fields have traditionally kept journals because the form encourages the creative process. The journal provides a place to deposit the first flash of creative imagination or experience. It allows you to capture the essence of the moment while it is vivid and fresh in your mind," said Tristine Rainer in her book *The New Diary*.[4]

A journal serves many purposes. It can be a trusted friend to confide in or a sounding board for solving problems. Privately releasing pent-up emotions frees you to write more openly.

Getting your feelings down on paper puts your life into perspective and gives you greater empathy with your readers and their needs.

Say, for instance, your spouse/friend has been overbearing lately. By internalizing this annoyance, you lose your concentration while you're working on your article. Write out a conversation between the two of you. Let him/her know how you feel. Be honest. After your tension is released you will be able to write. You're also better prepared to approach the person and discuss the situation.

Reflecting on your everyday experiences—raising children, establishing relationships, or coping with job stress—can not only be therapeutic but it can also be a source of ideas for writing projects.

That's what happened to Cathy Guisewite. She created the cartoon character "Cathy" as a reaction to her own work stresses in an advertising agency.

The conversations between "Cathy" and her coworkers and boss reflect the real Cathy's frustrations, hopes, and humor. She called them "doodles and dialogue" and had no intention of publishing her "doodle diary." Her mother encouraged her to submit them to Universal Press Syndicate which published them in a comic strip that is widely syndicated in newspapers and magazines around the country.

Your journal can contain blank pages for illustrations and writing. When trying to describe a house in a story, you can sketch one or cut a picture out of a magazine and paste it in your journal. It doesn't have to duplicate your description; it's just a stimulus to get you started.

A journal depicts a panorama of people, pictures, and experiences. One technique that helps capture their significance is descriptive writing. It can also improve your powers of observation and your writing style significantly.

Looking at a tree and seeing more than just a Birch tree, Robert Frost described his impressions in his poem "Birches."

Michael Blake used the journal in his novel *Dances with Wolves* as an effective way of describing John Dunbar's thoughts about living on the frontier;

his relationship with the Comanche Indians, especially Kicking Bird, the chief; and Stands With A Fist, the Indian woman he grew to love. You can do the same thing in your short story or novel.

Try this practice exercise in descriptive writing. Before beginning do the Write-Now exercise for writing rough drafts on pages 27-28. Select one person to write about. You can choose your best friend, neighbor, spouse, or a celebrity, historical figure, etc.

For five minutes write down in your journal only words that pop into your mind that describe the person. For another five minutes (or longer) write complete sentences using some of the words from your list. Be as descriptive as possible. Discuss the physical features as well as personality traits. What are his/her interests? Does he/she have a sense of humor? A sense of honor? Try to capture the real essence of the individual.

While giving you practice in writing it could also result in a character for your story. Real people often form the basis for fictional characters in many novels. Journal entries like this one allow your mind to incubate the information for later use.

If descriptive writing presents a problem, try a form of mind flow writing. Do the first three steps of the Write-Now method on pages 22-23 and write about whatever comes into your mind.

Maybe you're thinking about the movie you saw last night or how funny you must have looked on Saturday trying to ride your bike again after ten years.

Perhaps you've been considering some personal goals you'd like to reach. Write down a few of them, e.g., the kind of job you want to have in a year; what you want your weight to be in six months; and the activities you plan to do with your family next summer—camping, vacations, etc.

Now what are some of the things you need to do to achieve your goals? Take some courses to update yourself in your profession. Sign up for an exercise class. Start buying camping equipment. Write down your plans for making your goals a reality.

This type of "stream of consciousness" writing allows you to know yourself better. By communicating openly and honestly, you get a sense of the "real" you; the part of you that might be difficult to share with others.

Answer some of these questions in your journal: Are there any people in your life who intimidate you? Who do you genuinely admire? If you could change lives with someone for a week, who would it be and why? What is your favorite season of the year? How do you think you've changed in the last five years? What three things are you afraid of? Why? What do you think is one of the worst injustices in this country? How would you solve the unemployment and health insurance problems?

Make up your own list of questions and write several descriptive paragraphs about each one. Let your anger, apathy, or enthusiasm surface. Probing types of questions, especially personal ones, help clarify your thinking.

While writing, don't be editing simultaneously; it will interfere with the flow of your ideas. The novelist and critic, Virginia Woolf, felt that many writers inhibit themselves as they write. "Invisible censors," as she called them, have a negative effect on writing.

Journal writing should be spontaneous without concern for the mechanics of writing, e.g., spelling and punctuation, etc. By not being judgmental, the "invisible censor" will be eliminated.

Keeping journals private is a concern of most writers. Not wanting someone else to read material written for the purpose of self-awareness, personal growth, or other reasons is normal.

To insure the privacy of your journal, lock it inside a drawer, filing cabinet, or small safe. Designate a trusted friend or relative to destroy it after you pass away.

Journal writing allows you to witness your growth as a writer. When re-reading an entry made in the past, you'll notice the refinement in your style; regular writing makes this possible. You don't have to write a great deal; just write something every day.

Marjorie Holmes, author of numerous books and articles, and mother of four children, said when asked how she found time to write with her hectic schedule, "There were thousands of times when I thought I would go mad, mad, mad with interruptions and frustrations. Yet no matter what happened I managed to turn out a little something almost every day. Even a scrap of an idea or observation."

Professional writers need quality time to produce quality writing. To overcome interruptions and avoid writer's block, many of them record their thoughts in a journal or diary before working on their manuscripts.

John Steinbeck kept a journal from January 29 through November 1, 1951—the time he was writing *East of Eden.* The journal was written in the form of letters to his editor, Pascal Covici, at Viking Press. In the journal, letters to Covici appeared on the left-hand pages of a large notebook; the text of the novel appeared on the right-hand side.

Until the first draft was completed, Steinbeck wrote his editor a letter every day before resuming work on the novel. It was his way of "getting my mental arm in shape to pitch a good game." It was his way of thinking through the book; the letters were a kind of "arguing ground for the story."[5] Each letter was a warm-up exercise that prepared Steinbeck to write about 1,500 words of the novel each day; when the book was finished, he gave the journal to Covici. (Though Steinbeck didn't write the letters for publication, the journal was later published.)

Getting started is sometimes the hardest part of a writing project/session. Steinbeck's practice of writing a letter to a good friend (as he describes Covici in the journal entries) is a fine way to relieve the emotional stress writers sometimes feel as they confront a manuscript.

The fears and self-doubts that can creep into your thinking create stress as you begin to write: "Will this article be as good as the last one that was published?" "I can't seem to get my character off the ground; what's the matter with me ?" "What will my boss think when he reads this report?" A letter to a trusted friend may help you confront these fears openly so that you can deal with them. You need not mail or give the letters to anyone to experience the benefit of having written them.

Cecilia, a former student in my Write-Now workshop, writes articles about teenagers and their problems. Before beginning a piece, she writes letters to her niece and nephew, who are high school students. The letters help her picture her readers and their needs; they help her express her ideas in a way that would interest teens. Cecilia's unmailed letters allow her to empathize with teenagers facing decisions about whether to try drugs, alcohol, or sex because of peer pressure or poor self-image.

Cecilia's letters give her a chance to air her views about a subject without fear of criticism. They are a warm-up exercise that lets her test her own reactions to a subject before presenting it to her readers. Writing about a topic extensively in a letter stimulates Cecilia to think of different approaches for developing and writing her article.

Keeping a journal or diary or writing letters may be especially helpful if you're having trouble developing an idea. Write your letters or journal entries in a notebook; if you type your rough drafts, you may want to take Steinbeck's approach and divide your paper in half. Jot down on the left side the journal-type entries—your thoughts about the subject as well as your mood and perceptions at the time. Type the rough draft of your story or article on the right.

When I began teaching creative writing, I asked my students if they kept a journal. Only a few said they did. I suggested that during the first fifteen minutes of each class they try recording their random thoughts and experiences in a journal format. I encouraged them to be candid, personal, and descriptive because no one else would read these journals. It wasn't long before they admitted that all kinds of insights surfaced on those pages—as did characters, plots, and subjects for articles.

By keeping a journal, many of my students learned how to deal with the growing pains of being a writer. They wrote about what it felt like when they didn't feel like writing. They worked through some of the excuses ("I can't think of what to write about") that kept them from writing. They also learned that you don't write a perfect piece in the first draft; sometimes it takes four or five before you get it right. They learned, too, that your writing ability, like your body, must be exercised every day for maximum efficiency.

There were some students who initially had trouble coming up with ideas for writing projects. After a few months of consistent journal keeping, they resolved that problem. "Now I just go to my journal and read what I've written," said Bonnie, describing how she gets her ideas. "Usually the things that bother me the most—like violence, war, and poverty—serve as themes for my poems."

Journal writing isn't a new way to stimulate the Muse. Nor does it yield similar results for everyone. Though no two journals are alike, keeping one will likely influence your writing—if not today, then years from now.

Over twenty-four years, Henry David Thoreau kept thirty-nine journals. Some of his works, including *Walden,* were written from them. Journal writing heightened his awareness of himself and his sensitivity to nature. Through his journal entries, Thoreau transformed himself from "a parcel of vain strivings held by a chance bond together" to a person who kept pace with the sound of his own drummer for direction.[6]

After reading several of Thoreau's journals, I decided I'd keep one whenever I traveled. One year we drove to the West Coast from Philadelphia; in my journal, I described not only the places we visited and the people we met, but also my emotional reactions to the experiences. The Texas sky at sunset will remain in my memory forever. As we drove west into the setting sun, the sky surrounded us. No mountains or trees blocked the view; the sky met the ground at the horizon. As it grew darker, falling stars like fireworks lit up the heavens. I had the sense of being in outer space and feeling an incredible oneness with the universe. In my journal I included moods, feelings, and thoughts just as I had seen Thoreau record his. Ten years later, I still glean ideas for writing projects from my West Coast journal.

A "Working" Notebook

Best-selling author Phyllis Whitney keeps an elaborate journal notebook. But she hasn't always. In a magazine article written twenty years ago, and reprinted in *The Writer's Handbook,* Whitney explained why she keeps such a record. Early in her career, her students asked her how she planned her books. She realized then that her "planning" was actually a haphazard filing-away of character sketches and plot ideas. She also realized that there were long stretches of time when she didn't write. She decided to organize her time and writing materials. It was then that she made up her mind to keep a notebook—which she feels is the reason she became such a prolific writer.

Whitney's notebook is a 5½ x 7½-inch large-ring, loose-leaf binder—small enough to fit in her purse. She uses a separate notebook for each book she's working on. When she finishes a book, she removes her notes from the binder and files them away.

Whitney's "working" notebook is sectioned off—organized—in the following way:

1. Work calendar

This keeps her on a six-month schedule—two months for plotting, two months for writing the first draft, and two months for revising and typing the manuscript. To stick to her schedule, she draws a line down the center of each page. To the left is the number of pages she wants to do for the day; to the right, the actual number reached on that date. (Her normal pace is eight pages a day.)

2. Title ideas

She checks *Bartlett's Familiar Quotations* or reads poetry to get ideas.

3. Chronology

From her research, she records dates of historical events pertinent to her story and the time sequence of each chapter as it develops in the book.

4. Situation and theme

Listed here are difficulties that brought a particular character to the situation they're in. Without a conflict, you don't have a story. Whitney believes readers want a story to *say* something. The theme pinpoints what she wants to say through her characters.

5. Problem

Plot ideas are entered and developed here. The conflict the main character has to face is given; it must be a conflict he/she can handle. Whitney looks at the problems characters must face as goals that suggest action.

6. Development

Random notes concerning all possible angles of the story. When outlining her story, Whitney checks these so she recalls certain details accurately.

7. Characters

She lists characters' names and writes a sketch of each one. The descriptions change continuously throughout the book as the characters develop.

8. Additional

Rather than having to go back to Chapter 1 to make a change while she's writing Chapter 5, Whitney makes a note in this section that a deletion or addition is needed in Chapter 1. Later, when it's convenient, she makes the change in the actual chapter.

9. Bibliography

Whitney lists the books and other resources she used in her research.

10. Research

She records any topic she has researched and plans to use in that project.

11. Background

This is a list of scenes based on places she has visited. (Whenever she visits a place, she takes detailed notes on it in a small notebook.) Any of these might be used in her story.

12. Diary

Whitney uses a diary to get inside the head of a character who is hard to develop. On these pages, she lets the character talk in the first person.

Before she writes a word of her story, Whitney fills sections of her notebook; she "maps out" potential routes to her destination. This information gives her subconscious material to work with. While she's describing one scene, a plot idea might occur to her; she can record it in the appropriate section. She can thus work on different elements of the story at the same time. The blank spaces she experienced early in her career when she had trouble developing her stories began to fill up when she began her journal notebook. For Whitney, the notebook is a part of the first step of the creative process—getting an idea, gathering information about it, and analyzing it (preparation stage). From there, the creative process is on its way.[7]

Warm-Ups For Writing

Keeping a journal, diary, or notebook prepares your mind for incubation. There are other activities listed below that may also effectively serve as prewriting activities. Many of my students have found that these warm-up exercises help break the ice—so that after doing them, they can plunge into their writing with vigor and confidence.

Spend a minimum of fifteen minutes doing a warm-up exercise for each hour that you plan to write. (For a half-hour writing session, take about eight minutes for warm-up.) Do the exercises either in your writing notebook or in your journal. If, after four minutes, you decide that you've said all you can say about one exercise, choose another one. If you want to write longer, go ahead. These aren't rigid, timed exercises; rather, their purpose is to get your creative juices going.

Your writing during the warm-up exercises should be as free-flowing as it is in your journal or dream notebook. Don't worry about sentence structure, spelling, or punctuation: just start writing. Immediately after the exercises, begin working on your writing project.

These exercises help you overcome that empty feeling of "What should I write about?" as you stare at a blank sheet of paper. The warm-up writing differs somewhat from the kind of writing you do in your journal or dream notebook in that it's done immediately before your scheduled writing session.

☛ Write-Now Exercise ☚
Warm-Up Exercises

1. Pick a word that defines your mood at the time you're writing—e.g., sad, happy, romantic. Write several paragraphs about how you feel and why. This exercise can act as a catharsis to clear away emotional blocks that could inhibit writing.

   Let's say you're depressed when you begin your writing session. In your warm-up exercise, write about how you feel and why you feel the way you do. By doing this you recognize your depression and explain your reaction to it. The feeling will be out in the open and you'll be better able to take positive action to correct the situation.

2. Read a favorite poem or quotation and write your reaction to it. A literary "shot in the arm" or an insightful comment can stimulate an

idea. It can cause you to recall an experience, a person, or an emotion you may be able to write about.

3. If you're hoping to write a story during your regular writing session, use journalism's 5 W's to help you figure out what to say:

   Who—is the story about? List the characters.

   What—is the story about?

   Where—does it take place?

   When—does the story happen, i.e., time of day, year, era in history?

   Why—are you writing it? What is its theme? Moral?

   Before you begin your regular writing session, write a rough outline based on the 5 W's.

4. Review the research notes, character sketches, and plot outlines in your journal or notebook. This information has been incubating in your subconscious mind. The idea you're looking for may pop into your mind as you review your notes.

5. If you're keeping a journal, assign a separate page for each new day and put the date at the top of the page. You can write each entry in the form of a letter, as Steinbeck did to prepare for his writing sessions.

6. Picture the world through the eyes of your family pet or some other animal. What do you think he/she would say if he could speak? Let your imagination run free. You can write a dialogue in your journal between you and your pet. This exercise could result in a children's story.

7. Look at your high school yearbook picture (or one taken when you were seventeen or eighteen). Write down how your priorities in life have changed. What did you want to do when you got out of high school? Did you do it? How have your goals changed? Did you marry the type of person you dated in high school? What did you like about high school? Dislike about it? How do you think high school is different today compared to when you were a student? Write your answers in your journal. Do they suggest possible ideas for future stories or articles?

Like a car in winter, your creative muscles work more efficiently if you warm them up. You'll find it's easier to start a writing session if you've already aired your feelings or written freely about whatever's on your mind at the time.

Quality Writing Time

Once you've prepared yourself for writing, you want to ensure that your writing time will be quality time. Doing the next Write-Now exercise before a writing session will help relax your mind and body, both during the warm-up and writing periods. Even though you might feel tense when it's time to write—because of job or family pressures or a series of rejected articles—you can condition yourself to relax while you write. By suggesting to yourself that you're relaxed and by picturing yourself at ease, your attitude about writing will change.

It's important to be relaxed while writing because tension and anxiety can block your ability to express yourself. If you're worried about what your boss said to you at work, you're not going to be able to effectively write the opening paragraphs of your article.

Write-Now Exercise
Feeling Relaxed
While Writing

Goal: To be relaxed while you write.

1.
2. Do Steps 1-3 of the Write-Now exercise as outlined on page 79.
3.

4. Picture yourself at your desk. You have a relaxed and contented expression on your face. You're doing something you like—something you do well—writing. Your mind and body feel relaxed. Writing gives you a pleasant mental break from problems that might be disturbing to you. Focus on your story/article/book/poem. You feel as refreshed after a writing session as you do after a nap. You feel an inner peace.

5. Say to yourself ten times: "I am a relaxed writer. As ideas come to me I'll express them with ease. When I open my eyes, I'll feel good and I'll write with ease. I'll feel a sense of inner peace that enhances my

ability to express my ideas. I'm experiencing less and less stress, more and more inner peace."

Write-Now exercises help you value your writing time, and they help you relax, so the time is productive. They also help you develop mental discipline to stick with a writing schedule that allows you to complete projects without negative stress. (Not all stress is negative, of course. It depends on how it affects you. For some people, being a surgeon would be extremely stressful because of the risks involved; others—aware of the stress—may also be stimulated by the challenge. A certain amount of stress is necessary to motivate us—e.g., you put on a heavy coat when it's cold outside because of the elements stressing your body. More on stress and how it affects writers in Chapter 5.)

The Element Of Discipline

The secret is not to let stress keep you from developing your potential as a writer. To assume that potential, you need self-discipline.

Writers don't automatically acquire the habit of self-discipline after doing the Write-Now exercises a few times: it's something they have to keep working at. And as they do, they learn that managing and committing to their writing time are indications that, for them, writing is a serious business.

It's time for your writing session. To resist stretching out on the bed or sofa for just forty winks (which could easily become forty minutes) takes self-discipline. But then, so does anything else that's important to you—that you want to be successful at. Raising children requires self-discipline: sometimes you have to deprive yourself of free time or material goods so the children can have your guidance and the necessities of life. Likewise, doing a job well requires self-discipline. You may have to work late or take on new responsibilities in order to be successful in your work.

"Self-discipline was always the hardest part of writing for me," said Jack, a fiction writer. "But since I set up my writing schedule, I know I'll be at the typewriter from 7:00 to 7:30 each evening. I know I can quit when the time is up. I'm getting stories finished, and it's getting easier to stick to my schedule."

Most successful writers have had to struggle with self-discipline at some time in their careers. Even Erma Bombeck, whose writing seems so effortless, knows the rigors of disciplining herself to make time for writing. She understands that those writers unwilling to make the commitment may wait a long time for a byline.

> Some of them don't want to pay their dues—they want to get their house cleaned first, then write when they feel in the mood—or they want to wait until they're inspired. That's no good! I tell them they

have to have discipline. That's the only way, and it's serious business. My column appears three times a week, and I'm fighting for that space all the time.[8]

Thomas Thompson, author of the novels *Serpentine* and *Celebrity*, agrees that a genuine commitment to writing is a prerequisite to success.

You can't be a dilettante writer. So many people come up to me and say, "I'm going to write a book about my great uncle." I always encourage them, but talking about writing a book and actually writing a book are just incredibly different things. Nobody can write unless he makes a total commitment. You can't write on Tuesday night because there's nothing on television. Or on Thursday morning because you got up an hour early. Or on Saturday afternoon because it's raining. You have to write the same time every day. You have to get a routine going. Routine becomes a rhythm. I write every morning from eight to noon.... I write from wherever the story is when I last left it. If I can't get it going some morning, I'll go back and re-type three or four paragraphs from the day before. So if I'm stuck, I hope to build enough momentum to get over that hurdle . . . [I write] ten pages a day.[9]

A Table To Write On

Once you've disciplined yourself to the point of carving out a special time for writing, you should find a place (a table—the second "T" of the Write-Now 3-T approach to organization) where you feel comfortable. It should be a place relatively free from interruptions. If you're lucky enough to have a room where you can set up a table or desk, jump at the chance; however, if you must work in the basement or attic, that will do as well—as long as it's apart from the constant flow of people-traffic and distractions.

Get a desk or table with enough drawers for your supplies. This helps you stay organized so that when you need something during a writing session, it's readily available. A desk or table with drawers or compartments for your writing tools is as important as a closet or dresser drawers for your clothes. Everything is handy in your bedroom when you're getting dressed. (Imagine how disorganized and frustrated you'd be if your shirts were in one room, jackets in another, and your shoes scattered around the house.)

If you're using a writing table without drawers, you might feel the same frustration. If your own table doesn't have drawers, consider getting a children's bureau to put beside it for your writing supplies. A kitchen-drawer silverware divider can also solve the problem; it's a convenient holder for pencils, pens, erasers, paper clips, and tape.

A two-drawer file cabinet is also a good investment. It will help you physically delineate your writing space in a room. (Sometimes you can buy a file cabinet at a garage sale for a few dollars.) Round out your writing place with a straight-backed chair that gives your back the necessary support. Have a shelf nearby for your reference books.

Creating A Writing Place

The psychological impact of having your own place for writing is quite real: you begin to associate your desk with producing ideas and finishing manuscripts.

Carolyn is a children's writer who one day realized that her "desk" was the sofa, floor, bed, backyard—wherever she decided to write. "I was always looking for a dictionary or pen," she said. "I still write in those places occasionally, but now I have a desk equipped with everything I need. Once I realized how important a desk was, I decided to convert my sewing room into a writing room. I used to spend half of my writing time trying to find supplies and a quiet place to work."

My own experience with creating an optimal writing space was different from Carolyn's. After refinishing our basement, I added a desk, filing cabinet, and bookshelves. It was the perfect place to work during the day. But if I wanted to write at night, I was too far away to hear the children if they woke up or called for me.

I still keep my desk in the basement. But to solve the problem of where to write in the evenings, I use the dining room table. I have a large, sturdy canvas bag (similar to a shopping bag) in which I put all the supplies I need: paper, pens, paper clips, research notes. The bag is roomy enough to accommodate a dictionary, thesaurus, and a few other books pertinent to my writing. If I plan to write at night, I put these things in the bag during the day so I won't waste time looking for them when I'm ready to write. At the end of my evening writing session, I return the materials to my basement office for the next day.

This portable canvas "table" arrangement is also convenient if you want to write outside or in other parts of the house. If you want to work in bed, the canvas bag will bring your work "table" there; a lap board or sturdy tray can serve as a writing surface. Everything you need is in the bag. And if your writing project takes you far afield to a library or some other place, you can easily take the bag (filled with your "must have" supplies) with you.

Many variations are workable, but whenever possible, designate a table or desk as base. Before long, it will feel like home; you will develop an attachment to it. This sense of belonging is evident in John Steinbeck's journal description of *his* writing space.

> *February 12, 1951*
>
> *My first day of work in my new room. It is a very pleasant room and I have a drafting table to work on which I have always wanted—also a comfortable chair given me by Elaine. In fact I have never had it so good and so comfortable . . . I think my house is in order.*[10]

Keeping Writing Tools Together

Your "house" will also be in order if it holds the equipment you need—if it keeps all the tools of your trade *Together* (the third "T" of the 3-T method of organization). Little irritations such as not having the right book to look up a footnote or the right postage to make a deadline can annoy even the most dedicated writer. Worse yet, these minor aggravations might cause you to postpone your writing. As John Steinbeck wrote, "The cosmic ulcer comes not from great concerns but from little irritations."[11]

The checklist below is a brief rundown of some of the *basic* materials you should have at your desk or in your writing space. Keep in mind that this is a bare minimum for some writers. For more detailed information about the specifics (kind, cost, size, availability) of these items, consult appropriate writing titles in the bibliography at the back of the book.

1. *Block calendar*—Get a large wall calendar with plenty of room to record how long you write each day, when manuscripts are due, etc.

2. *Typewriter*—Get one that suits your needs. (You probably don't need an electronic model if someone else does your typing.) Even if you rarely type anything yourself, you may want to have a working typewriter on hand in case you want to see how a paragraph looks in type.

3. *Typing paper*—For rough drafts, use an inexpensive paper. For the final copy, buy a good grade of white bond paper (20 lb. with a high cotton fiber content—25 percent would be appropriate).

4. *Stationery*—If you can afford it, buy good-quality, white bond stationery that has your name, address and telephone number on it. Otherwise, use plain white bond for correspondence.

5. *Envelopes*—Use large (9x12-inch) manila envelopes for mailing manuscripts; long, white envelopes for correspondence.

6. *Carbon paper*—Unless you plan to photocopy manuscripts before mailing them, always make a carbon copy. Making copies of correspondence with editors (query letters, follow-up letters, etc.) is also a good idea.

7. *File cabinet*—A file cabinet will help you feel—and *be*—organized. Fill it with clearly-labeled folders containing newspaper and magazine articles that may stimulate ideas, enhance character profiles, and suggest plot possibilities and story themes.

8. *Postage scale*—This will save a lot of trips to the post office. Keep stamps handy so letters and manuscripts can be weighed and mailed from home. Be sure you have a chart of current postal rates.

9. *Bulletin board*—This helps you *stay* organized. Put your calendar on it, as well as reminders to yourself, outlines of plots you're developing, quotations or poems that motivate you, notices of writers' conferences, titles of books you plan to buy, etc. Use the bulletin board only for writing-related information.

10. *Miscellaneous supplies*—Keep the following supplies in your desk drawer: pens, pencils, pencil sharpener, rubber bands, paper clips, 3x5-inch cards, stapler, staple remover, ruler, reinforcements, notebooks, yellow legal pads, erasers, correction fluid and tape, mailing labels, scissors, cellophane tape, and an address book.

11. *Books*—*Webster's Third New International Dictionary* and *Roget's International Thesaurus* are the barest of essentials. You will, of course, fill your shelves with titles appropriate to your particular writing needs.

Being Organized

Be sure to get whatever supplies you need *before* you start a writing session. That's part of being organized.

The 3-T method of organization—Time awareness, Table, Together— puts you in charge of creating your optimal writing environment. The following

Write-Now exercise can be used with the 3-T approach to help you *feel* more organized—because you will be.

 Write-Now Exercise Organization Skills

Goal: To keep yourself and your writing materials organized.

1.
2. Do Steps 1-3 of the Write-Now exercises as outlined on page 79.
3.
4. See your desk or writing table in good order. Everything is organized so that it is accessible to you. You have all the supplies you need.
5. Give yourself the following suggestion ten times: "When I sit down to write, everything will be in place. I am an organized person and will keep my desk and materials orderly."

   If you do this exercise during the day, say, "When I open my eyes I'll feel great."

   If you do the exercise at bedtime, drop off to sleep.

June, a freelance writer, did this exercise for a month and soon began to notice a change in herself. "For a long time, I thought of myself as a disorganized person," she said. "But it never really bothered me until I realized how much time I wasted looking for things. I used to toss everything that I wanted to save into my desk drawer. After spending forty-five minutes one afternoon searching for some research notes I needed, I knew I had to get my things in order. After doing the exercise, I began to feel more organized. I was more conscientious about filing notes, keeping my desk reasonably neat and my supplies together. It took awhile to straighten things out, but in the long run I have more time for writing."

"We always have time enough, if we would but use it aright," advised Goethe. For writers, perhaps that should be gospel. The time for writing is available. By using the Write-Now 3-T method of organization, you'll find that time. You will also discover that suddenly your writing life isn't just organized, but productive, too.

Notes/Chapter Four

1. Alex Osborn, *Applied Imagination* (New York: Charles Scribner's Sons, 1963), p. 135.

2. Dennis Hensley, "The Time of Your Life," *Writer's Digest,* Vol. 62 (August, 1982), p. 20.

3. Arturo F. Gonzales, Jr., "Guess Who Writes 70,000 Words a Week, Publishes 24 Books a Year and Says 'Me Tarzan You Jane' Works Best in Sex Scenes," *Writer's Digest,* Vol. 59 (June, 1979), pp. 22-24.

4. Tristine Rainer, *The New Diary* (Los Angeles: Jeremy P. Tarcher, Inc., 1978), p. 292.

5. John Steinbeck, *Journal of a Novel, The East of Eden Letters* (New York: Viking Press, 1969), p. vii.

6. Odell Shepard, ed., *The Heart of Thoreau's Journal* (New York: Dover Publications, 1961), pp. ix-x.

7. A.S. Burack, ed., *The Writer's Handbook* (Boston: The Writer, 1970), pp. 26-35.

8. John F. Baker, "Erma Bombeck," *Bookviews* (March, 1978), p. 10.

9. Christopher Meeks, "Thomas Thompson, Celebrity," *Writer's Digest,* Vol. 62 (October, 1982), pp. 26-27.

10. John Steinbeck, *Journal of a Novel, p. 7.*

11. Ibid., p. 3.

CHAPTER FIVE

Dealing with Distractions and Obstacles in Your Writing Life

*The only limit to our realization of
tomorrow will be our doubts of today.
Let us move forward with
strong and active faith.*

Franklin Delano Roosevelt

CHAPTER OVERVIEW

1. How can the Write-Now method help you reduce the stress and fatigue that inhibit writing?

2. How do the Write-Now exercises help you block out noise and minimize physical discomforts that can hinder your writing efforts?

3. Why is it important to develop an attitude that nurtures your desire to write?

THE FINEST WRITING SUPPLIES, the most inspired setting for a desk, and all the free time in the world won't by themselves make you a successful writer. There's a great deal more that comes with the territory—not the least of which is learning how to deal with the distractions, annoyances, and day-to-day realities of the writer's life. In this chapter, we'll discuss ways that you can meet daily distractions and real problems head-on—and, in the process, develop a new confidence in your writing and in yourself.

Think about some of the distractions that interfere with your writing. What are the things that keep you from finishing (or starting) a project?

Over the years I've asked many writers in my Write-Now workshops the same question. Their answers reveal that they face both mental and physical distractions—some of which really threaten creativity. Lack of time and poor organizational skills, two hazards to writing discussed in the previous chapter, are mentioned frequently. The other major problems that regularly confront both novice and professional writers are these:

1. job stress

2. fatigue

3. noise and interruptions

4. illness

5. loss of confidence and poor self-image

To completely eliminate these real-life obstacles, we'd have to disassociate ourselves from earthly existence, but it's a realistic goal to learn to manage these problems and many writers have done it. H.G. Wells recognized it as not only an aim for success, but for survival.

> *If man did not soon learn how to adapt himself to the changes wrought in his environment by his scientific discoveries, he would become as extinct as the mammoth and dinosaur, who could not learn how to adapt to their changing world.*[1]

Allowing yourself to become distraught over disturbing situations and not finding a way to adapt to daily trials may even result in the extinction of your desire to write. Adaptability is *that* important to a writer's life.

Stress As A Writing Obstacle

Dr. Albert Schweitzer learned to cope with the distractions of his jungle surroundings and the stress of a hectic hospital schedule in order to write. In the book *The Africa of Albert Schweitzer*, we get a glimpse of the working conditions Schweitzer endured while—in his seventies—he labored on the third volume of *Philosophy of Civilization*.

> *Late at night, under the flickering light of a kerosene lamp, the Doctor labors at the writing table in his tiny study-office-bed-room.... As he finishes chapters, he piles them on the top shelf above his head. Chapters on which he is still working are hung by strings to nails behind him.*[2]

When asked how he managed to accomplish so much, Dr. Schweitzer claimed that he learned to use minutes because free hours never came.

The key to getting things done is to maximize the minutes and minimize the minutiae. The Write-Now method maximizes writing time and makes it quality time; the exercises in this chapter will show you how to minimize the minutiae—the distractions and interruptions that stand in the way of your writing.

Stress and fatigue are part of life. Part-time writers who work full time at other jobs often have a difficult time dealing with job-related stress and fatigue. These two serious distractions can whittle away at a writer's creative urge and writing time alike. Salespeople, secretaries, and executives all need something after their nine-to-five routine to alleviate stress and recharge their energy levels.

To reduce anxiety, some of them may turn to alcohol or other unhealthy diversions (or even to healthy diversions that nevertheless keep them from writing).

Lyle, an accountant in one of my classes, explained the exasperation of trying to work and write successfully: "It's usually a ten-hour day at the office. With all the deadlines, especially around tax time, and the heat from my supervisor, I'm really tense by the end of the day. I have a few martinis before dinner to unwind. Afterward, I usually fall asleep on the sofa. I just don't seem to have the energy or peace of mind to write."

High absenteeism, alcoholism, and job alienation that exist today in corporate and other work environments clearly reflect the stress and career pressures experienced by employees like Lyle.

Another kind of emotional strain is job burnout as seen among teachers, counselors, and others in the helping professions. These professionals sometimes have trouble detaching themselves from their emotional involvement with students, clients, or patients. When they get home, they're still thinking about work; this kind of preoccupation doesn't allow for the emotional release essential for creative work.

Jenny is a third grade teacher who knows well the all-encompassing aspects of her job. "I leave school every day at 2:30, but my mind stays there. I worry about whether the kids understood the spelling lesson or if I was too rough on them for forgetting their homework. It's hard to switch off emotionally at the end of the day and concentrate on writing."

Some of the writers in my workshop who were also teachers could easily identify with Jenny. They wondered about the feasibility of maintaining their jobs and pursuing their writing. How can people in high-stress, emotionally involving jobs muster the energy to write?

Dealing With Stress

To be effective as a teacher, business executive, or writer, you must reduce the stress precipitated by your job. By decreasing stress, your performance on *and* off the job will benefit. According to psychologist Robert Hicks, too much stress can kill creativity because it often keeps people from sleeping. Stress interferes with the R.E.M. period of sleep, the dream state in which our minds collate and sort through material. And a reduction of R.E.M. can result in a person's inability to think creatively.[3]

Both Lyle and Jenny found their creativity stifled by the stresses of their careers. By practicing the Write-Now exercise below they were better able to overcome the job-related tensions that had been keeping them from writing. The exercise will help *you* change your attitude about writing (even when you're tired); moreover, it will help you keep your peace of mind during a stressful day. Before beginning the exercise, read the first verse of Longfellow's "The Day Is Done."

> *The day is done, and the darkness*
> *Falls from the wings of Night,*
> *As a feather is wafted downward*
> *From an eagle in his flight.*[4]

See in your mind the vivid picture his words paint. The darkness descends gently, quietly, as it "Falls from the wings of Night." Think about the ending of a summer day: the sky retains the last tinge of rose as the sun lowers itself on the horizon. Nature readies itself for nightfall. Think of this scene for a few seconds before doing the exercise at bedtime.

Write-Now Exercise Dealing with Stress

Goal: To feel relaxed in a stressful situation.

1. Get comfortable in bed. Stretch out on your back and close your eyes. Noise should be at a minimum. Take three or four deep breaths. Inhale through the nose. Take the air down to the diaphragm. Count to three; exhale through the mouth.

2. Imagine the sun setting. Darkness is "falling from the wings of Night." See all of nature preparing for sleep. The night air is refreshing, and you breathe in and say five times, "I feel very relaxed." Sense the serenity. You feel very peaceful.

3. Push your heels down on the bed. Feel the tension; relax them. Do the same thing with your calves, hips, buttocks, spine, shoulders, hands, and arms: push down; release. Tighten and relax the facial muscles while taking three deep breaths. Silently repeat ten times, "I'm becoming more and more relaxed." (The main objective is to relax your mind and body so that the subconscious will accept your suggestions.)

4. See yourself during a working day—i.e., at the office, at home, on the road. Think of some of the things that cause tension and pressure—

e.g., asking for a raise, planning a budget, driving through traffic. Now see yourself reacting calmly in one of these situations. You visualize yourself having a discussion with your supervisor about getting a raise. You calmly present the reasons why you're entitled to a raise. (Substitute a scene appropriate for your situation.)

5. Say to yourself ten times, "I will think of the serenity of nightfall and my mind will be relaxed and at peace when I'm confronted with a stressful situation."

Drop off to sleep.

Problems With Fatigue

Fatigue is another barrier to writing that may or may not be related to your job and its stresses. If, for whatever reason, you associate writing with fatigue, then writing will make you tired.

"After sleeping late and wasting most of the day," began Mark, in one of my workshops, "I decided to go to the library and do some research on my article about the Phillies. But the thought of sitting there going through microfilm and newspapers to get the statistics on the players made me drowsy. The more I thought about it, the sleepier I got. Then a funny thing happened: Some friends dropped by and we played cards until 2:00 in the morning. I didn't feel tired at all."

Mark's negative association between writing and feeling tired kept him from accomplishing his writing project. Later, to break that association, Mark practiced every night for three weeks the same Write-Now exercise Joan (in Chapter 1) used. When he thought of sitting down to work on his article, he immediately thought of how energetic he felt when he played basketball. Gradually, his attitude about writing changed. (To refresh your memory of the visualization [picture] and suggestion for the Write-Now exercise dealing with fatigue, see Joan's progress check on page 14.)

Developing a good attitude about writing is important, because fatigue can be an effective deterrent to writing. To see why, think of activities that you associate with fatigue. They're jobs we all have to do, but try to put off: washing the kitchen floor, bathing the dog, and cleaning out the garage are favorite fatigue producers. (Add to that list: cleaning out the kids' closets.)

Now let's imagine that someone promises to pay you $100 every time you wash your dog. Who do you think would have the cleanest pooch in town? How would your attitude about the chore change? Undoubtedly, you'd (almost) look forward to sudsing up your mutt because there'd be a payoff—$100.

In the same way, the thought of writing won't ever make you tired if you focus on the payoffs—e.g., mental stimulation, ego satisfaction, money. Your attitude about writing will change. As with any other activity, if you're getting something positive from it, you'll look forward to doing it.

Sometimes, even when you enjoy writing, it's natural to feel tired when you have to do it. When I have a deadline for an article or book chapter, I occasionally feel this way. I know I'm not physically tired, but the thought of a long writing session triggers that "maybe I'll just take a nap" feeling. At those times, I do the following Write-Now exercise just before I start to write, and I feel energized.

The secret to making this exercise work is to see your writing project as already completed. Picture the month, day, and year that it's due. If you have no particular due date, just visualize the project completed.

Write-Now Exercise
Fatigue Associated
with Writing

Goal: To reduce fatigue associated with writing.

1.
2   Do steps 1-3 of the Write-Now exercise as outlined on page 101.
3.

4. Picture yourself standing in line at the post office counter. You have your completed manuscript all finished and ready to send to an editor. You feel pleased with yourself that you have met your (insert date) deadline.

5. Say to yourself ten times: "My article/story/book will be completed by (state the month, day, and year). I am able to meet my deadline."

When you finish the exercise, say, "When I open my eyes, I'll feel great."

Living With Noise

Sure to inhibit the flow of ideas for many writers are two other major distractions—noises and interruptions. Learning how to minimize these potential diversions and put your mind to your writing is the secret to dealing with them.

How do you do it? In just the same way that you can ignore background noise when you're caught up in a good book: you devote yourself to the story. To have the same keen focus on your own writing, you must block out annoying sounds and sharpen your concentration. Successful writers regularly do both of these things.

William Faulkner was able to ignore the constant ear-splitting noise of a dynamo as he wrote *Sanctuary* during his midnight-to-4:00 A.M. shift in the boiler room of a power plant. Shirley Jackson learned to target her concentration as she managed active careers as a writer and the mother of five children.

By using the Write-Now method, you, too, can rise above the din. What are the noises that disturb you? Loud music? Ringing telephones? Crying children? Whatever the source of your noise, imagine the following scene:

> *You've been sitting at your typewriter for twenty minutes. Finally, you get an idea. As you begin to type, the telephone rings. When you get back to your desk, your mind is preoccupied with the conversation you just had. Suddenly, outside sounds interrupt the silence. The neighbor's dog begins barking at the kids playing baseball in the backyard. You're distracted and mentally begin listing all the things you could be doing (mowing the lawn, cleaning the basement, etc.). You wonder why you've wasted the last twenty minutes writing.*

Sound familiar? Try the next Write-Now exercise. Before long, you'll be writing pages instead of paragraphs in the same amount of time it would take to enact the above scenario.

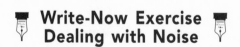

Write-Now Exercise
Dealing with Noise

Goal: To shut out noises while you're writing.

1.
2. Do Steps 1-3 of the Write-Now exercise as outlined on page 101.
3.

4. Picture yourself totally absorbed in your work. All around you is a glass wall. Large curtains cover the glass. When the curtains are open, you hear bothersome sounds; when they're closed, the disturbing noises go away. You feel very comfortable in the room, and you're pleased that you can't hear the distracting noises. It's so much easier for you to write without the annoying sounds.

5. Say to yourself ten times: "I am totally absorbed in my (article/story/book/report/etc.). The curtain shuts out all outside noises while I'm writing."

   When you complete the exercise, say, "When I open my eyes, I'll feel great."

Do this exercise right before a writing session for about three weeks. After a while, background noises won't interfere with your writing.

A variation of this exercise for writers who don't feel comfortable with the curtain imagery is to substitute the following for steps 4 and 5 above:

4. Picture yourself totally absorbed in your work. There is a large switch on the side of your desk marked "VOLUME." When the noises inside or outside your home/apartment/office distract you, turn the volume down. See yourself turning the volume down and shutting out the disturbance. You're very pleased that you can't hear the noise any more. It makes writing so much easier.

5. Say to yourself ten times: "I am totally absorbed in my (article/story/book/report/etc.). The volume is turned down and I am unaware of any noise. It's easier and easier for me to write under these conditions."

Ben is a real estate salesman who used the first "noise" exercise each day for two weeks to block out telephone and office conversations that went on during lunch—the time he set aside to work on his book dealing with buying property. "I could hear people talking," Ben told our workshop group, "but I wasn't interested in what was being said after I pulled the imaginary drapes while I typed."

The second Write-Now noise exercise worked for Shelly, who used to spend half an hour writing before breakfast every day. After taking a teaching job at the junior high school, she found that her mornings were too hectic to stick to her old writing schedule. Because she was determined to write, she decided to do so in her classroom before the students arrived. After doing the exercise, she found that the children's voices in the hallway didn't annoy her. In fact, the creative activity first thing in the morning seemed to put her in a positive frame of mind for the day.

The Incessant Telephone

It's possible that one person's noise may be another's inspiration. But one kind of distraction sure to interrupt your train of thought or surge of momentum is the ringing of the telephone. Yes, it *could* be an editor with an assignment, but more often than not, it's a neighbor, a solicitor, or someone calling to compare his math answers with your son's.

If telephone calls upset your writing schedule, you don't have to sit idly by and succumb to the miracle of telecommunication. You have workable alternatives that can ensure some quiet time for writing.

During your designated writing time, ask your family (or coworkers, if you write during breaks or lunch at work) to answer the phone and tell the caller that you'll telephone later. (This is what you'd do if you were watching the Super Bowl or washing your hair.) Do the same thing when you're writing: time on the phone can cause you to lose momentum.

Another option is to invest in an answering machine. This is a terrific idea if you or other members of your family get lots of calls. There's nothing more annoying than to be going full steam at the typewriter and have to stop in mid-sentence to answer the phone four or five times—especially if the calls are for someone else.

Several other ways to deal with Ma Bell and her competitors are to work in a room without a telephone in it or without one nearby. Another possibility is to write in a place far away from a phone. Occasionally, I go to a nearby park and write at a picnic table; I've yet to hear a phone ring there! You can also block out the sound of a ringing telephone with another sound. (See the Write-Now exercise on page 107.)

The key is to stay in control of your surroundings by establishing a firm telephone policy. Value the time you set aside for writing.

Neutralizing Noise

Sounds and noises in and of themselves aren't necessarily distractions to writing. In fact, you can actually use noise to minimize noise. Many writers find that it's easier for them to concentrate on their writing if there's a steady noise (e.g., an electric fan, an air conditioner) to drown out brash sounds such as those made by a budding musician practicing the trombone in the next room. Loud sounds that you can't eliminate (traffic, telephones ringing, dogs barking, carpenters hammering next door) can be neutralized with a steady sound.

Vicki, a mother of three, has learned to neutralize potentially disturbing clamor. "If I'm not responsible for the noise, I don't let it distract me," she told us in class one day. "There must be fifty kids in our neighborhood. If they're playing out in the front of the house and my husband is watching our children, the noise they make doesn't affect me. It becomes like the sound of the air conditioner running in the background."

If you can write peacefully with the washing machine agitating, a computer printer tapping away, or the dishwasher gurgling, you might consider "reacting" to other sounds—distracting noises—in the same way. The following Write-Now exercise will help you recast the sounds that interrupt your writing. Try the exercise when you want to write in spite of the racket around you. If you do the exercise for a week, you'll begin to see how useful some sounds can be to block out undesirable noises.

Write-Now Exercise Neutralize Noise

Goal: To neutralize distracting noises with acceptable, steady sounds that don't interfere with your concentration.

1.
2. Do steps 1-3 of the Write-Now exercise as outlined on page 101.
3.

4. Picture yourself at your desk. The noise that you hear in the background doesn't bother you. It's much like the sound of (name an appliance or something that doesn't negatively affect you) which doesn't disturb you when you're writing. You feel that the steady sound of the (name the appliance or whatever) will neutralize the loud noises and that your ability to concentrate will improve.

5. Say to yourself ten times: "The noise created by (give the type of sound) is like that of (name the appliance). It is not interfering with my concentration. When I open my eyes, I'll feel good and nothing will block my concentration."

The Power Of Your Imagination

You have the power to concentrate in even the most adverse writing environments. Consider the following story:

> *Many years ago, when prisons were much worse than today, a man was thrown into a cell with another prisoner. The newcomer looked about the dark, vermin-infested cell and cried, "I don't think I can survive in this miserable cold place!"*
>
> *The other prisoner, sitting at a table, writing by the feeble light of a candle, asked, "How long are you going to be here?"*
>
> *The newcomer replied, "Six months." The man who was writing smiled and said, "I have already been here for twelve years." He turned back to his writing. It was John Bunyan, who was working on his immortal* Pilgrim's Progress.[5]

John Bunyan didn't allow a dark, dingy prison environment to deter him from his creative work. He was able to see and write beyond his sordid surroundings. You, too, can imagine your present writing environment free of major distractions, then look for a way to make that vision a reality. The decision to do this strengthens your will and lets you experience a high energy level; indecision can weaken your will and produce tension in your body.

William James recognized the force and power of an energy born of desire.

> *The normal opener of deeper and deeper levels of energy is will. The difficulty is to use it, to make the effort which the word volition implies. It is notorious that a single successful effort of moral volition, such as saying "no" to some habitual temptation or performing some courageous act, will launch a man on a higher level of energy for days and weeks, will give him a new range of power.[6]*

The power of desire lets you take control of your life. When you want something strongly enough, the desire becomes imprinted on your subconscious mind. The emotion is transmitted to the nerves and muscles of your body, and you move swiftly in the direction of achieving your desired goal.[7] If you're hungry and you want a sandwich, that desire will cause you to make one for yourself.

Likewise, the greater your desire to write, the more creative energy you'll generate. Picture your writing goal clearly in your mind while doing the Write-Now exercises. With practice, eventually, you will attain it. The creative imagination has the power to change even an undesirable situation—as it did for John Bunyan.

The strength of your imagination can also lead you in new directions. The last two lines of this passage from *A Midsummer Night's Dream* by Shakespeare reveal how he understood the impact of the imagination on one's mental state.

> *And as imagination bodies forth*
> *The forms of things unknown, the poet's pen*
> *Turns them to shapes, and gives to airy nothing*
> *A local habitation and a name.*
> *Such tricks hath strong imagination,*
> *That if it would but apprehend some joy,*
> *It comprehends some bringer of that joy.*[8]

If you first think about joy and happiness, then you think about ways to find someone or something to bring that to you. In other words, you find people and situations that fit your mental picture of being happy. The visualization of your goal comes first, and the physical action follows. If becoming a better fiction writer will bring you happiness, then select Write-Now exercises to help you improve your fiction-writing skills. Practice the exercises, and you'll find new success in your work.

Creativity In The Face Of Illness

Your will and desire to write have a tremendous impact, not just on what and how you write, but also on your ability to write in the face of such obstacles as illness and loss of confidence.

Many great writers suffered poor health during their careers. Thomas Mann, Noel Coward, Katherine Mansfield, Ralph Waldo Emerson, and Henry David Thoreau are just a few who have battled physical ailments while they wrote. Their creative imagination was so strong, however, that they were able to write as a diversion from illness.

Despite his battle with tuberculosis, Robert Louis Stevenson wrote short stories, articles, and novels while lying in bed.[9] James Thurber, author of twenty-five books and hundreds of stories and articles, was blind in one eye. As a child, he endured several operations to save the sight in his "good" eye. As he grew older and his vision deteriorated, he could no longer see to type and had to use a crayon to write in large letters on yellow paper. At that point, Thurber could not draw the famous cartoons that were his trademark. Out of necessity, he learned to dictate his stories to a secretary. His desire to keep writing throughout his visual troubles may actually have enhanced his output; some critics claim that Thurber's writing improved in his later years when he was completely blind—when his total concentration was focused on the words.[10]

Psychologists suggest that being creative can serve as a positive distraction from illness. They cite seriously ill or handicapped writers who felt better because of their healthy, creative minds; it's possible this was why they continued to write despite the pain and inconvenience they suffered. Helen Keller was able to overcome the severe handicaps of deafness and blindness. Instead of succumbing to self-pity, she awakened her senses through her creative imagination. She wrote four books and maintained her creative abilities throughout her life.[11]

Dr. Elmer Green, a research scientist at the Menninger Foundation, has studied the healing effects of creativity on the body and mind.

> *Creativity in terms of physiological processes means physical healing, physical regeneration. Creativity in emotional terms consists, then, of establishing, or creating, attitude changes through the practice of healthy emotions—emotions whose neural correlates are those that establish harmony in the visceral brain.*[12]

(Helen Keller is an excellent example of how creativity heals emotions and establishes a healthy attitude toward life.)

The "illnesses" most of us battle are usually colds and headaches. These distractions can too easily deter us from pursuing our writing—if we let them. Why not write in the face of physical discomfort? The sense of satisfaction you derive from transforming a rough idea into a well-defined form can make you feel better both physically and mentally.

Stress-Related Illnesses

There are, of course, other illnesses—such as heart disease, high blood pressure, back pain, and arthritis—that can disrupt your writing. Some of these ailments may be caused or compounded by unresolved stress.[13] To keep writing while suffering from these illnesses takes stamina, strong will, and an understanding of what's causing or contributing to the ailment. To get that understanding, you should consult the physician best able to determine the cause of whatever is interfering with your writing. If the doctor determines that your discomfort is stress-related, you may be able to ease some of the pain with the help of a Write-Now exercise.

Lisa, a columnist for a local newspaper, went to her doctor about the abdominal pains she suffered whenever her deadline drew near. She explained that the discomfort persisted until she mailed a column to her editor, then it subsided—until about a week before the next column was due. The doctor conducted various upper and lower gastrointestinal tests, after which he was able to rule out the possibility of an ulcer or some other illness. He diagnosed her condition as stress-related.

Lisa did the Write-Now exercise every day before she began working on her column. Within a month, the stomach pains caused by her anxiety about the deadline disappeared.

It's not likely that *one* Write-Now exercise will "cure," or even alleviate, every stress-related malady. Before doing *any* stress-relieving exercise, you should consult your doctor about the cause of your health problem. If your physician determines that stress *is* a contributing factor in an illness, the next step is to identify exactly where in your body the tension is.

Most people, like Lisa, know the feeling of "butterflies in their stomach." Many of them have experienced a stomach "tied in knots." Quite often, neck and face muscles tighten to reflect tension and stress. Once you've identified the stress points, either by yourself or with the aid of your doctor, you're ready to do the next Write-Now exercise. (Let your physician know you're doing the stress-reducing exercise and get his or her approval; if the doctor recommends another way to alleviate your anxiety, be sure to follow the advice.)

Before doing the Write-Now exercise, think of the tense part of your body as completely limp. (Lisa imagined that as she typed her column, her stomach muscles were as relaxed as warm, wet noodles.) You can imagine yourself as limp as a rag doll or as flexible as modeling clay. Do the exercise before a writing session or at bedtime. After several weeks of practice, you should begin to feel less tense and better able to write.

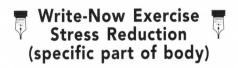

Write-Now Exercise
Stress Reduction
(specific part of body)

Goal: To reduce the stress in specific parts of your body so that you're completely relaxed during your writing session.

1.
2. Do steps 1-3 of the Write-Now exercise as outlined on page 101.
3.

4. Picture your back (or whatever part of your body is tense) as you're sitting at your writing desk. As you bend from side to side, you feel the tension moving out of your back. Tighten the muscles in your back. Hold to the count of two. Do this five times. See yourself relaxed. There is no longer any tension in your back. You feel healthy and look healthy.

5. Say to yourself ten times: "The tension in my back is leaving. I can feel it moving away from my back and out of my body. My back feels good. I feel relaxed and ready to write. I feel very healthy."

   If it's bedtime, drop off to sleep. If it's daytime, complete the exercise and say, "When I open my eyes, I'll feel great."

Developing A Success Consciousness

Many men and women have had to overcome major problems in their lives before they excelled in their chosen careers. These people wrestled too with the same irritations that plague everyone: stress, fatigue, distractions . . . fear of failure. Yet successful people circumvent the negatives in their lives and offer something positive to the world. Their lives present some valuable lessons for writers.

How do they do it? Are they geniuses? Do they have some special ability?

Napoleon Hill, author and consultant to major corporations, interviewed many successful individuals in depth. In his book *Grow Rich with Peace of Mind*, he discusses a common trait among them.

> *In my hundreds of interviews with men who had made fortunes, I noticed how well their minds were focused on success.... many eminently successful men do not possess any greater intelligence than most other men possess. Yet their achievements are such that we may say that these men have "genius." Surely it is the positive mental attitude of these men which makes their brain power, not greater, but more efficient and more available than most others. When I spoke to such men as Henry Ford, Andrew Carnegie, and Thomas Edison, I spoke with minds free of any fear or doubt that they could do anything they wished to do.... What was it then*

which impelled their minds to seize upon great goals, then winnow all the circumstances of life and make use of what could help them achieve their ambitions? It was a success consciousness.[14]

Thomas Edison had this success consciousness. He conjured up mental pictures that gave him the impetus to work persistently on inventions until they were perfected. The storage battery was one of the most difficult and challenging; after 9,000 experiments, his laboratory assistants tried to discourage him from continuing the battery research. He responded optimistically, "Those are not failures. That is 9,000 things we have learned that won't work; 9,000 things we won't have to do over."[15] Edison did 41,000 *more* experiments before he had a workable storage battery.

When people called Edison a genius, he was quick to define the term. "Genius," he claimed, "is 90 percent perspiration and 10 percent inspiration."[16] His expanded vision, reinforced with the belief in his success, spurred him on to explore, create, and develop over 1,000 inventions.

Though many people know of Edison's triumphs as an inventor, few know of the handicap he overcame: a childhood accident had caused him to lose most of his hearing. Edison could easily have used his disability as a rationalization for not leading an active life; instead, he turned his liability into an asset. Deafness was, in fact, a great help to him. "It cuts out the outside noises and useless chatter of people that amounts to nothing and leaves me free to concentrate on things worthwhile," he once said.[17]

Elaine was a deaf student in one of my Write-Now workshops; she, like Edison, had success consciousness. She was determined to learn to write fiction. Toward that end, she brought her husband with her to the workshop so that he could verbally communicate her ideas to the group after she first used sign language to express them to him. He, in turn, signed to her the comments and suggestions of other writers.

Leonardo da Vinci, Julius Caesar, Napoleon Bonaparte, Franklin Delano Roosevelt, and Albert Schweitzer also had success consciousness. In fact, they shared many traits—unusual powers of concentration, an unfailing confidence in themselves, and the ability to mentally relax under pressure—all of which helped them achieve their destinies.

Dealing With Rejection

"Destiny is not a matter of chance," claimed the great orator, William Jennings Bryan. "It is a matter of choice." It is not something to be waited for, but something to be achieved. In attempting to achieve it, writers often become discouraged and lose confidence in themselves. Maybe you're not improving in your craft as quickly as you'd hoped; maybe you're facing what seems like constant rejection from editors and publishers. These circumstances can undermine your self-assurance and produce a major distraction to your writing.

A barrage of rejection slips can trigger a writer's block that freezes your productivity. When your manila envelope regularly returns in the mail, the fruits of your imagination unpicked by a hungry editor, depression sets in. As a result, you may lose confidence.

Anxiety is a characteristic of someone mired in self-doubt. Left unchecked, this state of mind could inhibit your writing for weeks, even months. If your thoughts become preoccupied with failure, it's impossible to relax and write. Unfortunately, many writers begin to lose confidence not just in their writing, but in themselves, when their work is rejected. In their minds, a rejection slip means "I'm no good" or "I'm not a creative person because the story wasn't accepted." Rejection affects not only their will to write, but also their self-image. They begin to believe that self-worth is dependent on getting published. In fact, their self-worth *should* be defined by the courage they show, both in writing and trying to sell what they write.

Dr. David Burns, clinical professor of psychology at the University of Pennsylvania, believes that you cannot earn self-worth through what you do. Achievements bring satisfaction, but not happiness. Self-worth based on accomplishment is a false type of esteem—not the real thing.[18]

Granted, it's a good feeling to have your writing accepted. But if it's *not* accepted, and you become devastated by that, you could become depressed. As a result, your creativity may be transformed into something malignant because it undermines your confidence and distorts your self-image.

Becoming emotionally addicted to approval from an editor (or someone else) in order to define your self-worth is a hard habit to break. It's similar to having an enormous craving for sweets: after you eat a candy bar, it triggers a sugar-insulin imbalance in the body. As soon as the initial rush of sugar hits your brain, you sense a quick energy lift—but then a sudden drop in the sugar level takes place. This quick drop produces mood swings, irritability, and nervousness. Until you get your next "fix," your body has trouble adjusting to the change.

In the same way that you can become vulnerable to sweets, you can also come to depend on approval from editors and critics. Most parents wisely control the sugar intake of their small children so they don't develop a craving for sweets. Likewise, it's necessary to control the craving for praise and acceptance. Enjoy achievements and rewards for what they are, but don't let them distort your self-image. Otherwise, your whole system will be out of kilter; your writing won't be an exciting adventure, but rather, a terrifying test of your worth as a human being.

That's what writing had become for Greg—a terrifying test he was sure he'd failed. "After getting my sixth rejection slip yesterday," he told a few of us after class one evening, "I've decided to give up writing and get into something I'm good at. I spent three months doing research on my physical fitness craze article, rewrote it at least four times, and figured I had something an editor would like. I guess I just don't have what it takes to write."

"Are you saying that you're letting six people's rejection convince you that you shouldn't be a writer?" Bob asked in disbelief.

I could see that Greg was depressed and confused, but was thinking about what Bob had just said. I suggested that before he made any final decision, he should try a Write-Now exercise every day for a month to help bolster his self-image. He said he would try it but didn't think it would help.

I can't tell you how delighted I was when Greg enrolled in my fiction-writing workshop three months later.

A Positive Self-Image

If your self-image has been negatively affected by rejection and confusion about your ability as a writer, try the next Write-Now exercise, the same one Greg did every day for a month. This exercise will fortify your self-image. You'll feel good about yourself whether your writing is accepted or not.

Write-Now Exercise
Confidence/Self-Image

Goal: To realize that acceptance or rejection of your writing doesn't determine your self-image.

1.
2. Do steps 1-3 of the Write-Now exercise as outlined on page 101.
3.

4. See yourself as you are—intelligent and successful in various areas of your life. Select one area in which you feel confident—e.g., work, relationships, volunteer activities. Hold the picture in your mind. Feel good about yourself. You are a unique person with many fine qualities. Your self-image is becoming stronger and stronger.

5. Say to yourself ten times: "I'm am an intelligent, confident person. I feel good about myself. My self-image is positive. I have many talents and abilities. Writing is one of them. Whether my work is accepted or rejected, I'll still like myself."

    If you're doing this exercise during the day, say, "When I open my eyes, I'll feel great." If the exercise is done at bedtime, drop off to sleep.

You may feel the suggestion you give yourself in the above exercise is boasting. It's not: you're just building a new attitude about yourself as a writer.

The only people who really fail are those who never try anything. They fail themselves because they don't seize the opportunity to grow through a new experience. The courage to take the risk, even though you might fail, marks the truly successful person.

Greg proved he had the courage to try again. He also had the determination to change his attitude about himself in relation to his writing. "If editors like my writing, that's fine," he told me later. "If they don't, that's okay, too. I like it and plan to stay with it. What I think of myself doesn't depend on how they feel about my articles." With that kind of attitude, Greg will likely become a confident, relaxed writer. The confident writer expends less energy on worry, and therefore has more energy to keep writing.

"Every act rewards itself," said Emerson.[19] Write a page and believe that since you did it once, you can do it again. Suddenly, pages start to increase and your project is completed. When you believe in yourself, your writing and your outlook on writing get better. Emerson realized that too often, instead of recognizing it for its merit, we don't value our own work simply because it's ours.

> *To believe your own thought, to believe that what is true for you in your private heart, is true for all men—that is genius. Speak your latent conviction, and it shall be the universal sense . . . the highest merit we ascribe to Moses, Plato, and Milton, is that they set at naught books and traditions, and spoke not what men but what they thought. A man should learn to detect and watch that gleam of light which flashes across his mind from within, more than the lustre of the firmament of bards and sages. Yet he dismisses without notice his thought, because it is his. In every work of genius we recognize our own rejected thoughts: they come back to us with a certain alienated majesty.*[20]

Writing For Its Own Sake

If you look at writing as an opportunity to share your ideas with others, you will see other merits in the craft. You'll realize that your words have the power to make readers laugh or cry. Because of your writing, readers may learn something or be motivated to take action on an issue important to them.

For many writers, however, the most important benefit of writing comes from the writing itself. They enjoy being actively involved in the creative process. Taking the thread of an idea and weaving it into a recognizable pattern—poem, essay, story—stimulates and satisfies them. Getting their work published is a secondary consideration.

To help you feel the intangible exhilaration of writers who value their work in this way, do the next Write-Now exercise, which allows you to appreciate writing for its own worth. This exercise can be done anytime—at bedtime or during the day.

Write-Now Exercise Intrinsic Value

Goal: To appreciate writing for its own intrinsic value.

1.
2. Do steps 1-3 of the Write-Now exercise as outlined on page 101.
3.

4. See yourself totally involved in your writing. You feel stimulated by the thought of developing an idea into a finished product. You can express any emotion, any feeling when you write and create a poem, character, or (other) for your enjoyment. Writing can be a catharsis for you when you need an emotional outlet, a good friend when you need to talk to your inner self. You're happy to be a writer not for the monetary rewards, but for the personal rewards.

5. Say to yourself ten times: "I'm glad I'm a writer. It gives me the chance to get in touch with my feelings, create new word pictures, and develop a deeper appreciation of the creative process in my life."

If it's bedtime, drop off to sleep.

If you're doing the exercise during the day, complete the exercise and say, "When I open my eyes, I'll feel great."

Valuing writing for its own sake and valuing your own work for the satisfaction it gives you aren't just egocentric goals: they are two excellent ways to strengthen your commitment to writing—to write in the face of all distractions and obstacles.

In this chapter, we've seen how such factors as job stress, fatigue, health problems, noise, and lack of confidence can, if you let them, narrow your writing horizons. Armed with the belief that writing has value, you can deal with these troubles in a realistic, positive way. By constantly nurturing a healthy attitude and by practicing the Write-Now exercises, you'll keep moving—forward. With a strong and active faith in your ability as a writer, and a willingness to work hard to be one, you *will* realize your potential.

Notes/Chapter Five

1. Anthony Norvell, *How to Control Your Destiny* (Hollywood: Wilshire Book Co., 1957), p. 39. (Current publisher, David McKay Co., Inc: New York)

2. C.R. Joy and M. Arnold, *The Africa of Albert Schweitzer* (New York: Harper and Bros., 1948), p. 32.

3. Tom Mach, "How to Cope with the Stress of Living," *Writer's Digest,* Vol. 61 (July, 1981), p. 23.

4. Hazel Felleman, ed., *The Best-Loved Poems of the American People* (New York: Doubleday & Co., 1936), p. 115.

5. Anthony Norvell, *How to Control Your Destiny,* p. 37-38.

6. Ibid., p. 72.

7. Anthony Norvell, *The Million Dollar Secret Hidden in Your Mind* (New York: Barnes & Noble Books, 1973), p. 51.

8. William Shakespeare, *The Complete Works of William Shakespeare,* ed. by George L. Kittredge (New York: Ginn and Co., 1936), p. 251.

9. Ramon P. Coffman and Nathan G. Goodman, *Famous Authors for Young People* (New York: Dodd, Mead & Co., 1943), p. 125.

10. Ravina Gelfano and Letha Patterson, *They Wouldn't Quit* (Minneapolis: Learner Publications, 1962), pp. 22-25.

11. Anthony Norvell, *How to Control Your Destiny,* p. 18.

12. Sheila Ostrander and Lynn Schroeder, *Superlearning* (New York: Dell Publishing, 1979), p. 191.

13. Barbara Brown, *Stress and the Art of Biofeedback* (New York: Bantam Books, 1977), p. 227.

14. Napoleon Hill, *Grow Rich with Peace of Mind* (New York: Fawcett World Library, 1968), pp. 17-18, 40. (Latest edition, E.P. Dutton: New York)

15. Robert C. Halcrim, *The Edison Record* (Fort Myers, FL: Historical Society of Fort Myers, 1972), p. 32.

16. Ibid., p. 33.

17. Ibid., p. 22.

18. David D. Burns, *Feeling Good: The New Mood Therapy* (New York: New American Library, 1980), pp. 288-291. (original publisher, William Morrow and Co: New York)

19. Ralph Waldo Emerson, *Essays First and Second Series,* ed. by Ernest Rhys (New York: E.P. Dutton & Co., 1906), p. 62. (Current publisher, J.M. Dent & Sons, Ltd.)

20. Ibid., p. 30.

CHAPTER SIX

How to Write Better Fiction

To create a memorable story with characters who will engage the emotions of the reader is the ultimate goal of the storyteller.

Laurie McBain

CHAPTER OVERVIEW

1. What makes fictional characters memorable?

2. How can the Write-Now method help you develop successful plots?

3. How do you awaken your senses to create vivid settings?

4. How do you know what part of your fiction needs improvement?

WHO IS THE MOST UNFORGETTABLE fictional character you've ever met? I always get a variety of answers when I ask the students in my Write-Now fiction workshops: James Bond, Scarlett O'Hara, Anna Karenina, and Sherlock Holmes are some of their favorites.

When I probe further and ask them why a particular character made such a lasting impression, they're quick to reply: "He was just like a real person," or "I could identify with his problem," or "She reminded me of myself at that age," or "I loved his zest, his humor."

What makes a story and its characters memorable?

"I wish I knew," said Barb, the branch manager of a bank. "The plot and characters in my short story seem unrealistic, and I can't figure out why. Yet I'll remember a book that holds my interest to the last page. I know what I like, but it's hard for me to write a story that keeps my attention."

Creating believable characters and plots is a challenge for most fiction writers. In fact, manuscripts are regularly rejected by editors because of the cardboard characters and contrived plots they contain. The third element that can make or break a story is its setting. Painting vivid, appropriate surroundings for your characters to live in is essential to successful fiction.

This chapter focuses on these elements—character, plot, setting—as basic components of fiction. By visualizing fully drawn flesh-and-blood characters caught up in a well-paced plot taking place in a realistic setting, you engage the emotions of your readers and create a memorable story. The Write-Now exercises in this chapter will help you, as they did Barb, meet the challenge of that task. In other words, after studying this chapter, you'll understand the makings of a good story—and have a decent idea of how to write one.

Characters That Capture Readers

Think of a character whom you enjoy watching on TV. Perhaps it's Krystle Carrington (Linda Evans) of "Dynasty." Close your eyes. Picture her in your mind's eye. Describe how she looks: the color of her hair and eyes, her height, her outstanding features. Use three words to sum up her total look—statuesque, broad-shouldered, meticulous.

Now describe her personality in two words—sympathetic, charming. Why do you think she was cast for the part? What qualities does she project? Do you empathize with her? Do you want to see how she copes with all the problems that threaten her happiness? Why?

You enjoy watching Krystle because you care about her as a character. You need that same concern when developing your own characters: unless *you* care about them, make them unique and believable, and keep them involved in the story, your readers will tune them out.

Trudy, a secretary who attended a fiction-writing workshop, told us that she could identify with Irene, a character in a friend's story. Irene had rejoined the work force after a thirty-year hiatus. "Many of the problems Irene had adjusting to the working world after so many years of being at home and raising kids were the same kinds of things I went through," Trudy said. "Office politics were something I didn't expect. I found Irene's way of handling it—by squelching rumors—interesting. I wanted to keep reading to find out how she dealt with other situations.

Faith Baldwin believed that this kind of caring is essential in writing:

> *Just about the most important thing to a writer is what we call reader identification. If the reader is going to like a book or story, he must in some way identify himself with the situations and the characters.... The reader identifies himself in more ways than one. He can say, "This happened to me" or "If this happened to me, how would I react?"*[1]

While producing an average of two books a year, Baldwin was skilled in achieving this kinship between her characters and her readers. A *New York Times* critic once wrote that the key to Baldwin's popularity was that she could get lonely, working people of all ages to identify with her glamorous and wealthy characters by showing readers that problems and preoccupations in love and friendship are shared by everyone.

Reader identification is uppermost in the minds of anyone trying to create a particular image or make an appeal to a designated audience. Before a casting director auditions actors for a commercial or a play, he or she has a clear mental picture of the right kind of person for the role. The "young mother" type sells soaps, diapers, cereals, or anything of interest to mothers and wives. The "Walter Cronkite" image, on the other hand, projects authority and advertises insurance, real estate, and magazine subscriptions. The "ingenue" look is chosen for shampoo, suntan lotion, perfume, and soft drink ads.

All these types project certain messages. Casting directors know that selecting the right person is vital to selling the product. If a real-life mother identifies with the actress mother who tells how healthy her brand of peanut butter is for kids, she'll buy it.

Think like a casting director when you're creating characters to play certain roles. The important thing is to conceive of your main character, the protagonist, as a real person. If you write about someone ambitious and strong, but you don't give him the qualities that make him credible in the role, then he's miscast. The reader won't identify with him.

Creating "Real" Characters

To think of your characters as genuine individuals, you must know them intimately. Writer Marilyn Durham once explained how she nurtured this understanding of characters:

> *Before I knew what was going to happen to them, I was thinking about them. I began putting them in everyone else's situation. As I'd watch TV, I poked my heroine, Catherine, into every heroine's place, contemporary, western, spy story.... I immediately imagined what Catherine would reply, how she would react.... I found that I could do it by thinking about an actress—actresses are supposed to play parts—and Julie Adams became Catherine. I'd seen her on television and in old movies enough so that I knew how she walked, how she talked, how she would phrase things. Yet it was possible for me to think of her as Catherine and still give Catherine the freedom to be herself without thinking of her as Julie Adams.*[2]

Selecting a real person who has some of the same traits as your fictional character can help you, as it did Durham, visualize the character in your story. Try to see your character (who may even remind you of someone you know) in a number of real-life situations. How would your protagonist react if he discovered that his daughter had a drug problem? How would he react if he had just gotten fired from his job?

Another way of getting to know a character inside out is to let him or her be your house guest for a few days. How does the character fit in with your family? Is he bored with your lifestyle? Does she like your kids? What does she do to unwind? Does he complain much? What kinds of food does he like? "Seeing" your character "up close and personal" makes describing him or her much simpler.

Some characters are easier than others both to envision and create because their roots actually lie in the being of another person. Indeed, many authors draw their characters from people they have known.

Every character created by British author R. F. Delderfield, who wrote *To Serve Them All My Days,* had not one living prototype, but many.[3] In fact, it's common for writers to envision characters that are composites of several people they know.

"I have two aunts who were the prototypes for my main character, Darlene," explained Rob, an auditor, during one of my workshops. "One of my aunts has been married four times. The other has never been married, but because of her wealth, she's had a lot of proposals. Darlene has some of the characteristics of both these women, yet she has her own identity. It's fun to pick personality traits from a few people and combine them with other qualities and come up with a new character."

If you use a person from real life as a prototype for a fictional character, be sure that the two aren't carbon copies of each other. It's fine to use certain aspects of the actual person in your created one, but it's a good idea to change names and all other easily identifiable traits and circumstances.

"If my aunts recognized themselves in my story, they'd disown me," Rob admitted. "When I developed my main character, I kept that in mind so they wouldn't think Darlene was really them."

Using real people's features and attitudes in fashioning fictional characters is one way to make characters believable. To make them realistic, they must have genuine human qualities. They can neither be so admirable that readers see them as too good to be true, or so bland that readers can't muster up an ounce of feeling for them.

Some years ago, *Time* magazine had these thoughts on just how "real" one writer's characters seem.

> *Joseph Wambaugh's characters have altered America's view of police. His Los Angeles officers are neither the lone eagle heroes of*

> *reactionary fantasy nor fascist mercenaries.... They are, instead,*
> *ordinary, besieged working men and women whose lives are*
> *presented with war zone humor.*[4]

To capture this kind of realism, your characters need not be autobiographical. But you should be able to feel some of their joy, pain, depression, or confusion. It's not uncommon for writers to draw characters from their own personalities; they often infuse their characters with personal traits, wishes, and fears.

Characters may also evolve from a writer's needs: your hero's motivation to become wealthy might stem from your own desire to have a lot of money. If writers recognize and admit to certain flaws and strengths in themselves, they may be able to exhibit some of these features in their fictional characters.

Try to get close to the people in your story. Feel compassion and concern for them. Find out what makes them unique. Give them some of your own traits—but not too many, since you want them to retain their own identity.

Biography Of A Character

How can you make your characters come alive on the page? About ten years ago, I devised the following biography exercise for students who had difficulty transforming their fictional characters into "actual" people with whom readers could identify. Before you begin a biography of your character, think of a real person you know very well—e.g., a family member, spouse, friend, neighbor. Then draw a line down the center of a sheet of paper. In the left-hand column, put the person's name; leave the right-hand column unlabeled. Keep that real person clearly in your mind as you write the answers to the following questions in the left-hand column.

1. What does the person look like? Describe him as though he were a suspect and you were describing him to a police officer. Include height, weight, color of hair, eyes, etc.

2. What are some of the person's character tags? (Wears a lot of jewelry, always looks at watch, stutters, etc.) Any noticeable physical flaws or assets?

3. Did the person finish high school? College? Is he wise, or does he parrot what he's learned to impress others? Does the person speak slowly? Fast? Does he have a good vocabulary? What does his voice sound like?

4. Does the person have a good sense of humor? What kind? Vulgar? Absurd?

5. What are his beefs? Work? Politics? Money?

6. What does he like about people? Hate about them?

7. Does this person lie? Why? What proof do you have?

8. Is the person honest? Does he trust people?

9. What does the person do for fun? Sports? Movies? Gambling? Can he relax enough to have fun?

10. Is this person capable only of superficial relationships? Why?

11. If he won the lottery, what would he do with the money?

12. What are his priorities? Status? Money? Family? Religion?

13. How does he define love? What is his relationship with his spouse? Others? Describe the person's home life.

14. What do you like/dislike about this person? Does he/she have some of your good/bad traits?

Now try to visualize your own main character as you did the real person. Keeping your character in mind, answer the same questions in the right-hand column. Having thought about a real person first, you'll find it's much easier to describe an imaginary one in this kind of biography.

Before doing the next Write-Now exercise, read over the biography questions and your answers as they relate to your character. The Write-Now exercise will help you focus on how your character looks and acts. (You can, of course, do the exercise in conjunction with any character—not only the protagonist—in your story.)

Write-Now Exercise Characterization

Goal: To create believable characters who have positive and negative traits and who speak and act like real people.

1. Get comfortable in bed or an easy chair. Noise should be at a minimum. Close your eyes. Take three or four deep breaths. Inhale through the nose. Take the air down to the diaphragm. Count to three. Exhale through your mouth.

2. Imagine that you're lying on the beach (or in a garden, park, or anywhere you feel at peace). If you imagine the beach, you feel the sun warming your face. The salty air invigorates your senses. You feel relaxed and peaceful. All of nature is in harmony. You, too, feel that your mind and body are in harmony.

3. You push your heels down in the sand. Feel the tension; now relax them. Do the same thing with your hips, back, shoulders, neck, head, arms, and hands: push down, then release. Tighten and relax the muscles while taking three deep breaths. Repeat silently ten times: "I'm becoming more and more relaxed." (The main objective is to relax your mind and body so that the subconscious will accept your suggestions.)

4. As you turn your head to the right, you notice Alan Alda (or another actor). You see his facial features, the color of his eyes and hair. See him clearly in your mind. Include as much detail about his physique and personal appearance as possible. You overhear his conversation with someone else. You become aware of his sense of humor, his warmth, and his ability to relate to others.

   Now see the person he's talking with just as vividly as you see Alan Alda (or whatever actor you've chosen). See the other person's facial features and physical characteristics. This person is the main character in your story. Notice his ease or tenseness during the conversation. What type of personality does he have? Is he shy, talkative, witty, reserved? Try to see in your mind's eye the total person—just as you saw Alan Alda.

5. Silently repeat the following suggestion ten times: "The characters in my stories talk and act like real people and have positive and negative traits. I can picture them clearly in my mind."

   Drop off to sleep. If you're doing the exercise during the day, complete the exercise, and say, "When I open my eyes, I'll feel great."

Do the above exercise for seven days. At the end of the week, list as many physical characteristics and personality traits as you can for the main character in your story. (Put your list in your writing notebook, which is separate from both your dream notebook and your journal. If you keep dream notes, journal entries, and writing exercises in the same notebook, divide it into three separate sections.) Write several paragraphs describing the character in detail. Include the information you gleaned from the Write-Now exercise, as well as the facts you noted earlier in your character's biography. (You may also want to refer to your dream notebook for notes you may have made after practicing the Write-Now dream exercise on characterization on pages 48-49.)

Margaret Mitchell described the characters in *Gone With the Wind* so vividly that readers get a clear mental picture of each one. Melanie Wilkes' physical characteristics—e.g., frail, tiny, plain—reveal some of her personality traits. She is timid, simple, shy; but she has dignity and sincerity.

Scarlett O'Hara's appearance is in sharp contrast to Melanie's. Her square jaw and flirtatious green eyes coincide with her personality. She is willful, has a zest for life, enjoys men, and is often repressed because of social mores.

Making characters different from one another draws attention to them. By consciously making your characters distinct, the positive or negative qualities you want to emphasize become apparent. Although both women in Margaret Mitchell's story have certain physical attractions, there is a sharp difference in their personalities. Melanie is loving and ever the lady. Scarlett is sweet when it's to her advantage; she is shrewd, charming, and fun-loving.

Naming Your Characters

In addition to distinguishing your characters by their individual personalities, you make them real by giving them appropriate names. In their *Fiction Writer's Handbook,* Hallie and Whit Burnett make several suggestions for naming characters. They believe that giving a character the wrong name can interfere with his or her development. To avoid confusing readers, they suggest that you not assign two characters surnames that sound the same or begin with the same letter. Likewise don't use similar first names for two different characters in the same story—e.g., Chuck and Charlie, Liz and Liza.[5]

Margaret Mitchell knew the importance of giving the right names to her characters. The name Scarlett suggests a fiery, vibrant personality; the name Melanie connotes softness, almost like background music (melody).

Readers often draw inferences about characters based solely on their names. If the name doesn't complement the physical description or personality of a character, she doesn't seem believable. Would a beautiful, vivacious heroine seem real if her name were Hortense?

To get a better idea of how names (for whatever reason) suggest certain images, consider performers. Actors and actresses, too, know the value of having just the right name. They may legally change their real names to new ones that create a certain image in an audience's mind. They prefer names fans can remember, names linked to their personality.

For instance, Norma Jean Baker changed her name to Marilyn Monroe, which seemed more in line with her sex-goddess image. Similarly, Roy Rogers sounds more like a cowboy than does Leonard Slye, his real name. Mary Collins doesn't necessarily evoke the image of a "10" the way Bo Derek does. Leslie Hope preferred the more masculine sounding "Bob." Can you picture Loretta Young opening the door as she did on her 1950s television show and introducing herself as Gretchen Belzer?[6] Indeed, there's *something* in a name.

And it's as important for a fictional character to have the proper name as it is for an actor. A character's name should reflect how you want him/her to be portrayed, received, and understood by your reader. What do the names Millicent, Floyd, Pearl, and Gidget suggest to you? Write down the first impression (both physical and personality) that comes to mind when you read each one and say it aloud. Do any of these names have a negative association for you? Would readers likely react the same way? Does the name Millicent, for example, suggest a conservative, prudish person? Why or why not? *Why* you feel a certain way about a name doesn't matter; what does is that you're aware of whatever impression a name evokes in you, and that you name your characters with purpose.

Telling Readers About Characters

Writers have options for unraveling aspects of their characters' personalities. There are many ways to show readers who and what your characters really are. One of the most common is to show them in action: you can put your characters in situations that test their mettle, or have them make simple decisions that uncover their positive and negative traits. You can also point out the many sides—sometimes contradictory—of a particular character. Under the right circumstances, a selfish character might show a side of his personality that suggests he really isn't totally self-centered. Another seemingly likeable character might perform a good deed for ulterior motives.

Consider the pair of situations below. Notice how the characters' actions can mean two different things when presented in two different ways.

Situation #1

"Poor old guy. He'll get a heart attack if he tries to change that tire himself," Allan thought as he pulled over to the curb.

"Hi, Mac," he hollered as he jumped out of his car. "Can I give you a hand?"

Situation #2

"There's old money-bags Jones with a flat," Allan thought as he pulled over to the curb. "I bet he'll give me ten bucks if I change his tire."

"Hello, Mr. Jones," he called politely as he jumped out of his car. "Looks like you've got a problem. Let me help."

When you reveal a character's thoughts as well as his actions, your readers get insights into what the character really thinks about people, his job, his family, and life in general. Readers begin to feel as if they know that character. From watching him act and react, they can predict his future behaviors. (It's up to you to be sure a character acts consistently with how a real person might act.)

A protagonist in conflict with his surroundings may reveal by his thoughts certain foibles: Scarlett O'Hara trying to salvage Tara and win Ashley's love shows her ability to manipulate people to get what she wants. We, as readers, learn never to underestimate her will.

Stephen Crane revealed his main character, Henry Fleming's, thoughts about the Civil War in the *Red Badge of Courage*. As a young soldier he idealized it and yearned to be in combat. His views changed as he witnessed the harsh realities of death and destruction. Self-doubt and fear surface as his inner conflict with his surroundings mounts.

> *He had burned several times to enlist. Tales of great movements shook the land. They might not be distinctly Homeric, but there seemed to be much glory in them. He had read of marches, sieges, conflicts, and he had longed to see it all. His busy mind had drawn for him large pictures extravagant in color, lurid with breathless deeds.*

Later in the novel we see his attitude about war beginning to change.

The youth stared at the land in front of him. Its foliage now seemed to veil powers and horrors. He was unaware of the machinery of orders that started the charge, although from the corners of his eyes he saw an officer, who looked like a boy a-horseback, come galloping, waving his hat. Suddenly he felt a straining and heaving among the men. The line fell slowly forward like a toppling wall, and, with a convulsive gasp that was intended for a cheer, the regiment began its journey. The youth was pushed and jostled for a moment before he understood the movement at all, but directly he lunged ahead and began to run.

Learning to know how and what your characters think takes practice. Practice with real people. One of the best ways to discover what people are thinking is to study them: clues to their thoughts may be found on their faces. Body language, too, can reveal their inner concerns or delights.

The next time you're sitting in a restaurant, doctor's office, airport—or anyplace people gather—look at facial expressions and notice body language. Try to imagine what people are thinking about. Is that man shifting his weight from one foot to the other bored to death? Why? Does he seem contented? Does he have a vacant look? Is the chubby woman mentally counting the calories in the dessert she's about to consume, or might her sad expression reflect her depression about the death of a close friend?

To be believable, fictional characters, too, must reflect their inner strengths and weaknesses. The character E.T. expressed what he felt through his voice and eyes; you could tell what he was thinking. As much as he wanted to go home, he was still sad to leave his friend Elliott, who had shown his love by risking so much to help him. Your character descriptions should suggest to readers what your characters are thinking, how they're feeling. The portrayals must be genuine and appropriate; otherwise, they may send confusing messages to your readers.

Dialogue That Says Something

Dialogue is another important way to provide pertinent information about characters in a story. Think of novels you've read. How often could you tell whether characters were educated, funny, sad, serious, depressed, self-assured, or obnoxious—just by what they said? How did they speak? To whom? Could you tell whether they'd be able to resolve the conflict in the plot? How did you know they were strong or weak characters? Dialogue written convincingly can suggest answers to many of these questions.

To write convincing, natural dialogue, listen to people talk. Catch the tone of their voices. Are they people-pleasers never treading on controversial subjects? Are they subtle needlers who like to make others feel inferior? How much of their conversation is polite banter? How much is meaningful dialogue? Notice their vocabulary, their grammar, and whether they speak in clichés.

Train your ears to hear the substance and style of conversation. The actual word-for-word conversations between people often digress from the topic and are usually replete with "ahs," "ohs," "hmms," and "you knows." When you write dialogue, you want it to resemble conversation without all of these distractions—unless the distracting features somehow contribute to establishing something about a character. (For example, if you're trying to show how a character is affected by an authority figure you may have him talking to a police officer about to give him a ticket for speeding. "I k-k-know, officer. I'm s-sorry. I guess I d-didn't realize I was s-s-speeding.")

Besides being descriptive and purposeful, dialogue should reflect your character's personality. Look back at your character's biography. Let him speak the way you imagined. By doing that, his dialogue will reveal something about himself and the characters in the story, and it will advance the plot. (More on plot later in the chapter.)

There are many activities for building dialogue-writing skills. After you write a conversation, you might record it on tape. Listen to the dialogue. Ask yourself, "Does this *sound* like the person I've created?" Try to role-play the characters in your story just as an actor would do rehearsing a play. When you become the character in role-playing, your tone of voice may change. Other personality traits (aggression, compassion, etc.) may surface; when you describe the character later, those traits may add a new dimension to the character.

Another good way to learn to write dialogue is to analyze the dialogue in other stories—there's plenty of it to study. According to some estimates, more than half of a short story or novel consists of dialogue, which is often crucial to a story's success.

The next Write-Now exercise focuses on letting conversation mirror your characters' moods and feelings. Try this exercise for five days before you work with dialogue in your writing notebook.

 ## Write-Now Exercise
Dialogue

Goal: To write realistic dialogue that reflects the moods and feelings of the characters.

1.
2. Do steps 1-3 of the Write-Now exercise as outlined on page 128.
3.

4. Think of a scene in your story. Who are the two people talking? What are they discussing? Is it something pleasant or depressing? Is it a sarcastic or a sincere exchange? Are they having a friendly or a heated conversation? (Whatever visualization you select sets the mood and is extremely important, because it will affect the tone of the dialogue.)

5. Repeat the following suggestion to yourself three times: "The dialogue I write is realistic and reflects the moods and feelings of my characters."

Immediately following the exercise, record (in play form) the characters' conversation you saw and heard in your mind's eye. Using the play format makes the dialogue less verbose; it allows you to concentrate on recreating the natural rhythm of the conversation. In your writing notebook, set up and complete a page with two people conversing.

Purposeful Dialogue

What your main character says isn't the only dialogue in your story that has purpose. Other dialogue gives information about your characters and contributes toward creating images about them. There is dialogue showing what others say to your main character; dialogue showing what they say about him; and dialogue that reflects his reactions to other characters.

Henry Fleming, the main character in the *Red Badge of Courage,* begins to doubt his courage and fears he might run from battle. He probes Jim Conklin, the "tall soldier" and a minor character in the story, to find out how he would react when his courage was put to the test. The dialogue reveals both characters' emotions and reactions to that moment of truth. Another character, the "loud one," shows how he feels about what is being said.

> *"Jim!"*
>
> *"What?"*
>
> *"How do you think the reg'ment'll do?"*
>
> *"Oh, they'll fight all right, I guess, after they once get into it," said the other with cold judgment. He made a fine use of the third person. "There's been heaps of fun poked at 'em because they're new, of course, and all that; but they'll fight all right, I guess."*

"Think any of the boys'll run?" persisted the youth.

"Oh, there may be a few of 'em run, but there's them kind in every regiment, 'specially when they first goes under fire," said the other in a tolerant way. "Of course it might happen that the hull kit-and-boodle might start and run, if some big fighting came first-off, and then again they might stay and fight like fun. But you can't bet on nothing . . ."

". . . Did you ever think you might run yourself, Jim?" he asked. On concluding the sentence he laughed as if he had meant to aim a joke. The loud soldier also giggled.

The tall private waved his hand. "Well," said he profoundly, "I've thought it might get too hot for Jim Conklin in some of them scrimmages, and if a whole lot of boys started and run, why, I s'pose I'd start and run. And if I once started to run, I'd run like the devil, and no mistake. But if everybody was a-standing and a-fighting, why, I'd stand and fight. Be jiminey, I would. I'll bet on it."

"Huh!" said the loud one.

The youth of this tale felt gratitude for these words of his comrade. He had feared that all of the untried men possessed a great and correct confidence. He now was in a measure reassured.

In this dialogue we hear not only what Henry Fleming and Jim Conklin say to each other, but we also know what they think.

It takes deftness to mesh these elements so that a conversation flows smoothly. The Write-Now exercise below gives you some practice in crafting convincing dialogue that reveals not only how your characters feel about each other, but other information as well. The exercise allows you and a friend to act as minor characters and exchange information about one or more major characters.

Write-Now Exercise
Dialogue Reflects Thoughts
About Main Character

Goal: To write dialogue that reflects what minor characters say and think about main characters.

1.

2. Do steps 1-3 of the Write-Now exercise as outlined on page 128.

3.

4. See yourself at a party. You know only the host and your best friend, who is sitting with you on the sofa near the door. No one can hear your conversation, so you're very candid about each guest. What is your first impression of each person at the party? What kinds of things (gossip, facts, opinion, criticism, envious remarks) would you say about the following people:

   (a) A handsome man/pretty woman—your type.

   (b) A very fat woman with a pencil-thin husband.

   (c) A poorly dressed young man.

   (You can make up and describe different guests at the party. These can be the major characters in your story.)

5. Silently repeat this suggestion ten times: "My dialogue will contain information about the characters in my story as well as the thoughts of some of the characters."

Immediately following the exercise, record in your writing notebook the conversation you had with your friend about these people (the major characters in your story). Be sure the dialogue includes your thoughts. Make it realistic.

The following is a sample dialogue showing how two friends reacted to and discussed one of the guests at the party:

> *"Look at that guy over there, Janie. Who does he remind you of?"*
>
> *"My God, he looks just like Paul Newman. I can't believe it. Did he come in with anyone?" she asked Sandy, hoping he was alone.*
>
> *"I don't think so," Sandy said, straining her eyes to see if she could spot a wedding ring. "I'm going over there." I wonder if Janie would mind, she thought as she started to get up.*
>
> *"What are you gonna say to him?" Janie asked. They both looked over at the handsome, broad-shouldered man who captivated them.*
>
> *Just then, a petite woman approached him.*
>
> *"Aren't you glad we didn't go over and make fools of ourselves? That's probably his girlfriend," said Sandy sheepishly.*
>
> *"You can say that again," agreed her friend.*

From this dialogue you can see that the women are nearly enchanted by the handsome man who resembles Paul Newman. They both want to meet him—one is even ready to take matters into her own hands and approach him. But their hopes are dashed when the petite woman enters the picture. You sense their relief that they never had a chance to follow the impulses that could have led them to sheer embarrassment.

Empathizing With Your Characters

One of the best ways to know your characters and then to portray them realistically is to live some of what they live. Hallie and Whit Burnett suggest that walking in your characters' shoes lets you see your characters with a new perspective.

> *Fiction writers must put themselves in their characters if their work is to have any value in interpreting and recording the state of man's mind and emotions; it is more necessary with some characters than with others. How else can we empathize, say with a fourteen-year-old boy guilty of telling a lie, than by somehow seeing ourselves as a child faced with the same threat of punishment.*[7]

To know how your characters would feel in certain situations, you must be able to empathize with them. You try to "become" them and experience your story situations as they would. Empathy plays an important part in creating characters with whom readers can identify.

How would your main character feel if he became an overnight celebrity? How would you feel? Would the attention, fame, and fortune go to your head? How would your life change? By imagining yourself in your character's situations, you can portray him with new insight that enables you to add feeling, realism, and depth to your descriptions of his experiences. To get in touch with a character in your story, do the next Write-Now exercise.

 ## Write-Now Exercise
Empathize with Characters

Goal: To empathize with a character in your story.

1.
2. Do steps 1-3 of the Write-Now exercise as outlined on page 128.
3.

4. Pick one of the characters in your story. (Let's assume your character is seventeen and mildly rebellious toward his parents and teachers.) Now picture yourself as a teenager. How do you like being told what to do, when to be in on Saturday night, and what things should be important to you in your future? Try to recall those resentments—the anger and frustration of your adolescent years. (Because time has passed, you can recall how you felt then without becoming tense and upset now.) Now see your character as you saw yourself. What bothers your character? What upsets him the most? Empathize with him. Feel what he feels.

5. Say to yourself ten times: "I will empathize with the character in my story. I'll feel the same way he feels in his situation and record those feelings in my story."

Immediately after the exercise write a few paragraphs that echo your reactions to the experiences your character faced.

After doing this exercise every night for a week, Hal wrote a dialogue that his character Mark had had with his mother.

> *"I'll be home a little late tonight," called Mark as he grabbed his lunch and headed for the door.*
>
> *"Where are you going? What time will you be home?" His mother interrogated him every time he said he'd be late.*
>
> *"Come on, Mom. Give me a break. I'm not a kid anymore."*
>
> *"That's what you think. Don't get fresh with me or you'll be grounded this weekend."*
>
> *He slammed the door, ran across the street, and got on the school bus.*

The conversation reminded Hal of a similar dialogue he once had with his own overprotective mother. Mark's dialogue was natural and convincing because Hal could empathize with his character's frustration and resentment.

True-to-life characters help make memorable stories. We've discussed several ways to make fictional people "real." As you read a novel or short story notice how the author makes a character unforgettable. Is the essence of a character revealed through dialogue, through thoughts or actions, or does the author let you know a character by inviting you to empathize with his or her needs? Perhaps it's a combination of these things that creates a memorable fictional character.

Essentials Of Plot

Somerset Maugham said that it is only through plotting that an author gratifies the reader's desire to know what happens to people in whom his interest has been aroused. In other words, once you've created memorable characters, you must weave them a story.

Aristotle defined plot as "an arrangement of incidents which must be whole, complete in themselves, and of adequate importance." Others have described elements of plot in different ways, and often the terminology is confusing. To simplify matters, think of plot as consisting of four parts (the 4 C's): Conflict, Complications, Climax, Conclusion. The 4 C's are easily identified if you ask a series of questions. First, what conflict (problem) does the main character have? This can usually be summarized in a question—e.g., "Will John give up drinking?"

Next, ask yourself, "What's happening in the character's life to complicate it?" (A complication is something that happens to a character that he doesn't want to have happen.) Potential complications might be undue pressure on the job, a demanding family, or a humdrum life. If the complications are too simplistic, the plot is shallow and the reader loses interest. Yet if there are too many, too convoluted, complications, you may lose the reader altogether.

Consider this question third: "Where is the turning point of the story?" This is the climax—the high point of the action—when the complications have been overcome and the reader finds out the answer to the original conflict question: "Yes, John will give up drinking," or "No, he won't."

The conclusion follows shortly after the climax. It ties together and explains any loose ends the story might have.

The major conflict in the novel *Jaws* is "Will Brody kill the shark?" Several complications contributing to the action include: a mayor who won't publicize the real danger the shark poses, lest the merchants of Amity lose their holiday business; Brody's conscience nagging him to tell the public—an action that would cost him his job; the public's panic when they find out about the "Great White"; the horror that Brody's son might have been killed; Brody's wife, her panic, and her involvement with Hooper; the men killed trying to destroy the shark.

The climax occurs when the major conflict is resolved—and resolved ingeniously. "Will Brody kill the shark?" "Yes, the shark is blown up." In the conclusion, Brody is greatly relieved that the conflict is over.

Universal Conflicts

There are three major conflicts in fiction: man against man (man vs. woman, woman vs. child, man vs. group of people, etc.); man against himself; and man against nature. These are universal conflicts because readers have likely experienced most of them and can therefore identify with them. These three broad conflicts provide the action that moves characters swiftly along to the story's climax.

In the man-against-man conflict, the main character wants something but another person is preventing him from getting it. One person is often pitted against another; because each wants his or her way, conflict arises. "Will Ted convince the escaped convict to free the hostages?" (Ted vs. the convict.) "Will Joe defeat Ray and keep the heavyweight boxing title?" (Joe vs. Ray.)

The man-against-himself conflict revolves around the main character's personal problem. It could be a major fear, a serious flaw, or some other characteristic she must wrestle with until the climax of the story. A woman trying to cope with her feelings of inadequacy after a divorce represents a woman-against-herself conflict.

Man against nature pits the hero against a life-threatening situation such as a hurricane, earthquake, tornado, fire, flood, drought, or ferocious animal. Will the deputy kill the shark? Will Mark survive the earthquake? A man-against-nature conflict occurs when a group of people are trapped in a ski lodge because of a dangerous blizzard.

Think about stories that have held your attention. Their plots likely posed intriguing conflicts and introduced enough complications to make them exciting. They were the stories that kept you guessing and kept you reading.

Did you want Scarlett O'Hara to keep Tara? As she struggled to raise money to pay the taxes, did you admire her, or think she was a calculating shrew? And what of Madame Bovary—were you hoping she'd chuck her country life and find happiness in the big city? Did you care if E.T. got home? Was *Jaws* so real that you had second thoughts about swimming in the ocean?

If you had an emotional reaction to these stories, they were successful. Their authors piqued your curiosity with the main character's conflict and led you over each barrier until the complications were eliminated and the conflict resolved. You were captivated by a compelling and dynamic plot.

Outlining A Plot

Thinking about the plot of your own story before you write it can save time and headaches. Sometimes writers have what editors refer to as a "slight" plot, which means the story line isn't fully developed or entirely believable. Frequently, these plots have too many or too few complications and a predictable climax.

The next Write-Now exercise can remedy a weak plot by showing you how to outline. You'll see how a main conflict is presented, how the complications progress and proceed logically to a climax and then a conclusion. Do the exercise about thirty minutes before you watch a television show that has a main character.

Write-Now Exercise
Plot Outline (TV Show)

Goal: To learn how to outline a plot that includes conflict, complications, climax, and conclusion.

1.
2. Do steps 1-3 of the Write-Now exercise as outlined on page 128.
3.

4. Picture yourself watching the TV program you've selected. You're able to identify the conflict and write down all the complications the main characters must overcome before the conflict is resolved in the climax. You note when the climax and conclusion occur. You are totally absorbed in the program.

5. Say to yourself ten times: "As I'm watching the TV show, I'll be aware of the conflict the main character must solve, and all the complications associated with it. I'll know when the climax and conclusion occur, and I'll record this information on my plot outline."

After completing the exercise, prepare to watch the TV show. During the program, identify the 4 C's of the plot. What is the main character's conflict? What complications must he go through before the story reaches its climax? Where/what *is* the climax? What happens immediately after the climax that leads to the conclusion? In your writing notebook, set up a page like the outline below.

The plot of _____(name the show).

1. Conflict: (state in the form of a question)

   Will Thomas Magnum learn who murdered the tennis player?

2. Complications:

   a. Tennis player took payoffs to lose matches.

   b. She had a drug problem.

   c. She and boyfriend broke up before she died.

   d. Someone wrote a scandalous, anonymous newspaper article about her and her connection with the underworld.

   e. She had made up her mind before she died not to take any more payoffs or throw any more matches.

3. Climax: Her ex-boyfriend killed her because she refused to take any more money to lose matches. He also realized she was in love with Magnum.

4. Conclusion: Ex-boyfriend goes to prison. Magnum understands why she took money—because of her drug habit.

Now you have a plot outline for the story you've just seen. Even though you might notice the components of the plot unconsciously as you watch the show, write them down in this way so you have a record of how the plot developed. You can later duplicate the process in your own work.

Colleen McCullough's novel *The Thorn Birds* sold millions of copies because people were enthralled with its characters and its central conflict. Let's review the story in terms of the 4 C's of plot. The basic conflict is with Father Ralph de Bricassart. He has an intense desire to experience the power and prestige of becoming a cardinal in the Catholic Church. Although he loves Meggie Cleary, he can't marry her and still remain a priest. De Bricassart is torn between ambition and love; his conflict can be stated in a question: "Will Ralph choose Meggie or the Church?"

Various complications add interest and depth to the story: Ralph's insatiable ambition to move up in the ranks of the Church; his desire for love and sexual satisfaction; his inability to understand the depth of feeling that Meggie has for him; his selfishness at trying to have both the Church and Meggie; his manipulation of Mary Carson to get her property to ensure his promotion; his loneliness; his quest for perfection and holiness; his indecisiveness.

The climax comes at the end of the story. Ralph chooses to remain a priest; then he dies. In the conclusion, we see that Meggie has accepted Ralph's decision.

Plotting Your Own Story

The 4 C's of plot provide a skeletal structure for any fictional work. The following Write-Now exercise shows you how to think of your own story in terms of the 4 C's of plot. Do it prior to your writing session. It will help you complete the plotting process just as you outlined it in the earlier exercise.

Before doing the exercise, be sure you've formed at least a very rough idea of your story—i.e., you have a character in mind, and maybe a problem for him to face along with some complications to overcome. Read over your rough sketches and story ideas right before the exercise. Familiarize yourself with the questions in Step 4 of the exercise.

Write-Now Exercise
Plot Outline (Story)

Goal: To set up a plot outline for your own story by using the 4 C's of plotting.

1.
2. Do steps 1-3 of the Write-Now exercise as outlined on page 128.
3.
4. Think about your story as you read over these questions. What is the conflict (problem) of the main character? State it in a question. Will it be interesting enough for the readers? If not, how can you make it more exciting? Next, consider the complications your main character has to surmount to solve the problem. Are they credible? Too complex? Too predictable? What is the climax? Does it answer/resolve the conflict question? If not, have you digressed too far from the problem? Does the ending explain anything not covered up to that point?

5. Say to yourself ten times: "When I answer the questions about my story pertaining to the conflict, complications, climax, and conclusion, I'll come up with a solid conflict (problem). I'll develop a solid plot. My conflict and complications will be believable and hold the reader's interest. I'll answer completely all the questions about the 4 C's of plot." Say, "When I open my eyes, I'll feel great."

Following the exercise, write the answers to the questions in Step 4 in your writing notebook. Go over the complications you've listed. Ask yourself:

"Have I made the conflict too easy? Too difficult to overcome?" (If you have trouble determining this, try the Write-Now empathy exercise on pages 137-138. It will help you put yourself in your character's place to see if it would be hard for *you* to overcome the obstacles and solve the problem.)

Next, write another rough draft of your story, keeping in mind the answers to the questions you contemplated in the exercise. You don't have to write a complete rough draft right after the exercise as long as you've answered the questions. Do try, though, to write a new draft within a day of doing the exercise.

As your plot unfolds and begins to flow in subsequent rough drafts you're not required to stick to a rigid outline or use every complication you've considered along the way. Some complications may change or be eliminated as you write. The 4 C's exercise helps you see the weak areas in your plot so you can improve them. It gives you a point of departure—so you can not only refine your plot, but also begin pulling it together in a well-thought-out rough draft.

Where To Find Plot Ideas

Where do authors get plot ideas? Undoubtedly, there are as many sources as there are writers. Some writers think first of a character and then give him a problem to solve; they consider all the complications the character must face and how they can build interest and tension toward the climax of the story. Other writers begin with an interesting problem and then develop a character who can solve it. Either way, writers who are especially keen at recognizing potential plot lines are those who've trained themselves to think in terms of conflict.

When you're tuned in to recognizing conflict, you realize that with the help of your imagination everything around you has plot potential. Therefore, you cultivate an exaggerated way of looking at reality. You pretend, for instance, that the old man at your neighborhood newsstand witnesses a hit-and-run accident—and if he identifies the person driving the car, it could cost him his life. Your imagination fills in the details.

Or take people you know and give them imaginary conflicts. Think of your spouse. "Will my husband/wife continue to be a drug dealer? Later, you can change the character—but by starting with a familiar person, you have some idea how that person naturally reacts to conflict. By turning in to the basic elements of conflict, you stimulate your creativity; the seed for a plot takes root.

For example, you think of an actual neighbor who creates a mild disturbance by playing loud music; you turn him into a fictional neighbor who's an arsonist. A writer's friend who gets a divorce becomes her enemy when she turns homewrecker. If you've trained yourself to think in terms of conflict, a tropical rain can become a killer hurricane.

Themes can also spark plot ideas. The way you feel about poverty, over-population, or the women's movement can be reflected in your writing. Themes are an author's insights about life. Trust, loyalty, change, adjustment—all can be themes that surface from characters, conflicts, and complication in a plot. Give your main character a conflict to solve that will reveal the theme of your story.

In looking for plot ideas, remember that truth is often stranger than fiction. Don't concoct a plot that's unbelievable or too involved; some of the most engaging plots actually arise from real-life happenings. Look at magazines and newspapers to suggest these plot ideas: tabloids such as *The National Enquirer* have huge circulations and publish a variety of intriguing, often bizarre articles. Imagine one of your characters burdened by some of the problems examined in tabloid newspapers!

A thought-provoking picture might also suggest a plot: a photo of a boarded-up old house (what happened?). A sketch of a young woman crying (will she find her child?). An oil painting of a professional woman (will she choose a career or marriage?). A black-and-white print of an old man (will he overcome his fear of death?). The answers to those questions may lead you to fascinating story-lines.

Just as you may apply some of your own personality traits to your characters, you can also draw from your own experiences for plot development. You can embellish and reshape your life events into new ones for your characters. Hemingway transferred his war experiences and love of hunting to his heroes. Shakespeare's and Chaucer's attitudes about life and fate permeate their works.

Alex Haley's *Roots* evolved from his intense desire to trace his family's origin. A major change in your life—moving to a new country, losing a loved one, having a sudden spiritual revelation—can precipitate a plot. So can your wishes and fantasies. Much science fiction is born from a writer's desire to explore outer space and meet extraterrestrial beings. Your own adventures, attitudes, and philosophies may be the vital substance or the energizing supplement for your fiction.

The following Write-Now exercise encourages you to seek out plot possibilities while you're reading, watching television, or simply being an observant bystander. Do the exercise every day for two weeks.

Write-Now Exercise
Plot Awareness in the Media

Goal: To become aware of plot possibilities for stories in newspaper articles, television shows, and other situations.

1.
2 Do steps 1-3 of the Write-Now exercise as outlined on page 128.
3.

4. See yourself reading an unfamiliar (perhaps an out-of-town) news-paper. As you go through each section, you see a number of possible ideas for plots. You scan the sports, business, world news, and features sections; you recognize several potential plots for stories.

5. Give yourself the following suggestion ten times as you read the paper (or perform any other activity where you are an interested by-stander): "When I'm reading or watching TV, I'll become aware of the possibilities for plots for my stories."

When you complete the exercise, say, "When I open my eyes I'll feel great." Record any plot ideas you get in your writing notebook.

Painting Believable Settings

Once you've created realistic characters and decided on an engaging plot, the next point to consider is how to paint a believable setting as a backdrop for the action in your story.

Think back to the scariest movie you've ever seen. *Psycho? Night of the Living Dead? The Birds? Halloween?* What made *Psycho* so terrifying? For you, it may have been the sinister Norman Bates. Or maybe the unexpected twists in the plot. Whether or not you realized it at the time, the setting, too, created an aura of fear: a woman alone at night in an isolated motel. The murder scene in the shower seemed twice as brutal because of the suspense preceding it.

Setting contributes to the total effect of a story. In the movie *Jaws,* the horror of each attack was so realistic that whenever the chilling music signaled another, people in the audience screamed. Remember how much terror the hundreds of live cobras in the snake pit scene of *Raiders of the Lost Ark* added to the adventure? With the right props, location, makeup, and special effects, Hollywood can create the illusion of horror, wealth, romance, mystery— whatever is necessary to capture the viewer.

In similar ways, writers must make their story setting both memorable and authentic. The scenes in historical and romance novels, for example, are particularly important because they provide a context for characters and plots both. The drama of the Civil War and its impact on the characters adds depth and color to *Gone With the Wind;* similarly, Drogheda, the sprawling Australian sheep station in *The Thorn Birds,* serves as a focal point around which the characters in Colleen McCullough's novel interact. A strong attachment to this land affects each of their lives.

In order to make a setting authentic, research is a must. It may mean frequent trips to the library, interviews, travel—even some sleuthing, perhaps—to get the information you need to paint an accurate picture.

If your story is set in Hawaii and you've never been there, your research is likely to be extensive and time-consuming. You'll have to find out about the climate, terrain, culture, and customs of the land; a travel bureau may be the perfect place to go for pictures and general information. Maps and atlases are also helpful when you're describing a place—the *American Automobile Association Tour Books* are a great resource. For sites in Europe, consult the *Michelin Guides.* Don't overlook a reference librarian as an excellent resource person to get you started, or at least point you in the right direction; the actual ferreting out of facts, however, is your job.

If you plan to set your story in the United States, *The American Guide Series* is a good reference to the individual states. Writer Marilyn Durham has found this series valuable in her own research.

> *I discovered the state guides when I was looking for a place for the story to happen. When I found the Wyoming guide, it was so good that it decided me on Wyoming. Then I took the state guide, and an Atlas, and a couple of maps, and started to lay out the setting for my story. I looked very carefully through Mrs. Spring's book and made a list of all the trees, shrubs, and flowers that grew in places where my story was going to happen.... My sort of research takes what is available instead of wearing itself out trying to find out everything.*[8]

Colleen McCullough certainly did her homework for *The Thorn Birds:* her description of Drogheda is vivid and inviting.

> *Drogheda was the oldest and the biggest property in the district, and had been endowed by its late doting owner with a fitting residence. Built of butter-yellow sandstone blocks hand-hewn in*

quarries five hundred miles eastward, the house had two stories and was constructed on austerely Georgian lines, with large, many-paned windows and a wide, iron-pillared veranda running all the way around its bottom story. Gracing the sides of every window were black wooden shutters, not merely ornamental but useful; in the heat of summer they were pulled closed to keep the interior cool...Several acres of meticulously scythed lawn surrounded the house, strewn with formal gardens even now full of color from roses, wallflowers, dahlias, and marigolds.

How did the author take a fictional plot of ground, Drogheda, and magically turn it into a "real" place?

Sensory Settings

One way novelists accomplish this is to appeal to all five of their readers' senses, which play a vital part in determining whether a setting works. When readers can "smell" the roses and dahlias and "see" the austere Georgian lines of the house, their senses combine to form a mental picture that excites the imagination.

To become more aware of your own senses, take each one separately and dwell on it. Hold an apple in your hand. Look at it closely. Close your eyes. What colors do you remember? How big is it? How much do you think it weighs? What's unique about it? What could it symbolize? Open your eyes; try again to answer those questions you couldn't answer when your eyes were closed.

Pick up the apple again. Rub it with your fingers. What is its texture? How does it smell? Take a bite. What does it taste like? What sounds do you hear when you bite into it?

Now that you've isolated each of the senses, write one "sense" sentence for each of the five senses. For example:

The red apple is shiny.

It feels smooth except for five nobby bumps on the bottom.

It smells like autumn in my parents' orchard.

As I take a bite of the apple, I hear a loud crunch.

The apple tastes sweet and cold.

Practice keying in to your senses by writing one "sense" sentence for each of the following words. Try using each sense at least once.

1. spaghetti

2. a sandy beach

3. a lemon

4. toast

5. sunburn

6. a wet dog

Which sense was the easiest for you to describe? The hardest? Consciously practice using the one most difficult for you to focus on.

How well you create a visual backdrop for your story may reflect your own powers of observation. Developing those powers involves working with your senses and heightening your awareness to the stimuli around you. According to author Stephen King, what writers see and how they see is evident in their work.

> It's the imagery that makes the book "stand out" somehow; to come alive; to glow with its own light…. [the] story springs from the image: that vividness of place and time and texture…. Our eyes convey images to our brains; if we are to convey images to our readers, then we must see with a kind of third eye—the eye of the imagination and memory. Writers who describe poorly or not at all see poorly with this eye; others open it, but not all the way.[9]

Developing A Third Eye

How do you develop this third eye, this ability to picture in your mind the setting for your story and then enrich it with sensory observations? The following Write-Now exercise will get you started. To prepare for it, pretend you're in a restaurant. Be alert to the setting around you. Ask yourself these questions:

1. What is the most striking thing about the atmosphere of the restaurant?

2. When you walked in, what two things did you notice?

3. How does the restaurant smell?

4. What kind of music is playing? Do you hear any conversations?

5. How does the food taste? (Choose one dish.)

✒ Write-Now Exercise ✒
Settings

Goal: To use your five senses to describe story scenes so vividly that readers will "see" them.

1.
2. Do steps 1-3 of the Write-Now exercise as outlined on page 128.
3.

4. Imagine yourself in a restaurant. Concentrate on the setting. What are you wearing? Are you alone or with someone? Reflect on all the questions you studied in the preparation for the exercise. You experience with your senses the five situations the questions frame.

5. Repeat the following suggestion ten times: "When I describe scenes in my story, the reader will be able to see them clearly. I will use my five senses to make scenes vivid, authentic, and imaginative."

Immediately following the exercise, answer in your writing notebook all the questions about the restaurant setting. Recall as much detail as possible. Try to convey sense impressions about the restaurant scene.

After trying the Write-Now exercise three times with a restaurant setting, you may want to substitute a real scene from your own story accompanied by questions directly related to your setting.

Some writers have so nearly perfected their attention to sensory detail that they can successfully describe something they have never actually seen. Although the Civil War ended six years before his birth, Stephen Crane wrote about it so realistically in the *Red Badge of Courage* that veterans were convinced he had been there. His colorful descriptions are replete with sensory images.

> *The cold passed reluctantly from the earth, and the retiring fogs revealed an army stretched out on the hills, resting. As the landscape changed from brown to green, the army awakened and began to tremble with eagerness at the noise of rumors.*

Crane used his "third eye"—his vivid imagination—to "see" the battlefields, the armies, and the fear of dying on the faces of soldiers.

Getting In Touch With Your Surroundings

A writer's imagination is further stimulated by an awareness of his own surroundings. Unfortunately, it's not always easy to notice the very things, people, and places we take for granted—the squirrels chasing one another up one oak tree and down another, the woodpecker drumming in the yard, the gum-snapping TV repairwoman, the picnic table that wobbles in the crabgrass. Author William Saroyan suggests that many writers are missing out on a lot of stimulation by not tuning in to their immediate world.

> *Most people don't look at anything.... People never see the streets over which they move every day. To see a street one must look at it in relation to everything on it, near it, and over it—particularly over it. Not to see what is over things is to go, literally, closer and closer to the grave, which is never more than twelve or thirteen actual feet beneath the eye.*[10]

To get in touch with your surroundings and to open up your "third eye," try this Write-Now exercise for one week before describing a scene in your story.

Write-Now Exercise
Neighborhood Setting

Goal: To describe your neighborhood or a place nearby using your "third eye" to visualize it and your senses to describe it.

1.
2. Do steps 1-3 of the Write-Now exercise as outlined on page 128.
3.
4. Think about the street where you live. What color is the house or building across from you? Is the neighborhood noisy? Quiet? Are there any flowers, trees, or other natural things that make it attractive? What do you like about it? Dislike? What is your most vivid memory about your neighborhood?
5. Repeat the following suggestion ten times: "When I'm describing my neighborhood or a place near where I live, I will use my 'third eye' to visualize it and my senses to describe it."

In your writing notebook, answer the questions asked in Step 4 above. Write a description of your neighborhood or a specific place near where you live. Use as many of your senses as you can.

Several years ago, I spent six months at the University of California in Santa Barbara taking graduate courses. The campus overlooking the sea is breathtakingly beautiful. It was there that my own "third eye" was opened: each morning I went to the beach and watched the sun rise above the fog-shrouded mountains. As the air warmed, the fog gradually lifted. Gentle waves and salty breezes awakened in me a deeper appreciation of nature. The ocean was before me and a rainbow of tropical flowers scattered exotic scents on the rolling knolls bordering the beach. All my senses came alive.

Some time later, this scene provided the setting for a story I wrote about a blind girl who experiences this same place with all of the senses except sight.

Analyzing Your Fiction To Make It Better

Now that you know something about what makes good fiction and you know how to practice your fiction-writing skills, you may well be asking: "But how do I *know* what part of my story needs improvement? How do I *know* if the readers' emotions will be engaged when they read my work?"

One way is to honestly answer and critically evaluate your story with the checklist of questions below. Students in my Write-Now workshops have used the questions successfully to pinpoint the areas of their stories that need more work. The questions will help distance you from the story so that you can see it as your readers will. Your candid answers to these questions will give you clues about how to make your fiction better (and often, more salable).

Fiction Checklist

1. Are you "hooked" after reading the opening paragraphs of your short story or the opening pages of your novel? Do you feel as though you want to keep reading?

2. Are the 4 C's of your plot (Conflict, Complications, Climax, Conclusion) believable? Does the story drag? Or does it move quickly, thus keeping you interested?

3. Have you presented the conflict (problem) the main character has to solve early in the story? Do you have a clearly identified "viewpoint" character—from whose point of view the story is told?

4. Will your reader like or hate the main character? Is this the effect you want? Have you developed each character enough so he/she can be "seen"? Do they talk like real people? Will your readers empathize with or care about them?

5. Does something happen to the characters? Do you get into the action quickly to engage your reader early in the story?

6. If there is a theme or moral to the story, is it subtle or obvious? (If it's too obvious, you may turn off your reader. If there's a moral or a message, you want to weave it subtly through the story, allowing the reader to draw his own conclusions.)

7. Is the setting so descriptive that you can visualize the story's immediate surroundings (see, feel, hear the atmosphere of the story)?

At one fiction workshop, Barb (the bank manager mentioned at the beginning of the chapter) told us how she used the Write-Now exercises and the fiction checklist to improve her story about a bank employee, Sylvia, whose main conflict involves her discovery that Mr. Johnson, one of the bank vice presidents, is an embezzler.

After doing the biography exercise, I discovered why Sylvia had never seemed real to me. She didn't have any minuses. She was just too perfect, too unbelievable. I gave her a few of my bad habits. I began to "see" her during the character visualization exercise. That made it easier to get Sylvia down on paper. When she was talking to Alan Alda, she acted self-conscious about her chubby legs. She was afraid of what Alan might think of her. I kept this negative trait—lack of self-confidence—in Sylvia's personality. It shows up in her fear of what others might think of her if she turns Mr. Johnson in to the authorities.

I gave Sylvia fewer complications, but more exciting ones. I dropped the complication that she was trying to be the president of the company by day and super-wife and mom by night. I added the complication that Mr. Johnson was the person who hired her for the job when others told her she was inexperienced. She felt a sense of obligation to him for hiring her, and to make matters more interesting, she could even understand the reason he was embezzling the money. (His wife had a terminal illness; his medical insurance covered only a portion of the hospital costs.) Sylvia remembered her own grandmother's long illness and how it had depleted her parents' savings account.

In outlining my plot, I had Sylvia tell Mr. Johnson that she knew what he was doing. He begged her not to say anything for at least forty-eight hours. She promised that she wouldn't. Because he had embezzled only $3,000, he decided to ask his wealthy sister for the money and used it to replace the stolen funds. After his wife's death a year later, he resigned from the bank; Sylvia never divulged his secret.

Barb had chosen a setting that was familiar to her. She could describe the bank's atmosphere authentically because she had worked in a similar situation for twelve years. Because she started with a setting she knew, Barb concentrated mostly on the characterization and plot elements to improve her fiction. "By working through the plot and characterization exercises, I had a good idea of what I had to do with my fiction to make it ring true," she said.

By practicing the combination of Write-Now fiction exercises, and using the fiction checklist presented in this chapter, you, too, will develop your fiction potential. With both your imagination and your memory in high gear, you'll visualize plot, "see" your characters, and judge for yourself whether they're real or mere imitations. You'll hear your characters speak and through their dialogue watch them reveal their feelings. Finally you'll successfully project a scene from your story onto your own mental screen, thereby making it easy to describe. In the process, you'll begin to understand, as Barb did, how convincing characters, plots, and settings work together to create a story your readers will remember.

Notes/Chapter Six

1. A.S. Burack, ed., *The Writer's Handbook* (Boston: The Writer, 1970), pp. 143–144.

2. Virginia Thrasher, "Exclusive Interview with Marilyn Durham," *Writer's Digest,* Vol. 53 (March, 1973), p. 34.

3. R.F. Delderfield, "Confessions of a Long-Distance Writer," *The Writer,* Vol. 84 (Sept. 1971), p. 12.

4. J.D. Reed, "Those Blues in the Knights," *Time*, Vol. 117 (June 8, 1981), p. 76.

5. Hallie and Whit Burnett, *Fiction Writer's Handbook* (New York: Harper & Row Publishers, 1975), p. 55.

6. David Quinlan, *The Illustrated Directory of Film Stars* (New York: Hippocrene Books, Inc., 1981), p. 40.

7. Hallie and Whit Burnett, *Fiction Writer's Handbook,* p. 51.

8. Virginia Thrasher, "Exclusive Interview with Marilyn Durham," p. 35.

9. Stephen King, "Imagery and the Third Eye," *Writer's Digest,* Vol. 60 (October, 1980), pp. 11-13.

10. Belle McKenzie and Helen Olson, *Experience in Writing* (New York: Macmillan Co., 1962), p. 60. (First appeared, *Theatre Arts Magazine,* March, 1941)

CHAPTER SEVEN

How to Write Nonfiction with a D-i-f-f-e-r-e-n-c-e

A writer's problem does not change.
He himself changes and the world he lives in
changes but his problem remains the same.
It is always how to write truly and
having found what is true, to project it
in such a way that it becomes a part
of the experience of the person who reads it.

Ernest Hemingway

CHAPTER OVERVIEW

1. How can Write-Now exercises stimulate ideas for nonfiction projects and expedite the research necessary to develop and complete an article or book?

2. What is the d-i-f-f-e-r-e-n-c-e technique and how can it increase your chances of getting published?

3. How do you know when your article or book is the best it can be—and ready for an editor's scrutiny?

HOW DO YOU WRITE NONFICTION that "becomes a part of the experience" of your readers? It's a lofty goal that Hemingway sets for us. Just as a solid piece of fiction must be carefully planned and developed (Chapter 6), so, too, must the writing of nonfiction be a deliberate process. A publishable article is rarely written off the top of your head: the bylined articles that you enjoy in the *Atlantic, Esquire,* or *Ladies' Home Journal* are there because they've been thoroughly researched, carefully written, rewritten—perhaps even re-rewritten.

This chapter explains the nuts and bolts of good nonfiction.* The chapter covers both the components and the know-how you need to write the kind of nonfiction Hemingway was talking about. By doing the Write-Now exercises, you'll develop the proper attitude for creating interesting, informative nonfiction. You'll see how and where to get ideas for articles and how to research them completely and efficiently. And with the help of the "difference" technique, your nonfiction will be ready for its audience.

Why Nonfiction

Why do people read nonfiction? They want to be informed, or to improve some part of their lives. Readers may want to be stimulated to think or act, or they may simply want to be entertained.

---

* *Though the chapter focuses on articles and short nonfiction pieces, all the elements of nonfiction discussed here apply to books as well.*

Articles and books that tell readers how to be healthy or wealthy, appeal to the opposite sex, or overcome personality problems are in huge demand. Have you visited a bookstore lately? There you can find titles promising to improve your appearance, self-image, creativity, and general quality of life. Likewise, magazines cover everything from fitness to photography, food to finance.

Consider some of the major categories of books as listed in the *Subject Guide to Books in Print. (Books in Print* is the annual roundup of all in-print and forthcoming titles from more than 15,000 publishers. Its volumes are arranged by author, title, and subject.) Skimming the *Subject Guide,* you'll find broad topics such as popular psychology, how-to, self-improvement, cookbooks, health, business, communications, sex, and women's and men's liberation. It's clear that readers are hungry for information on whatever interests or intrigues, aggravates or amuses them. (Keep in mind that what I've capsuled in this paragraph is just a sampling of the subjects people want to know about.)

Still, writers continue to ask: "What should I write about?" Many believe that unless you have a fascinating job, the freedom to travel, or an abundance of time and money, you won't have anything to say. The truth is, you could be bedridden, poor, and *still* come up with at least ten ideas a day. Impossible? Not at all. Consider what in your own life might stimulate your imagination to cater to some reader's needs. Your work, hobbies, family, lifestyle, and community involvement are just the beginning.

Ideas From The Newspaper

What about the daily newspaper? It pulls you into a whirlwind of emotions and events. Crime, death, advice, and laughter are discussed, documented, and delivered to your doorstep. Reading the paper can be just a routine exercise—or a powerful idea generator.

If you're an active reader, you tackle those pages pen in hand and question in mind: "How can I use this in my writing?" You make notes in the margins as you read; you put checkmarks next to articles you plan to clip and file for future use.

As you read about the man who unexpectedly inherited three million dollars from a distant cousin, your active mind asks, "How will this change his life?" "How would the average person spend that much money?" "What would I do with it?" The answers to these questions could be explored in articles of your own.

The newspaper's "Dear Abby" and "Ann Landers" columns suggest a host of potential article topics. What kinds of pieces could be developed from questions such as "How do I deal with jealousy/a workaholic husband/a runaway daughter/a terminal illness?"

Even comic strips can spark ideas to be developed into articles on contemporary issues. "Cathy," the character created by Cathy Guisewite, evolved from the cartoonist's own working experience—situations that she found other women shared.

A caricature suggested a workable idea for one of my students. "I saw a cartoon in a magazine that gave me an idea for an article," said Marie. "It was a picture of a little girl, probably around seven, sitting at a table with three of her dolls, each in a separate chair. Her mother has just come in; she looks around and assumes her daughter is having a tea party. The little girl says, 'It's not a tea party, it's a board meeting.' I started to wonder if the women's movement had influenced the way most young girls thought of themselves, and if so, how that might come out in the way they played traditional games. I've started doing research on the subject."

The TV-Radio Connection

Television and radio are other potential idea factories to which you have easy access. If you're an active viewer, or listener, you take notes on shows whenever they trigger a reaction from you. (If you react to a subject, chances are other people will, too.)

What about the TV movie you watched last night—the story about a football player who ran seventy yards for a touchdown during a playoff game? How will the football hero adjust to life when the applause fades into forgotten seasons? Do other professionals have difficulty adapting to ordinary life when their careers are over? What does a violent, competitive sport do to a person's sensitivity?

News shows ("60 Minutes," "20-20," "Prime Time Live," for example) motivate you to explore in depth some of the high-interest stories they cover. They usually present enough information on both sides of an issue to get you thinking.

What about children's programming? What positive and negative effects do cartoons have on children? Does "Sesame Street" make learning fun and exciting for kids? Or are they so distracted by the characters and fast pace that learning becomes secondary?

Talk shows are another resource. Interviews on shows like "Oprah," "Lifestyles of the Rich and Famous," and "The Tonight Show" can give you insight into why people strive for recognition. These shows provide stimuli for articles on motivation, perseverance, self-confidence, and goal-setting. The "Donahue" show might introduce you to a new way of looking at a familiar problem that could be a springboard for an article—maybe even a book.

Becoming An Active Reader/Viewer

The following Write-Now exercise will help you become an active reader and viewer—someone alert to recognizing ideas around him. Try the exercise every day for three weeks. You'll begin to notice how ideas for nonfiction projects occur to you as you read or watch television.

 ## Write-Now Exercise
Nonfiction Ideas

Goal: To be open to ideas for nonfiction writing as you read newspapers, magazines, and books; watch TV; and listen to the radio.

1. Get comfortable in bed (or an easy chair if you're doing the exercise during the day). Noise should be at a minimum. Close your eyes. Take three or four deep breaths. Inhale through the nose. Take the air down to the diaphragm. Count to three. Exhale through the mouth.

2. Imagine that you're lying on a lounge chair near a pond. It's a pleasantly warm fall day. The surrounding trees reflect the reds, greens, and golds of their leaves in the water. All of nature is in harmony. You, too, feel that your mind and body are in harmony. (You can substitute another scene especially pleasing for you.)

3. Push your heels down on the chair/bed/floor. Feel the tension; now relax them. Do the same thing with your hips, back, shoulders, neck, head, arms, and hands: push down against whatever surface they're touching, then relax. Tighten and relax the muscles while taking three deep breaths. Silently repeat ten times: "I'm becoming more and more relaxed." (The main objective is to relax your mind and body so that the subconscious will accept your suggestion.)

4. Picture yourself getting up and preparing to start your day. If you read the newspaper at breakfast, see yourself going through each section, thoroughly enjoying what you're reading and taking down ideas for your own writing projects. Now see yourself going through a

magazine with the same enthusiasm. Next, visualize yourself sitting comfortably watching TV. As your favorite show comes on, you take out a 3x5-inch card and jot down any article ideas it suggests to you. (If you listen to radio talk shows more than you watch TV, you may want to substitute that scene.)

5. Say to yourself ten times: "As I read newspapers, magazines, and books, I'll be an active reader. As I watch television or listen to the radio, I'll be an active viewer and listener. I'll be open to ideas for my own nonfiction writing. I'll make note of ideas that come to mind."

If you're doing this exercise during the day, say, "When I open my eyes, I'll feel great." If you're doing the exercise at bedtime, drop off to sleep.

Once you become an active reader, you'll look at article titles with new awareness, new curiosity, and begin to ask questions. The titles below contain kernels of thoughts that could be developed into other articles; they suggest questions you might ask yourself. I've included a few questions to show you what I mean. The answers to those questions suggest projects you might pursue.

1. "New Drug Fights Depression"

   What depresses people? What depresses me? Are there alternatives to antidepressant drugs? Is depression common in children? Do men get more depressed than women?

2. "Twice as Much Love"

   What can we learn from people with twins? What is life like for widows who remarry? How does a family decide to adopt children?

3. "Incredible Clothes of the Future"

   What are disposable clothes? Skirts . . . for men? What's the future of the three-piece suit?

4. "Food Facts"

   What isn't the FDA telling us? How can you quench your thirst with impure water? What does it mean when even lab rats won't eat hot dogs? Can pesticides on fruit make you sick?

Robert Frost believed that "an idea is a feat of association." The four provocative newspaper headlines listed above can stimulate endless ideas. Write down two of your own for each title.

Pam, a dietitian in one of my classes, came up with several ideas after reading the list. Looking at "Food Facts," she thought, "What we don't know *will* hurt us," and proceeded to research a piece on harmful food preservatives and additives. For "Twice as Much Love," Pam planned to write an article about stepchildren who have the love of two sets of mothers and fathers.

Start With What You Know

As you can see, the major sources for nonfiction writing projects are easily available; you're limited only by your imagination. The old adage "write what you know" is good advice, but don't stop there. Let what you know lead you to explore the unfamiliar. Each month, read at least two magazines you've never read. The library has hundreds of periodicals from which to choose.

"While browsing in the library, I noticed a magazine called *Success* that I haven't seen on the newsstands," remarked Bart, a basketball coach in my writing seminar. "I looked through the back issues and liked the upbeat and practical advice on setting realistic goals. I got the idea to do an article about how kids are happier when they set their own goals than when they rely on their parents or me to do it for them."

Brainstorming

Another successful technique to generate ideas is brainstorming, a popular method used in industry, education, community affairs, and other sectors to come up with advertising slogans, new products, and solutions to complicated problems. Alex Osborn, the founder and chairman of the Creative Education Foundation, developed the brainstorming technique in the 1950s.

There are generally five features common to any brainstorming session: 1) it's done as a group activity; 2) people in the group call out every idea they have on a subject; 3) no idea is made fun of or discarded—group members feel free to offer any suggestions; 4) ideas are quickly written down so they can be referred to later; 5) ideas are evaluated after the session.[1]

Though brainstorming is usually a group activity, you can use it on your own to get a slant on a subject you're interested in. If you're having trouble finding a topic, think about what people want to know; review some of the major categories of nonfiction books. Better yet, skim through *Subject Guide to Books in Print* when you're in the library; you'll be confronted with more possibilities than you can imagine. Such a bombardment of stimuli often results in flashes of insight.

When you've hit on a topic, write it at the top of a sheet of paper. For five minutes, quickly write down anything related to that subject that comes to mind.

Don't make judgments about what you've written; don't correct grammar or spelling. Jot your ideas in a paragraph, a phrase, or an unnumbered list. There's no set formula to follow.

Let's say, for instance, that you picked the stock market as your topic. What words, phrases, concepts, ideas does "stock market" suggest to you? After five minutes of brainstorming, you may have a list that looks like this:

Wall Street	preferred stocks
risks	broker
money	options
complicated	bull
common stocks	bear

Now be judgmental. Ask yourself: "What fascinates me about the market? Who else might be interested in knowing about it? Who would read an article about the stock market?" Cross out anything that either doesn't appeal to you or that you anticipate won't interest others. Circle those items you'd have to research in order to write knowledgeably about.

By quickly writing down everything that pops into your mind about your topic, you'll explore the subject in depth and bypass your inner critic—your conscious mind with its judgmental interjections. Afterwards you'll be able to decide what and how many points to develop in your writing. It's important to do this *early* in the writing stage because it's frustrating to finish an article only to realize that you should have picked an additional main idea to develop. A brainstorming session gets all your ideas out in the open. At the outset of planning your article, you can select the two or three major points you'll cover. This helps to reduce the possibility of getting sidetracked in your research.

Try the next Write-Now exercise before a brainstorming session to get optimum results. It will unleash associations and ideas about your subject and give you an in-depth look at your topic.

Write-Now Exercise
Brainstorming

Goal: To relax your mind so it has free rein to come up with ideas during the brainstorming session.

1.
2. Do steps 1-3 of the Write-Now exercise as outlined on page 161.
3.

4. See the subject you're writing about written in large letters on a blackboard in front of you—in this case, the stock market. Think of anything that relates to it. As you do, the words appear on the board under the topic.

5. Say to yourself ten times: "When I'm involved in brainstorming my topic, my mind will be relaxed. I'll list freely anything that pertains to my subject. I won't pass judgment on the list for five minutes (longer if you need more time). Afterward, I'll briefly outline each of the main points I plan to use in my writing."

Say, "When I open my eyes I'll feel great."

The S-O-S Outline

After the Write-Now exercise and your subsequent brainstorming session, write down the three major points (or more or fewer depending on the length and depth of the article you plan to write) you want to discuss in your article. List the points in outline form. The S-O-S outline I've devised isn't a detailed plan, nor is it an outline such as you learned in high school, where the structure rather than the substance was often emphasized. The S-O-S outline is a brief, rough sketch. Its purpose is to provide direction, not digression, as you proceed down the writing road

S—Say what you're going to say.

O—Outline what you're going to say.

S—Summarize what you've said.

The S-O-S outline is appropriate for nonfiction writing because it suggests a logical pattern. All writing has three parts: beginning, middle, and end. In the beginning, you tell your readers what it is you'll be writing about. In the middle of the article or book, you discuss the topic in detail: you use quotes, statistics, anecdotes—anything that will help you make your point. At the end, you briefly summarize what you've said. A strong concluding statement is important to make your readers feel they've profited in some way from what you've written.

If you plan to write about the stock market, first envision who your readers will be. (You should know before you write the article what magazines you plan to market it to.) Based on how knowledgeable you think your readers are about the subject, you'll know what to cover and in what depth. If you plan to write an article for stockbrokers, you wouldn't have to include basic background on the stock market. Let's suppose instead that you've decided to target your article to women (with families) interested in learning the basics of investing money.

Now you're ready to set up your S-O-S outline:

S—How to shop in the stock market. Types of stocks to buy and how to buy them.

O—Types of stocks to buy

1. Common stock—definition
   - advantages (quotes)
   - disadvantages (statistics)
   - cost (statistics)
   - anecdotes from investors
   - good and poor companies for investment

2. Preferred stock—definition
   - advantages over common stock (quotes)
   - disadvantages (statistics)
   - cost (figures)
   - anecdotes—investors
   - good and poor companies for investment

3. How homemakers can invest as a group
   - how to organize an investment group (anecdotes, quotes, facts)
   - capital needed (figures)
   - which stock is best (quotes, facts, figures)
   - dividends to expect (statistics)

S—Summary statement

1. Make a recommendation to the readers.

2. Conclude with a strong statement. Readers should want to get involved in the stock market or just be glad they read the article.

Having thought through your proposed project, you can flesh out the outline so you have a solid article. (Of course, if you're writing a book, your outline will have more depth and a broader purpose.) In fleshing out your outline you give it substance. Under each main point you note how you plan to support or substantiate it. Will you use quotes, facts, figures, anecdotes, or some other verifiable information to give your article both relevance and credence? (See the first main point—common stock—in the S-O-S outline above. The kind of supporting material you might use in developing this point is listed in parentheses following each feature of "common stocks" you plan to discuss.)

The D-I-F-F-E-R-E-N-C-E Technique

Facts, figures, and quotes alone do not an article make; waves of facts can capsize your readers into a sea of statistics from which they emerge not informed, but confused. There are, however, many things you *can* do to ensure that your writing is not just informative, but interesting as well.

Think of the word D-I-F-F-E-R-E-N-C-E to make your writing distinctive. I developed the "difference" technique when I was teaching two Write-Now workshops. Students in one class were learning the basics of article writing; the other class had taken other writing courses and had had some of their work published. After a few sessions with each group, I realized that the second group needed a refresher course on some of the basic factors of vital, valid nonfiction.

I suggested the "difference" technique as a way for them to approach and follow through with their nonfiction projects. It's a guide that will help you distinguish your writing from that of novices, and will thus help you write nonfiction that gets published. The technique consists of tending to the following elements:

D - Description

I - Introduction

F - Facts

F - Figures

E - Evaluate

R - Readers

E - Editing

N - Narratives

C - Compare and Contrast

E - Ending

After we discussed and practiced the technique in depth, Donald, a student in the second group, told us how it helped his writing. "I've been freelancing for five years," he said, "but I never realized until now how much you need narratives and anecdotes in articles so readers can identify with someone in the same situation. Now I let real people reveal information by their actions instead of telling it to the readers myself."

Of course, not all ten elements are needed in every article. For Donald, being aware of the effectiveness of narratives made the difference. Which factors pertain to *your* writing project will depend on the length of the piece, the topic, and your readers. However, most articles should include at least four or five, though not necessarily in the order discussed here.

Good nonfiction always includes these basic elements: an introduction, an ending, reader identification, facts, and description. The "difference" technique serves as a quick check to see if you've done enough to ensure that these elements make the article appealing to the reader.

For beginning writers who often forget to substantiate their claims with telling statistics and opinions from experts, the two F's in "difference" suggest what may be missing in their articles. For seasoned writers, the "difference" technique draws their attention to the ingredients of good nonfiction and reminds them that enhancing or refining one particular element might make an article salable.

By paying attention to the "difference" technique, your nonfiction will capture and keep the attention of your readers.

D—Description

According to Rudyard Kipling, "Words are the most powerful drug used by mankind." As a writer, part of your task is to project vivid word pictures to the reader to let him or her "see" whom or what you're writing about.

Description, once more common to fiction than nonfiction, has now become important to most types of nonfiction writing, where it enhances rather than upstages the information so essential in factual writing. An inviting travel article about the Napa Valley, for example, contains enough detail that the smell of the vineyards seems real.

What helps writers create colorful images? In my workshops, I suggest two things in particular: using strong active verbs and studying poetry.

In the classic writing resource *The Elements of Style*, Strunk and White offer this suggestion: "Write with nouns and verbs, not with adjectives and adverbs."[2] Strong nouns and verbs produce dynamic word pictures. In addition, verbs in the active voice—the subject of a sentence does the acting—keeps momentum flowing. A conscious effort to use the active voice in your writing gives your words immediacy and relevance.

Studying poetry can also improve your powers of description. Poetry sharpens your awareness of strong nouns and verbs; it emphasizes the importance of selecting the right word—and the right amount of words—to communicate your ideas.

To stress the value of writing concisely and finding the right word to express an exact meaning, I have my students read and discuss the poems of Robert Frost, Carl Sandburg, and other writers.

Les, a mechanical engineer in one of my seminars, told me how studying poetry helped him with the prose he had to write. "I write reports all the time. Reading poetry made me see why I should pick a couple of vivid words to get my point across instead of saying the same thing in two or three sentences."

Using The "Best" Words

Samuel Coleridge described prose as "words in their best order" and poetry as "the best words in their best order." The following well-known poem by Robert Frost is elegant in its statement; it also suggests the implication in Coleridge's words—specifically, that there is a power in well-chosen, carefully placed words.

The Road Not Taken

Two roads diverged in a yellow wood,
And sorry I could not travel both
And be one traveler, long I stood
And looked down one as far as I could
To where it bent in the undergrowth;

Then took the other, just as fair,
And having perhaps the better claim,
Because it was grassy and wanted wear;
Though as for that the passing there
Had worn them really about the same,

And both that morning equally lay
In leaves no step had trodden black.
Oh, I kept the first for another day!
Yet knowing how way leads on to way,
I doubted if I should ever come back.

I shall be telling this with a sigh
Somewhere ages and ages hence:
Two roads diverged in a wood, and I—
I took the one less traveled by,
And that has made all the difference.

Robert Frost[3]

The beauty of poetry is that it's subjective and can be interpreted in different ways by different readers. You don't have to know what a poem *meant*—only what it means to you. Let's look at one subjective interpretation we might give of Frost's poem. The diverging roads could symbolize a career choice or other major decision. There's a suggestion of doubt about it—"Oh, I kept the first for another day! . . . I doubted if I should ever come back." But the last line implies that whatever misgivings involved in the decision have been resolved—"I took the one less traveled by,/And that has made all the difference." If you were writing an article about making decisions and how painful it can be not to know which "road" to choose, you might open your piece with "The Road Not Taken."

Note, too, Frost's economy of words. He describes a "yellow wood"; if he'd spent three lines depicting the woods, they wouldn't have had the same impact. Two well-chosen words are enough. What do you see when you envision a yellow wood? The fact that you *can* see it is evidence that Frost has succeeded in communicating an image.

Figurative language—the substance of poetry—can add color and texture to nonfiction. Metaphors and similes are two common literary techniques writers use in description. A metaphor is the comparing of two unlike objects to suggest a resemblance: "The eyes are windows of the soul" compares the function of the eyes with that of windows; a "peaches and cream" complexion compares someone's face with the color and perhaps texture of a delicate dessert. Metaphors such as these stimulate the senses and make them more acute: the poet wants the reader to have a sensory experience.

A simile is the same thing as a metaphor with one exception. The words "like," "as," and sometimes "seems" and "than" are used to make the comparison. Wordsworth's "I wandered lonely as a cloud" compares the aimless wanderings of a person with the seemingly directionless motion of a cloud. "Joan is as gentle as a lamb" uses a simile to give us a definite impression of Joan's personality. (We could have used the metaphor "Joan is a lamb" to accomplish the same effect.)

Now you've seen how figurative language creates atmosphere and effect in poetry. In the same way, it breathes freshness and vitality into nonfiction: if your readers can associate an abstract concept or an unfamiliar subject with something concrete or familiar, they'll have a deeper understanding of it.

If you were writing an article about today's children wanting their independence at a young age, you might use the line "a boy's will is the wind's will" to help your readers identify with the topic. The line is from Longfellow's "My Lost Youth"; it could serve as either a title or an introductory sentence. If you were analyzing the issue of mid-life career change, you could use Frost's "The Road Not Taken" to symbolize the experience. A reference to the poem might help you explain why a surgeon suddenly decides to take the career he bypassed in youth and pursue acting.

Using Your Own Figurative Language

Before making up your own metaphors and similes, learn to recognize them in poetry. Select some of your favorite poems; then read other, unfamiliar poems by the same writer. Next, read poems by different poets. Read one poem a day for a week. Write down the metaphors and similes and your interpretations of them.

When you become tuned in to recognizing figurative language such as this, you'll be ready to write some of your own. Think of the pairs of words below. What similarities can you discover between the two elements in each pair? Compare them and see if you can create a metaphor or simile to express the resemblance. (If any article ideas occur to you in the process, write them down.)

1. flower—baby

2. computer—person

3. book—boat

4. money—mask

5. thoughts—seasons

6. child—building

7. self-image—tape recorder

Make up your own list of words or word pairs, or use the list above. For a week, take one pair of words each day and do the Write-Now exercise below. Record in your writing notebook any vivid metaphor or analogy you think of during the exercise. (If you're doing the exercise at bedtime, record your ideas the next day.)

Write-Now Exercise
Similes, Metaphors, Analogies

Goal: To develop an awareness of how metaphors, similes, and analogies make nonfiction writing more colorful and descriptive.

1.
2. Do steps 1-3 of the Write-Now exercise as outlined on page 161.
3.

4. Think of one word—e.g., flower. Try to get a vivid picture of a particular type of flower. What kind is it? What is its scent? What does it remind you of? Hold the picture in your mind for a minute. Now think of the other word in the pair—baby. What does the baby look like? Is the baby happy? What does he/she remind you of? Is a flower like a baby? How are they similar? How are they different?

5. Silently repeat this suggestion ten times: "When I think of certain words or word pairs (whatever the pair you've chosen to analyze on a certain day), I'll visualize them. I will notice different aspects of the word(s) and see if they can be used as a metaphor or an analogy. I'm developing word awareness."

    If it's bedtime, drop off to sleep. If you're doing the exercise during the day, say, "When I open my eyes, I'll feel great." Then get busy recording your images in the writing notebook.

"Since I've been doing the Write-Now word awareness exercise," said Angela during one of our seminar discussions, "I'm beginning to see not just the word, but a word picture. Reading my articles was a little like looking at a black-and-white movie. Now that I've become aware of the richness of word images, my writing is more colorful."

Liz, another student in the seminar, discussed how the exercise made her more aware of similes and metaphors.

> *I used the two words "building" and "child" during the exercise.*
> *First, I thought of my own two-year-old, Teddy, and everything*

about him: brown-eyed, chubby, cute, innocent, dependent, angry. I thought of all the guidance, love, and values my husband and I would give him to strengthen his character as he grew. Then I thought of a building—concrete, office, skyscraper, foundation. Next, I considered similarities: both need a good foundation, good materials to build upon, and someone else to provide them with materials—a child needs parents; the building needs workers.

I wrote the following analogy in my notebook: A child's character is similar to the foundation of a building. A child needs a solid set of values, guidance, and love to provide strength during each stage of his life. A building needs a solid foundation made of quality materials to support each story that will rest on it. The workers provide this, just as loving, caring parents provide a solid base for a child.

About three months after Liz wrote this entry in her notebook, she used the analogy in an article about the early developmental stages of children. Recording analogies, metaphors, and similes in your notebook is important. Though you may not use them in a current writing project, they'll be there when you need them for a future piece.

Edgar Allan Poe described poetry as "the rhythmical creation of beauty in words." The ideas and figurative language you glean from poems and from your imagination will heighten the emotional response and enjoyment of your readers. Whether you're aiming for the bestseller list or writing an article for a local magazine, your readers must see the word pictures you've painted.

Description also plays an important part in making nonfiction more salable. Editors know that a dry display of facts and figures is sterile writing. Readers want the facts—but they want them presented in a pleasant, palatable way. Vivid descriptions of factual information won't just inform readers, but interest them as well.

I—Introduction

Getting the reader's attention in the beginning of an article is of paramount importance. The introduction is similar to the narrative hook in fiction. Often, it determines whether you've enticed your reader to read further. Any one of several approaches can make your introduction provocative and appealing: tell an anecdotal story; use a startling, alarming statistic; ask a rhetorical question; relate a humorous incident.

Anecdotes are often the most engaging introduction. People like to read about other people. While researching your piece, keep notes of relevant anecdotes you cover along the way.

Another way to pique a reader's interest in the introduction is to use an eye-opening statistic. "Sixty-one percent of the population in the United States drinks alcohol" could open a piece on alcoholism. "Cigarettes killed 340,000 people last year. Will you be their victim next year?" could introduce an article about the hazards of smoking.

The rhetorical question is another attention-getter. "How many of the 61 percent of the population that drink liquor in this country are potential alcoholics?" "Why do women outlive men?" "Is marriage becoming obsolete?" In this kind of introduction, the writer poses the question and then proceeds to answer (or at least explore) it in the ensuing article.

Sometimes humor best grabs a reader's attention. Getting him to chuckle or smile or laugh out loud puts the reader in a receptive mood and helps you set the tone for your article. It's important to choose an anecdote or joke that highlights your theme. The humorous side of the relationship between painters and their spouses, for example, could be illustrated by a remark Pablo Picasso's wife made: "If my husband ever met a woman on the street who looked like the women in his paintings, he would faint."

Similarly, John Steinbeck's statement, "The profession of book writing makes horse racing seem like a solid, stable business" might be an appropriate opener for an article about the sometimes volatile lives of professional writers.

Using Someone Else's Words

It's possible that someone has already written an introductory sentence for you. Quotations are a rich source for presenting ideas to your readers. An article on inaccurate news stories could begin with Mark Twain's comment: "The reports of my death are greatly exaggerated." Maybe it's a line from a poem or a direct quotation that focuses precisely on the essence of your topic. Somerset Maugham's observation that "only a mediocre person is always at his best" could effectively introduce your article on self-improvement. Because of your engaging introduction, you've captured the readers' interest in your topic. The next step is to give them some "telling" information about it.

F-F—Facts And Figures

To enhance credence to your ideas and opinions, you must substantiate your views with facts and statistics—the "meat and potatoes" of the nonfiction piece.

The facts and figures ingredients may well be the most time-consuming element of the "difference" technique. No nonfiction writer can afford to skip this part of the process.

But where do you get information on pygmy rattlesnakes in South Florida or on the Polish community in Chicago today? The greatest source of information about any topic is people. What they say, what they've written from their own research, what they've developed to prove a point—all this is fodder for the facts and figures you need. Here are some tips that will make your search for appropriate information both easier and more efficient than you may have imagined.

Your research will likely begin with books. Some you have on your own bookshelf; most will be in a library. Librarians are excellent resource persons; don't hesitate to enlist their help. But because they must share their expertise with every other researcher, take time yourself to become familiar with the reference books, directories, indexes, and government publications that might contain exactly what you need.

Some of the most basic information-finding tools used by nonfiction writers are readily available in large public libraries. These references include: *The New York Times Index; Poole's Index to Periodical Literature, 1802-1902; Reader's Guide to Periodical Literature, 1900-Present; Book Review Digest, 1905-Present;* and *Social Science Index.* If you're not sure *where* to begin your research, consult *Finding Facts Fast* by Alden Todd or *Knowing Where to Look* by Lois Horowitz. (Check the bibliography for other reference books for writers.)

Many of the reference tools listed above will lead you to other books and magazines, but if the particular source suggested to you by any information-finding tool described here is *not* available in your own library, don't despair. Computer access files are becoming more and more common in libraries around the country, making ever more material accessible to writers. A librarian can do a computer search for a book not available in your library, to see if another university, business, or city library owns that title. If the book is available elsewhere, your library can arrange an interlibrary loan. You may have to wait a few weeks to get the book, but then again, it could be just the one you need.

People Resources

The books and magazines you use in your fact-finding ventures often lead you to the people who wrote them. Quotes from experts in a particular field are cited in the materials you read during research and the university, organization, or corporation with which the experts are affiliated is always included. If an address is given, your job is easy; if not, ask a librarian to suggest an appropriate directory. If none exists, you may be able to reach your expert by writing to him or her in care of the author of the article that mentioned him, or in care of the publisher of his or her article or book.

Interviews by mail can be just as effective as those conducted on the telephone or in person. Always explain your writing project to the interviewee and ask for permission to quote. The number of questions you ask in a letter depends on how much information you need—but keep in mind that if you ask too many, the person might not take the time to reply. Ask very specific questions, not questions that can be answered with a simple yes or no. Avoid time-consuming, complex questions that might elicit no response at all. (When I interview an expert by mail, I try to limit myself to five questions that require just a one-paragraph answer.) In conducting this kind of interview, you may have to write a second time to get the specific answer you need. The advantage of a telephone interview is obvious: if you don't get a complete answer, you just ask for more details.

Let's say you're writing about the Big Brothers/Sisters of America. Check your local phone directory for a nearby office of the organization. There may be an "expert" in your own city. Call and make an appointment to speak to someone you can interview either in person or on the telephone. Prepare your questions in advance.

Another approach is to write a letter several weeks prior to when you want to meet and request a convenient time to get together. Describe the article or nonfiction book you're working on and how this person might help you. Any correspondence or telephone contact you have with the expert should reflect your professionalism as a writer—i.e., arrange to call at the expert's convenience; if you're writing, type a neat letter on quality paper or your business stationery. Always enclose a self-addressed, stamped envelope for a reply.

Prior to a phone or in-person interview, research your topic so you can ask intelligent questions. Make them open-ended so the response is more than a one-word answer. Have your questions written out in their order of importance. Since your time is limited during an interview (experts are usually busy people), try to focus on getting the most pertinent information first.

When I interviewed Dr. Henry Dyer at the Educational Testing Service in Princeton, New Jersey a few years ago, I wanted to know what he thought of I.Q. tests. I didn't go into what the consensus of educators' opinions was on the subject because his time was limited, and my preliminary research had already given me those answers anyway. I wanted a direct quote from Dr. Dyer on the subject of I.Q. tests and how reliable they are in determining a person's intelligence, so I concentrated on getting that information.

When you have an expert's statement that you want to use verbatim, read it back to him or her for accuracy. As long as there are no objections, consider using a tape recorder to avoid having to read quotes to the person for verification.

Throughout the interview, encourage the expert to share interesting anecdotes you can use to add dimension and reader appeal to your writing. Anecdotes make facts easier to digest.

In a face-to-face interview, it's important that the person you're talking with feel comfortable during the exchange. If you appear nervous, poorly prepared, or disorganized, you won't be at your best—and chances are, neither will your interviewee. To feel at ease during the interview, read over ahead of time the questions you plan to ask. Do the following Write-Now exercise several times before your appointment. It will help you prepare yourself to get the facts and figures you need.

Write-Now Exercise
Interview

Goal: To feel at ease during the interview and to get the information you need for your writing project.

1.
2 Do steps 1-3 of the Write-Now exercise as outlined on page 161.
3.

4. See yourself talking to a friend. You're genuinely interested in what he's telling you about his work. As he answers your questions, you encourage him to talk. When he relates stories, you find them fascinating. Now picture yourself talking to the person you plan to interview. Think about some of the questions you're going to ask. You are as genuinely interested in the answers he/she gives you as you were in your friend's comments.

5. Repeat the following suggestion ten times: "I'm looking forward to interviewing (Mr./Ms. fill in the name). I'll feel at ease during our conversation. I'll make a note of all statements and anecdotes that will help me in writing my article/book."

If you're doing this exercise during the day, say, "When I open my eyes, I'll feel great." If it's bedtime, drop off to sleep.

Research Time-Savers

Whether you're looking for experts, preparing interview questions, or doing the reading that research involves, you'll eventually feel the pressures of time. The volume of material to be read, assimilated, and reacted to can be so overwhelming that projects may never get completed. The following techniques will expedite your research and streamline your fact-finding: 1) overview reading; 2) skimming; 3) note-taking; 4) vocabulary-building.

Overview reading lets you see the overall content of a book or article *before* you read it. The technique is similar to glancing over an outline before reading an entire work: you save time because you know almost immediately if the material pertains to your topic. Your comprehension improves because you see how information is organized; therefore, it's easier to fit in details later when you read the entire article.

Overview Reading For An Article

1. Read all headings and subheadings first.

2. Read the first and last sentence of each paragraph (main ideas).

3. Read the first three introductory paragraphs of the article (identifies the topic).

4. Read the last three paragraphs of the article's conclusion (summarizes what has been said).

5. Ask yourself: "What's the article about?" "Will it give me the information I need?" "What facts, figures, anecdotes do I want to record in my notes?" If the article doesn't give you meaningful answers, go on to the next article. If it gives you the answers you want, record them in your writing notebook.

Overview Reading For A Book

1. Skim through the index first. Does it contain some of the subjects you want to cover? Next, read the table of contents and the introduction.

2. Read the first five pages of the first chapter and the last five pages of the concluding chapter.

3. Read the first three paragraphs of each of the remaining chapters. You should know by then if the book will be beneficial.

If you decide not to read the book but you want to check it for a few statistics and facts, you can skim through it.

Skimming A Book Or Article

1. First, make a note of exactly what you're looking for—i.e., anecdotes, quotes, charts, statistics on whatever the topic.

2. Mentally divide each page into three vertical rows. Each row consists of approximately three or four words. Let your eyes move down the page, quickly picking up the information you need. (You can cover up the remaining two-thirds of the page with an index card as you skim.) Let your eyes stop only once before moving to the next line.

Try the skimming exercise now. After doing Steps 1 and 2, see how many times you notice the word "the" on this page. It takes a little practice, but skimming will save a great deal of time later on.

Megan, one of my students, found the practice helpful. "I used to come home with five or six books on whatever subject I was writing about," she told our seminar group. "After spending hours reading through them to see if I could use any of the material, I was lucky if one book had what I needed. Now I do the skimming and overview exercises in the library. When I check out books, I know I'll use them."

Both overview reading and skimming let you grasp the essence of the books, newspapers, and other resources. To improve your reading comprehension so you can recall and record relevant information, do the following Write-Now exercise. As preparation for the exercise, read over the notes you took in your writing notebook in response to the questions asked in Step 5 of the "Overview Reading" exercise. "What is the article/book about? What are the main points? How were they substantiated and what information did I get to help me write my article?"

 Write-Now Exercise
Comprehension

Goal: To improve comprehension and recall salient facts pertaining to research material and take notes only on relevant information.

1.
2. Do steps 1-3 of the Write-Now exercise as outlined on page 161.
3.

4. You have just finished reading an article. You begin telling the person next to you about it. He asks you what the article/book was about. What were the main points and how were they supported? What did you learn about the subject you were researching? You answer all his questions knowledgeably. You feel confident about the subject.

5. Give yourself this suggestion ten times: "I am able to remember and recall significant facts about the material I've read. Overview reading and skimming helped me do this. My comprehension is getting better, and I'll take notes only on information I need."

If you're doing the exercise at bedtime, drop off to sleep after Step 5. If you're doing the exercise just before you read an article, prepare to read it following this exercise.

Students in my Write-Now workshops who had difficulty retaining, recalling, and taking notes while doing research did this exercise three times a week for two months. Many of them also had trouble concentrating while they read, so on alternate days, they practiced the Write-Now Concentrating on Research exercise on page 26. Both their comprehension and concentration improved significantly.

Concentrating on and comprehending the material you read doesn't automatically guarantee that you'll remember it. Notes are a must. The more skillful you become at taking notes, the more efficient you'll be at doing research. Keeping track of sources, quotes, and other data becomes relatively simple with this four-step note-taking technique:

1. Use a preliminary S-O-S outline to give your note-taking some direction. Write down the main points for which you want to find facts and figures.

2. On 3x5-inch cards write down the sources (books, magazines, newspaper articles) you plan to use. Record the author, title, publisher's name and location, and date of publication for each source. Write the word "bibliography" in the top left corner of the card; label each card B1, B2, etc., in the top right corner. These are your bibliography cards; keep them separate from your note cards (see #3 below).

3. Write each main point from your S-O-S outline in the upper left corner of a card. When using one of your sources and taking notes from it, put the bibliography number that corresponds with that source in the top right corner of the card on which you're actually taking notes; include statistics, facts, quotes, anecdotes that pertain to the main point

indicated on the card. In the lower right-hand corner, write the page on which you found the information. These are your note cards.

4. If in your reading you come across another main point you want to include, add it to your outline and enter it on a separate card. When you've read or skimmed and taken notes on all your material, clip together all the note cards that refer to the same main idea. Organize the note cards according to your outline; this is how you'll present your ideas in a rough draft. (When you have all your note cards in order, you may want to number them to eliminate confusion if for some reason they're dropped or fall out of sequence.)

Sample bibliography and note cards are illustrated below. (These could have been part of your research for the stock market article discussed earlier.)

Sample Bibliography Card

> **Bibliography** **B 1**
>
> Sloan, Harold S. and Arnold J. Zurcher. *Dictionary of Economics* (New York: Barnes & Noble Books, 1970).

Sample Note Card

> **Common Stock (capital stock)** **B 1**
>
> The permanently invested capital of a corporation contributed by the owners either at or subsequent to the time the corporation is organized. Capital stock is divided into shares; each share represents a proportionate ownership in the corporation.
>
> Capital stock is divided according to class: common, equity or ordinary stock and preferred stock.
>
> Common, equity or ordinary stock enjoys exclusive claims to the net assets and to the profits of the corporation if no other class of stock is issued.   (page 5)

Learning to take notes efficiently prepares you to write the first draft of your work. Another advantage is that while taking notes you can increase your vocabulary: research is an opportunity to build your inventory of colorful and unusual words and phrases. When you come across an unfamiliar word, write it down on a 3x5-inch card. Later, look up the definition and write it on the other side. You can also include a sentence to show how the word is used in context. After you've accumulated ten words, go through the cards and study them. If you have difficulty remembering their definitions, read each word and its meaning into a tape recorder before doing the Write-Now exercise below.

Write-Now Exercise   Vocabulary

Goal: To increase your vocabulary and become more aware of the importance of new words in your own writing.

1.
2. Do steps 1-3 of the Write-Now exercise as outlined on page 161.
3.
4. See all the words in your mind's eye as you listen to the tape. Visualize exactly what they symbolize. You know their meanings.

5. Repeat to yourself ten times: "My vocabulary is increasing because I'm becoming more aware of the meaning of words and their importance to my writing."

   If you are doing this exercise during the day, say, "When I open my eyes, I'll feel great."

   If you do it at bedtime, drop off to sleep.

Make it a practice to add seven to ten new words to your vocabulary while researching an article and a few new words per chapter during research for a book. If your research is minimal because you're very knowledgeable about a topic, you'll probably not come across as many new words as if you were researching a subject in depth for the first time.

E—Evaluate

After completing your research, read and evaluate the notes you've taken. Select the best anecdotes, statistics, and studies to support your views. Certain criteria will help you choose the most telling research notes to include in your rough draft.

Select the most current facts and figures. Quote only reliable and respected experts in a particular field. (With most readers, the simple fact that an expert is affiliated with an educational institution or national organization adds credibility to his statements.) For that reason, I included in my I.Q. article Dr. Henry Dyer's statement about I.Q. tests rather than a similar comment made by a high school counselor. Because of Dyer's years of experience in the field, his input on the subject was much more convincing.

Well-documented studies are an excellent way to support your views and premise. Sketchy research studies that don't give all the pertinent data or don't reach some clear conclusion should *not* be included.

One way to further evaluate your notes (to see if they really are what you need) is to fill in the body of your outline with the types of information you want to include in your article. (See the S-O-S outline on page 166.) Evaluate the notes you've taken for each main point by asking the questions below (let's assume you're writing about the stock market). When going through this list of questions for your own topics, use only the italicized words and substitute your own topic specifics for the stock market references.

1. Are the definitions for *common and preferred stocks* easy to grasp, or are they too technical? (Keep in mind the reader and his/her background.)

2. Do the *advantages and disadvantages* give the readers enough information to make an intelligent decision if they decide to *buy stocks*?

3. Have I included enough examples of *companies that issue common and preferred stock* to give the reader an idea of cost?

4. Are there enough anecdotes to enlighten the reader about *people who have invested in the stock market*? Since this article is slanted to women, are there stories about *women investors*?

5. Have I mentioned several reputable *brokers* who've suggested a few *companies for possible investment*?

If after going through your S-O-S outline and evaluating your notes as they relate to the above questions you don't have enough information—i.e., you still have unanswered questions or "gaps" in your notes—then recheck the sources listed on your bibliography cards and read more thoroughly.

The evaluation step of the "difference" technique is important because it makes writing the rough draft easier.

R—Reader

When you developed your rough S-O-S outline, you had a general idea who the readers of your article/book would be. Now you're ready to take a closer look at your readers.

Let's continue our discussion of "Shopping at the Stock Market," which you're targeting for women with families. What kinds of magazines would appeal to these readers? *McCall's, Ladies' Home Journal, Redbook, New Woman,* and *Woman's Day* might be likely choices. Check the current edition of *Writer's Market* to see if the readers you imagine for your article match with a particular magazine's reader profile. Also check each magazine's nonfiction requirements to see if your article would fit with a publication's style, content, and format. *(Writer's Market* is an annual directory that should be on your bookshelf if you intend to sell your writing. It gives the most up-to-date names and addresses of book publishers and magazine editors, as well as information relevant to submitting both fiction and nonfiction manuscripts. *(Writer's Market* will be discussed further in Chapter 8.)

If you checked the entry for *Women's Circle* in the 1993 *Writer's Market,* you'd find this information relating to the submission of nonfiction manuscripts:

> **WOMEN'S CIRCLE,** P.O. Box 299, Lynnfield MA 01940-0299. Editor: Marjorie Pearl. 100% freelance written. Bimonthly magazine for women of all ages. Buys all rights. **Pays on acceptance.** Byline given. Publishes ms an average of 6 months to 1 year after acceptance. Submit seasonal material 8 months in advance. Reports in 3 months. Sample copy $2. Writer's guidelines for #10 SASE.
>
> **Nonfiction:** Especially interested in stories about successful, home-based female entrepreneurs with b&w photos or transparencies. Length: 1,000-2,000 words. Also interesting and unusual money-making ideas. Welcomes good quality crafts and how-to directions in any media—crochet, fabric, etc.

With a keen eye set on your readers' interests, you realize that a *Women's Circle* article on the stock market would be quite different from one that appears in *Fact,* a money management magazine. *Women's Circle* would probably require a detailed explanation of the different types of stocks; *Fact,* because of the typical reader's knowledge of investments, would likely focus on market trends and predictions.

Knowing something about your intended readers and their unique needs/ wants in a particular publication helps you avoid sounding either condescending or complex. Besides, if your writing is appropriate for a particular audience, that magazine's editor will know you've done your homework.

After checking a magazine's own description of its readership in *Writer's Market,* get this year's back issues of the publication from the library. Study the table of contents for every issue to be sure the editors haven't recently published a piece similar to yours. Use the overview reading technique for half the articles in each magazine, but read the others completely. Analyze the advertisements, which will give you an idea of the age and background of the magazine's readers. You'll find ads for breakfast cereals, cakes, pies (and other food products), diapers, baby food, detergent, furniture polish, and floor wax in magazines geared to young women who are wives and mothers.

The Rough Draft

Imagine again what your potential reader looks like; you might even give him a name. When you begin writing your rough draft, keep that person in mind; pretend you're writing a letter to a friend. You wouldn't send him a letter filled with bland facts and unappealing information. See your reader the same way; realize and respect his needs and wants.

The next Write-Now exercise helps you "see" your reader. Do the exercise for three days prior to writing your rough draft.

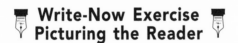

Write-Now Exercise
Picturing the Reader

Goal: To picture your reader so that your article is relevant to his/her needs.

1.
2. Do steps 1-3 of the Write-Now exercise as outlined on page 161.
3.

4. See your reader clearly while he's reading your article or book. He is totally absorbed in the article and underlines a few helpful hints while reading it.

5. Say to yourself ten times: "I'll write this article for (name the reader). He will learn something from it because the information in it is relevant to his needs."

> If you're doing this exercise during the day, say, "When I open my eyes, I'll feel great."
>
> If it's done at bedtime, drop off to sleep.

Now that you've identified your readers, written an S-O-S outline as a guide, and researched your topic, you're ready to write your rough draft. Its purpose is to get down what you have to say in some logical order. (This isn't the time to worry about spelling, punctuation, or other mechanics. That comes later, in the editing stage.) Rough drafts are an important part of the writing process; it's not unusual for professional writers to write four or more drafts before they get a final copy.

In your rough draft, use the facts, figures, anecdotes, etc., that appear on the note cards you organized from your S-O-S outline. Introduce each main point thoroughly. The Write-Now exercise on writing rough drafts in Chapter 2 (page 27) will help you write uninhibitedly. Try the exercise for at least two weeks. You'll begin to notice how much easier it is to do a rough draft for your article.

E—Editing

The editing aspect of the "difference" technique is discussed in detail after the final "e" (ending) is covered later in this chapter. Since editing takes place after the rough drafts have been written, we'll discuss it after all the writing steps are introduced.

N—Narratives

"The article demands anecdotes that make a given point, that illustrate, that tell a story . . . anecdotes are far and away the favorite device for sustaining reader interest in nonfiction subjects," claims professional writer Morton Sontheimer in the excellent book, *A Guide to Successful Magazine Writing*.[4] Narratives and anecdotes are effective either in the introduction of an article, or in the body or conclusion—as long as they illuminate your main points. A narrative tells a story. An anecdote is simply a short narrative. Both have the power to inspire, entertain, upset, or bore the reader, depending on how they're told and how relevant they are to your topic. When sharing an anecdote, pay attention to getting its sequence of events in the proper order; also be sure its tone is appropriate for the message you intend to communicate in your piece. Be descriptive without being verbose; let the reader experience the action of the story.

The article, "Looking Out for Number Two," by Denise Foley, appeared in *Prevention Magazine* in February 1984. The opening paragraphs contain two anecdotes. Notice in this excerpt how effectively dialogue pulls the reader into the body of the article.

Looking Out For Number Two

Vince Ward will be the first to tell you: High blood pressure can be one of the unwelcome perks of his high-tension job. Ward, 52, is advertising and public-relations director "flak-catcher" for one of the nation's largest telecommunications firms.

But Ward says his blood pressure is fine. In fact, everything is fine. He's fit, doesn't lose sleep worrying, "and my kids like me." In his spare time, Ward works with parolees from the Kansas State Penitentiary, raises money for a children's home and has donated more than 14 gallons of blood to the Community Blood Bank of Greater Kansas City. All in all, he says, "I'm a pretty happy guy."

When she was a child, they called her "Dummy." And Kay Arnold grew up believing they were right. But the 48-year-old homemaker knew she had musical talent and she knew she wanted to help people. Four years ago, she joined a troupe of entertainers called SENSE, in Newington, Connecticut, that performs for the disabled and elderly. Today, Kay Arnold has a different opinion of herself.

"This gives me a sense of worth I never had before," she says. "It's like therapy that works both ways." And she noticed something even more remarkable. "I have arthritis," she explains, "and when I perform, it seems to make the pain go away."

Vince Ward and Kay Arnold are more than just a couple of do-gooders. Their lives—full and healthy—illustrate a little-known corollary to the Golden Rule: Doing unto others can do wonderful things unto you.

Though there weren't stress tests and EKGs in the days of St. Luke, he was medically accurate when he wrote, "It is more blessed to give than to receive." We've always known that people with generous spirits tend to be happier, but now doctors are saying they're healthier and live longer too. Generosity comes naturally to us, they say. In fact, it may be nature's way of keeping us well.

Anecdotes like those used in this article can make an abstract concept easier for readers to comprehend.

Now consider the article "Like Sagging Muscles, Intuition Can Be Developed," by Stuart B. Litvak, which appeared in the October 1982 *New Woman* (excerpt from his book, *Use Your Head*). Intuition is also an intangible concept, but the anecdotes about Katherine and Bob make its meaning more concrete. Many readers unable to define intuition before reading the introductory paragraphs of the article can afterward identify with that "something told me not to do it" feeling. The anecdotes hook the reader and reel him gently into the subject.

Like Sagging Muscles, Intuition Can Be Developed

Katherine was a bright, young writer at a fairly large magazine. She was offered a high-paying, glamorous position with a relatively new advertising agency that boasted an impressive array of national accounts. The agency had a good reputation in town; the employees were all energetic and success-oriented. However, something told Katherine to hold up on her decision. She told the agency she would possibly be ready to make a move six months down the line. Within three months, the agency had folded.

Bob met a young woman who had everything he was looking for in the perfect mate. She was attractive, personable, intelligent—and had a good career. Though his acquaintances and friends kept assuming they would soon marry, Bob could not visualize their being together. Something just wasn't right. A year later, the woman was convicted of embezzlement.

Strange, how these people just knew what to do. And their knowledge certainly wasn't based on annual reports, computerized compatibility charts—or the use of metal detectors. They knew because they listened to those subtle little voices, if you will, within them that said, "Do this!" or "Wait this one out...."

Though the word "intuition" for some may conjure up visions of psychics running around, steaming up their crystal balls, intuition does exist even in the most conventional of minds. It's a way of thinking you know something, but you don't know how you know it. It's that sixth sense, that faculty of the mind that operates independently of reason and logic. And, like sagging muscles, it can be developed with the aid of a bit of practice.

So, you say to yourself smugly, if everyone has this so-called intuition, how do you put it to work?

1. Be aware of "soft" facts as well as "hard" ones. Hard facts are logical, objective, overt—the kind you tend to associate with lawyers and news reporters. Soft facts are less formal or obvious, such as impressions, feelings, inclinations, and vibrations. In most situations, both hard and soft facts will reveal themselves. Hard facts are obvious, conscious, tangible; soft facts are hunches, intuitive, invisible.

2. Learn to tune in to intuitive feelings. They can be distinguished by vague sensations of being "certain" or (more commonly) "almost certain."

3. Don't rely solely upon intuition; study the situation, use the other side of your brain, too. Research. After you've done your research, then let intuition guide you to your final choice. Intuition is something that is best used in conjunction with your logical, rational abilities.

4. Be true to your intuition. Extraneous factors will often intrude, such as social pressures, and so on, but don't let them alter your decision.

5. Those little voices don't like terminally tense people. Relaxation makes you more sensitive to intuitive experiences.

6. Intuition is developed through trial and error. Be patient. Through trial and error you will get it. And here's the clincher: You'll know when you've got it.

In my article, "Is School Ruining Your Child?" I used anecdotes to make the idea of ability grouping clearer for readers. The article opened with these paragraphs:

When Jimmy Andrews was a first grader in Chicago, he took an I.Q. test. He was classified as mentally retarded. Nine years passed. He was re-tested. "We made a terrible mistake," admitted the principal. "Jimmy isn't retarded. He lacks reading skills, not intelligence."

> *Each year, according to the Office of Education, unfair I.Q. and standardized tests doom thousands of children to the wrong ability group. The real tragedy is that many of these youngsters, like Jimmy, are convinced they are stupid.*

Another anecdote later in the article illustrated the negative effect that ability grouping had on Penny's self-image.

> *Penny was in a slow class for eight years. After spending several months in a remedial reading lab, I recommended her for a higher group. "How can I keep up with those kids," she argued. "I've been in the dummy class since grade school." After I reassured her, she agreed to try. Her attitude about herself began to change. She graduated with high honors and went on to college.*

Humorous anecdotes have enormous appeal in nonfiction. They draw the reader into the article in a pleasant, upbeat way. But these anecdotes must be chosen carefully. To be effective they must make a point and tie in specifically with your topic. They must be developed enough so readers get a sharp mental picture of the situation being described. Humorous anecdotes used excessively with only casual regard to tone or content can make an article sound like a comedy routine; choose them wisely and they'll add both clarity and levity to your writing.

In his book, *Classic Comebacks,* author Brian Herbert offers the following anecdotes to show how people have managed to find a quick reply to a snide remark.

> *On an airliner between Chicago and Las Vegas, a stewardess approached Muhammad Ali and told him to fasten his seat belt.*
>
> *"Superman don't need no seat belt," Ali said, winking.*
>
> *Unimpressed, the stewardess replied: "Superman don't need no airplane!"*
>
> *Lady Astor told Winston Churchill: "If you were my husband, I would put poison in your coffee."*
>
> *Said Churchill: "If you were my wife, I would drink it."* [5]

These anecdotes would perk up any article if the topic called for them. In fact, you can often get an idea for an article from an anecdote or narrative you hear at work, the supermarket, or at a party. Anecdotes derived from real-life experiences can also generate article ideas.

The next selection contains both a narrative and an anecdote. It's an excerpt from the article "Night Person/Morning Person," by Annie Gottlieb, featured in *McCall's* February 1983 issue. The piece is filled with dialogue, information, and humor. It moves swiftly and generates and maintains interest.

Night Person/Morning Person

My husband, Jacques, opens his eyes at 7:30 A.M., sees the sweet morning light and bounds out of our double bed, wide awake before his feet hit the floor. Humming to himself, talking to the cats, he bustles around the apartment—putting on coffee, dishing up cat food, even vacuuming.

I hear none of this. Head buried in the pillow, I am busy on a beach in Florida, reeling in a fish that turns into a manuscript. Annoyingly, someone is calling me, interrupting my concentration on the battle.

"Little Annie! Coffee!"

It's Jacques, standing in the dismal morning light with an incomprehensibly cheerful expression on his face, holding out a steaming cup that I will (horrors!) have to sit up to accept.

"Mmf," I tell him, waving an arm at the night table. "Pu' over there." And I turn my face back into the warm dark, rooting for my lost beach. It will be half an hour before I can drink the coffee, another half hour after that before I speak in complete sentences and to accept, much less look forward to, the day ahead.

By 11:30 at night, Jacques is finished. All washed up. In the hours since dinner, his optimism has gradually sagged, his energy flagged, his thoughts settled into a rut. Now he lies beside me, a snoring mountain, while the boxing match he struggled to watch blares on unnoticed. I shut off the TV with my big toe and turn the page in my magazine. My eyes are bright, my brain clicking. I'll still be reading and making notes at 1:30, when Jacques rolls over, peers at me, and groans, "What am I gonna do with you? You don't want to go to sleep, and you don't want to get up."

Except for the absence of children, this is a fairly typical scene from a marriage. With uncanny frequency, "morning people" and "night people" wind up married to each other. Of course, it doesn't always happen; plenty of couples are serenely—and to us mismatched types—enviably synchronized. They have breakfast together—or they both gag at the thought. They like to make love at the same times. They don't have those lopsided conversations in which one spouse is earnestly talking and the other is grumbling or snoring.

Take Sally and John, for instance. Both doctors in their early 30s in a small Virginia city, they are both morning people, like my husband—early to bed and early to rise. I imagine them springing out of bed in unison at 7:00 A.M., like a pair of trained Lippizaners. They have the time and lucidity to talk over a large, unhurried breakfast, the morning person's favorite meal. After a strenuous day's work, neither feels much like going out or staying up late. A nice dinner, good wine, and they're in bed—together—with lights out by 10:30.

Gottlieb makes you part of the action throughout the narrative. By blending dialogue and description she lets you picture Annie and Jacques dealing with the problems of night owl vs. early bird. This narrative is followed by an anecdote about morning people Sally and John. The remainder of the article is as interesting and fun to read as this beginning. It's chock-full of examples, insights, and information.

Whenever you read or hear an anecdote or narrative that you think is good, write it down or clip it out and put it in a file folder marked "Narratives." Though you may not be writing about the subject right now, it might be perfect for a future article—or as an idea booster when your Muse needs a shot in the arm.

Two excellent sources for anecdotes and narratives are the *Toastmaster's Treasure Chest* and *The Oxford Book of Literary Anecdotes*.

C—Compare And Contrast

Not all nonfiction writing lends itself to the technique of comparison and contrast. But when you discuss two similar yet different items, ideas, or philosophies, comparison and contrast is often an effective way to present them to readers.

When you compare two or more related things you show how they're similar to and different from each other. When you concentrate on showing how they contrast with each other, you stress their differences. There are two ways to compare things: to write about A completely and then B completely; or to examine a specific aspect of both A and B, then move to another point about both A and B, and continue in this way until you've completed the comparison.

Let's say you want to compare large cars with subcompact cars. (You may want to do this to stress the superiority of one car over the other. Or you may want to take an objective view of the pluses and minuses of driving/owning each car.) You decide to compare and contrast the advantages and disadvantages of owning a Cadillac and a Chevette.

If you've chosen the first compare-and-contrast method, you look at the Cadillac first. On the positive side, Cadillacs have plenty of leg and luggage space; they're comfortable, large, luxurious, and smooth riding. On the negative side, they get low gas mileage; they're expensive and costly to maintain; and they're hard to park. (You could add to both lists if you planned a lengthy article.)

You then do the same for the Chevette. Advantages to owning a small car include its low cost, high gas mileage, and ease of parking. Disadvantages are that it's uncomfortable to ride in for long distances; it offers little protection in an accident; it has little storage space.

If you decide to compare and contrast the two cars using the second method, you'd first look at a specific aspect of both the Cadillac and the Chevette—perhaps gas mileage. You'd compare the two cars' mileage, then move on to the next point—comfort. You'd then follow through with all the topics you wanted to discuss until the comparison was complete.

Readers benefit from the use of comparison and contrast. Besides allowing them to see at least two sides of an issue, the technique can help them understand an unfamiliar idea or concept—especially when it's compared to something familiar. The important thing to remember is that both items must be presented equally. You can compare and contrast Chinese and American cuisine, living in the city or country, or life imprisonment and capital punishment. But to be both effective and fair, you should show the pros and cons of each.

Look again at the "Night Person/Morning Person" excerpt on pages 191-192. How effectively does the author use comparison and contrast? In the opening paragraph she contrasts Jacques, a typical morning person, with herself, an average night person. While he's bounding out of bed, she's buried in her pillow, deep in a dream. And so on, throughout the article. The comparison and contrast works to show the differences and similarities in two types of people.

To practice seeing both sides of situations, compare and contrast the following: (You may have to do some research before you begin.)

1. The Scarsdale Medical Diet and the Weight Watcher's Diet

2. Owning your own business and working for someone else

3. Being single and being married

4. Living in Europe and living in the United States

Let's focus on being single vs. being married. To better picture the similarities and differences (and pros and cons) between both states, do the brainstorming exercise described on pages 164-165. Put the first subject (Being Single) at the top of a sheet of paper. Brainstorm all the pros and cons of the single life. Next, picture being married and go through the same brainstorming procedure. Afterwards, study both your lists. How might you compare and contrast these life options in an article?

Two people, let's say Brenda and Colleen, decide to brainstorm the pros and cons of being single. Based on their experiences, imaginations, lifestyles, and biases, it's likely their lists will differ. Some of Brenda's "pros" may be Colleen's "cons."

For Brenda, one of the positives of the single life is having complete freedom. Colleen, on the other hand, may equate this with loneliness; she may see it as a negative. Not having to divide her time between kids and a career might be a plus for Colleen, while Brenda could view this as a minus because she sees the responsibility of simultaneously raising a family and having a career as a stimulating challenge.

It's likely their lists on the pros and cons of being married would also differ. Subsequent articles they may write on the single vs. the married state would undoubtedly differ in tone and vision, yet both could be effective if, in researching their articles, they looked for quotes, statistics, case studies, facts, and anecdotes to reflect and support their individual views.

When you read articles where items are compared or contrasted, check to see whether the writer has created a clear mental picture of both things. If you can recognize the use of comparison and contrast in published writing, you'll be better prepared to know when to use it in your own work. To do a thorough job of comparing and contrasting topics, you'll have to do sufficient research. You must know both sides of the issue.

E—Ending

The ending of your nonfiction piece deserves as much consideration as the beginning. An abrupt conclusion to an article is like an abrupt ending to a conversation: it's neither expected nor appreciated.

How do you avoid the sudden ending? One good way is to refer back to your introduction. If you began the piece with a line from a poem, rephrase the line or blend it with a brief summary statement.

If (as mentioned earlier) you opened your article on career decisions with Robert Frost's lines "Two roads diverged in a yellow wood, And sorry I could not travel both," you could logically conclude the piece with the last two lines of "The Road Not Taken" and a brief statement about your decision:

> *My choice to give up my own business and become an artist was not what others expected. But for me it was the road "less traveled by and that has made all the difference."*

Another type of conclusion for nonfiction writing is a short summary of a plan or method you've presented. The key with this kind of ending is to be concise. It's not the place to reiterate the whole substance of the article, just its major points.

An anecdote is another way to effect a strong finish. It can be inspirational, informative, or humorous—as long as it relates to your subject.

If the purpose of your nonfiction piece is to get your readers to take action on your subject, you might end with an appropriate question or challenge. Make a plea for your readers to take a stand, heed your advice, or make a commitment, i.e., vote "yes" on the issue!

If you're having trouble deciding on a suitable ending for your article, do the following Write-Now exercise. It will help you visualize the entire article as though you were watching a documentary. Before doing the exercise, go over your S-O-S outline and read through your entire article, chapter, or book.

Write-Now Exercise
Endings

Goal: To write an interesting and appropriate ending for your nonfiction writing project.

1.
2. Do steps 1-3 of the Write-Now exercise as outlined on page 161.
3.
4. See yourself turning on the television. Your article is being shown as a documentary and you're looking forward to watching it. You're sitting in a comfortable chair; you begin to follow the sequence of events in

the documentary. They flow as smoothly as they did in your S-O-S outline. The ending of the documentary is logical, interesting, and summarizes the main points of the work. You're pleased with the outcome.

5. Give yourself this suggestion ten times: "The ending for my article/chapter/book will be a logical, appropriate conclusion. I will visualize my writing as a whole: beginning, middle, and ending."

If it's daytime, say, "When I open my eyes, I'll feel great."

If it's bedtime, drop off to sleep.

Do this exercise every day for two weeks. You'll soon begin to think of your ending as a continuation of the body of your manuscript instead of as something detached from it.

Studying Nonfiction That "Works"

Now that you understand the ingredients of good nonfiction, let's see how they work together in a finished piece.

"Will You Help David?" is a short article I wrote several years ago for a Philadelphia newspaper, *The News Gleaner*. It contains some of the components of the "D-i-f-f-e-r-e-n-c-e" technique. See if you can identify some of the elements as you read it.

Will You Help David?

David's dad died when David was nine. His mother works hard to support both of them. There is not much time to do things together. When David watches a football game or goes fishing, he is usually alone. What he and many other fatherless boys in the Philadelphia area need is a Big Brother.

Big Brothers are mature, concerned men who care about kids like David. The basic aim of the Big Brother program is to provide male identification and friendship through a one-man-to-one-boy relationship. The boys, who are between eight and sixteen years old, need a man's guidance and companionship, which is missing in their lives.

A Big Brother spends a few hours a week with his Little Brother doing things they both enjoy. It might be playing baseball, going swimming, or just talking.

No financial or legal responsibilities are assumed by the Big Brother, and there are no educational requirements. A Big Brother is a friend—not a father replacement.

The staff of professionally trained social workers at The Big Brother Association takes into careful consideration personality, religion, race, and mutual interests when matching Big and Little Brothers.

Jim Wilson is Bobby's Big Brother. They were paired on the basis of common interests.

"I try to be with Bobby one day a week," Wilson said. "We do special things now and then. We've gone on fishing trips and to the zoo, but mostly we just try to include Bobby in whatever the family happens to be doing. It's a good feeling to know the boy will confide in you. Many times Bobby asks me questions he thinks are stupid, but they aren't really."

Shared confidences and experiences are meaningful to young boys. One Little Brother agrees, "My Big Brother is nice. He takes me places, and he helps me with my school problems and all kinds of other problems."

A Big Brother's genuine interest and encouragement can help an insecure, lonely boy develop confidence in himself and overcome certain fears. One mother claimed, "Steve's interest has been the catalyst for a gradual but miraculous change in my son."

"The boy a Big Brother gives his time to is at the point when he most needs a man's encouragement. Helping him learn that life can be beautiful is a serious venture, but it's fun, too," says actor Jack Lemmon.

Won't you spend a little of your time with a fatherless boy like David so he will realize life is beautiful because someone cares about him?

Please call The Big Brother Association at 742-2930.

Write out a rough S-O-S outline for this article. How many quotes are used? Anecdotes? What are some of the facts and figures mentioned? Is there reader identification? Even though you're "working in reverse" (going from completed piece to outline), you will get an idea of how I came up with the finished product.

E—Editing

Editing is one of the most important stages of writing; you haven't finished your project until you've finished editing. After you've completed your research and written one or several rough drafts, you're ready to take up the editor's proverbial "blue pencil." It's time to take a good, hard look at your article or chapter—the way an editor would.

Many writers try to be both writer and critic as they do their rough drafts. That's like having a critic review a play as it's being written and rehearsed. Research and write first; edit later.

The following checklist lets you look critically at your manuscript. Read over each point and check your article (or individual chapters of a book) to see if you can answer "yes" to all the questions.

Ten-Point Nonfiction Checklist

1. Is your writing well organized? Did you follow the flexible S-O-S outline?

2. Does the introduction hook the reader? Did you get the reader interested by using anecdotes, surprising statistics, or some other arresting introductory element?

3. Did you develop the body of the article/book keeping in mind the elements of the D-I-F-F-E-R-E-N-C-E technique?

   D— Did you define terms and describe a process so the reader could visualize it?

   I— Did you get the reader's attention and keep it beyond the introduction?

   F-F— Do you have enough facts and figures to support your contentions?

   E— Have you evaluated and selected the best research information?

R— Did you remember the reader and his/her needs? Can you picture him/her? Similarly, have you evaluated the markets and selected the one that seems most likely to have readers such as the ones you intended to reach?

E— Have you caught errors in spelling, punctuation, logic, and form when you edited the second draft?

N— Are narratives and anecdotes included to make the nonfiction interesting?

C— Did you compare and/or contrast two things, if appropriate, to help the reader understand your point?

E— Is the ending effective? Will the reader benefit from having read it?

4. Did you keep within the required word limit of the magazine or publisher to whom you plan to send the manuscript?

5. Is your sentence structure varied enough? Have you used strong verbs and nouns and the active voice most of the time?

6. Are quotation marks, commas, semicolons, and colons used correctly?

7. Have you checked words that might be misspelled?

8. Are run-on sentences and fragments corrected?

9. Have you deleted clichés and jargon?

10. Do you feel you've covered your topic adequately?

Before you write and type the final draft of your article, take a critical look at every aspect of it. Distance yourself from it so you can see it as an editor would. After doing this Write-Now exercise for a week, you'll begin to see what key elements are still missing—what you can still do to make your work better.

Write-Now Exercise
Editing

Goal: To read your manuscript as an editor, keeping in mind the criteria for publication.

1.
2. Do steps 1-3 of the Write-Now exercise as outlined on page 161.
3.

4. See yourself as the editor of the magazine or publishing company where you're planning to send your manuscript. You're looking critically and objectively at your work. You have the final checklist in mind as you read the manuscript.

5. Give yourself the following suggestion ten times: "I'll read my book/ article as though I'm the editor at (name the magazine or publisher). I'll keep in mind the nonfiction checklist and the magazine's or publisher's criteria for publication. I will be totally objective and delete anything that is undesirable."

   If you're doing this during the day, say at the count of three, "When I open my eyes, I'll feel great."

   If it's bedtime, drop off to sleep.

After you've gone through the checklist twice and have done the editing exercise for a week, take yet another close look at your manuscript. Read it aloud in order to catch and correct ungrammatical constructions. Make any necessary revisions. If certain sections of the article or book still seem lean on facts and figures or other supporting material, do some additional research and add information where it's needed.

One word of caution: Don't over edit your work. Many professional authors who have written for years are *never* quite satisfied with their work even after it's published. There *is* a time to "let go" of your writing. Set realistic deadlines for when the editing job will be over, when the article/chapter will be typed, and when you'll send it to an editor. Then keep your deadlines. If you don't you'll spend too much time editing and not enough time working on new writing projects.

Your nonfiction can become "a part of the experience of the person who reads it," as Hemingway suggested, if after "having found what is true" you craft that truth into a well-organized, carefully researched piece of informative, engaging writing—the kind your readers can't put down. Use the Write-Now exercises and the ingredients of the "difference" technique to help you reach your goal of good writing. Then consult the next chapter for help on how to get your writing published.

Notes/Chapter Seven

1. Alex Osborn, *Applied Imagination* (New York: Charles Scribner's Sons, 1963), p. 210.

2. William Strunk, Jr. and E.B. White, *Elements of Style* (New York: Macmillan, 1972), p. 57.

3. Robert Frost, *The Poetry of Robert Frost*, Edward Connery Latham, ed. (New York: Henry Holt & Co., Inc., 1979), p. 105.

4. Society of Magazine Writers, *A Guide to Successful Magazine Writing* (New York: Scribner's, 1954).

5. Brian Herbert, *Classic Comebacks* (Los Angeles: Price Stern, 1981), p. 48.

CHAPTER EIGHT

Taking the Mystery Out of Marketing Your Writing

Literature is like any other trade;
you will never sell anything
unless you go to the right shop.

George Bernard Shaw

CHAPTER OVERVIEW

1. Why is it important to understand the workings of the writing business?

2. What questions should you ask before trying to market your writing?

3. How do you write a query letter that "sells?"

4. How can the Write-Now exercises nurture persistence in the writing marketplace?

MANY WRITERS SET THEMSELVES up for rejection by going to the wrong "shop" to sell their work. That's what Matt did a few years ago. He had written an article on legal deductions for the average taxpayer. "I can't seem to find an editor who wants it," he said. "I sent it to three of them and they all rejected it."

To get some clues as to why Matt's article may have been rejected, we consulted the current edition of *Writer's Market.* There we discovered that two of the three magazines that said "no" to his freelance article were staff-written. The third publication accepted unsolicited manuscripts of no more than 1,200 words, and then for only one of their columns; Matt's article was over 3,000 words. The editor had scribbled a note across the bottom of the standard rejection slip—"not slanted for our readers and too technical."

Matt was discouraged by his unsuccessful efforts to sell his work; he was convinced that his writing was poor. "After all," he said grimly, "if three editors rejected it, there must be something wrong."

There *was* something wrong. But it wasn't with Matt's writing; it was with his marketing.

After talking with Matt, I wondered whether his frustration with trying to sell his work was typical among writers. I asked students in my workshops about their experiences and discovered that they, too, faced similar problems. Marketing their writing seemed to be a mysterious process for them—one they approached with confusion and sometimes, dread.

I asked them how they decided where to send their material. Most of them claimed they selected magazines where they *wanted* to see their work published. They didn't know much about the magazines' basic requirements—length of articles, age and interests of readers, types of fiction and nonfiction featured, etc. The majority of them didn't use *Writer's Market, The Writer's Handbook,* or any other source that could readily give them this essential information.

Too, most of my students had only a vague idea about query letters and other marketing aids, such as writer's guidelines—tools that could have improved their sales records. (Writer's guidelines spell out a book publisher's or magazine's requirements for freelance submissions. These guidelines are usually sent on request—especially when the request is accompanied by a self-addressed, stamped envelope.)

When I saw that many of my students were in the dark about how to successfully sell their writing, I decided to include in my Write-Now workshops several sessions about marketing. That's the purpose of this chapter, as well. By practicing the Write-Now exercises presented here, you'll begin to see yourself as a confident participant in the writing business. By studying the markets discussed in this chapter, you'll learn how to analyze readers and their needs—and thereby ferret out appropriate outlets for your manuscripts. You'll learn how to contact editors, keeping in mind the do's and don'ts of query letters. You'll also see why it's important to view publishing as a business in which you must maintain a professional and persistent attitude about selling your work.

Buyers And Sellers In The Writing Marketplace

I've noticed that professional writers who regularly publish have developed both their writing *and* selling abilities. They nurture not only their work, but their chances of sharing it with an audience.

There are other writers who view having to sell their work as something akin to huckstering. They feel that marketing somehow diminishes their art. Unfortunately, this unrealistic attitude often keeps them from seeing their work in print. Selling ourselves is very much a part of our lives. If you're looking for a job as a computer programmer, you don't wait for an employer to call you, nor do you market your services to a fast-food restaurant. You go to a company where there's a good chance you'll be hired.

As a writer, you face a similar challenge every time you try to sell your work. You don't wait for someone to discover your writing ability. You contact appropriate editors—those who are in the business of buying and selling. They buy material from writers in order to sell their own magazines and books to readers. In effect, writers supply editors with material that their readers demand.

Before editors accept a manuscript, they ask themselves, "Would our readers like this?" To stay in business, they must satisfy their buyers or subscribers; they must select material that appeals to their particular readership. Whether they personally like, approve of, or enjoy your article or story doesn't matter; whether their readers will does. Therefore, editors establish and adhere to certain guidelines when deciding the fate of a manuscript.

For example, your 3,000-word article on the latest food fads might be well-researched and well-written, but if the magazine to which you submit it has just run a 5,000-word piece on the subject (or is planning a similar one), they probably won't buy yours. Likewise, your essay on Cabbage Patch dolls vs. Barbie dolls may be rejected—not because it lacks humor, but because the magazine doesn't publish essays.

It's important to understand this aspect of the writing business. How often have you thought, "If my article was good, they'd buy it anyway." The truth is, they'll only buy it if it's good for their readers. Would an editor at *Sports Illustrated* buy an article on cake decorating? The question isn't as outrageous as it sounds. Editors complain that too many writers don't even consider readers' needs and interests when they submit material for publication.

One editor offers this solution: "Reading the magazine regularly is the best way to find out what kind of stories *Redbook* is buying."[1]

To succeed in the publishing business, you must understand one of the basic principles of the marketplace: Find a need and satisfy it. The reality is that an editor is a buyer who needs good articles/stories (to keep readers content), and you are a seller (who supplies the editor with writing that will satisfy his needs for quality material). To nurture a positive business-like attitude about your role in the publishing marketplace, do the following Write-Now exercise. Practice it every day for one week before you begin actively searching for an appropriate editor/publisher for your work.

Write-Now Exercise
Writer as a Salesperson

Goal: To see yourself as a salesperson satisfying the needs of an editor by sending him/her a piece of writing that meets the readers' needs.

1. Get comfortable in bed or in an easy chair. Noise should be at a minimum. Close your eyes. Take three or four deep breaths. Inhale

through the nose. Take the air down to the diaphragm. Count to three. Exhale through the mouth.

2. Imagine that you're lying on a lounge chair near a pond. It's a pleasantly warm fall day. The surrounding trees reflect the reds, greens, and golds of their leaves in the water. All of nature is in harmony. You, too, feel that your mind and body are in harmony. (You can substitute another scene especially pleasing for you.)

3. Push your heels down on the chair/bed/floor. Feel the tension; now relax them. Do the same thing with your hips, back, shoulders, neck, head, arms, and hands: push down against whatever surface they're touching, then relax. Tighten and relax the muscles while taking three deep breaths. Silently repeat ten times: "I'm becoming more and more relaxed." (The main objective is to relax your mind and body so that the subconscious will accept your suggestion.)

4. See yourself selling a piece of furniture. You're confident that the person looking at it closely will buy it. The person is pleased with your sales presentation. He says that the dining room table is just what he needs and it will make his family happy.

5. Say to yourself ten times: "Because a magazine or publishing company is a business, editors must buy material to satisfy their readers. I'll keep this in mind when I'm analyzing the best market for my material."

Say, "When I open my eyes, I'll feel great."

Identifying Markets For Your Work

After doing the exercise, ask yourself several questions about the particular magazine or book publisher to whom you'd like to send your material. (If you hope to find some interested editors, you should ask these same questions each time you plan to market your writing.)

1. What are the particular magazine or book publisher's requirements for fiction and nonfiction? Does it buy both kinds of writing?

2. Who are its readers: what is their age range, educational level, etc.?

3. What major topics are likely to interest these readers?

4. What is the word count of the articles, stories, books the editor needs?

5. Does the editor accept unsolicited manuscripts? Are writer's guidelines available?

6. What is the name of the editor to whom you should send your material?

Don't assume *anything* about a particular market. The answers to these questions are important because few markets are exactly alike. Magazines and book publishers, like specialty restaurants, have their own unique characteristics. You wouldn't go to a Chinese restaurant for Mexican food; nor would you send an article on high fashion to *Field and Stream*. But are you aware that *Good Housekeeping* doesn't want the same kind of material as *Mademoiselle*, though both magazines are for women? Even magazines that print the same kinds of articles or stories have subtle differences in treatment of subjects, writing style, or article length. The only way to know if your writing is appropriate—if it has a chance to be accepted—for a certain magazine is to find out its particular needs and requirements (and to read several recent back issues with an analytical eye).

Back issues of magazines are usually available in libraries. And the answers to the six marketing questions listed above are available in the current edition of *Writer's Market*. Published annually, *Writer's Market* contains information and advice from more than 4,000 editors, all looking for good writing. Many professional writers use *Writer's Market* as their main marketing guide. Individual entries for book publishers and magazines capsule editors' needs, readers' interests, and requirements for manuscript submissions. (The guide also lists production and theater companies interested in scripts, cartoonists looking for gags, and syndicates buying freelance material.) Information in the appendix includes specifics on how to set up a manuscript page, what type of paper to use, and how much postage you'll need. Other tips explain how to give your manuscript the "professional" look that shows editors you know the trade.

In the Write-Now workshops, I ask students to bring in two kinds of articles or stories: those they're ready to send to an editor, and those that have been rejected by an editor. Using *Writer's Market* as a source book for editors' names, addresses, and manuscript submission requirements, we do a marketing analysis of the students' written work. The analysis usually yields potential markets for newly completed manuscripts. It frequently reveals that many of the rejected works were really "misdirected" submissions.

You can follow this same marketing procedure before sending out your own work. To increase your awareness of the special requirements of potential buyers, and to relax while searching out the best match of markets to material, do the Write-Now exercise below. The exercise helps to alleviate the tension and frustration that often occurs when you're looking for something and can't find it immediately. You'll begin to scrutinize magazine and publisher requirements more carefully than ever—and in the process you'll uncover previously untapped outlets for your work. Try the exercise before your next marketing session.

Write-Now Exercise
Appropriate Magazine/Publisher

Goal: To select the most appropriate magazine/publisher for your writing.

1.
2. Do steps 1-3 of the Write-Now exercise outlined on pages 206-207.
3.

4. See yourself looking for a dress or a suit for a specific occasion—a wedding, dinner-dance, etc. It must be just the right color, size, style, material. You want your dress/suit to be appropriate for the occasion.

5. Say to yourself ten times: "I'm very capable of marketing my writing. I will check *Writer's Market* (or another source) and select the most appropriate magazine/publisher for my work. I'll keep in mind the marketing questions I must answer to target my material. This will increase my chances of getting published."

   Say, "When I open my eyes, I'll feel great."

After doing the exercise, briefly review the questions on pages 207-208. You may get some clues as to where to initially send your manuscript, or where to re-submit it for a greater chance of acceptance.

Analyzing Specific Markets

Jean, a homemaker in the workshop, wondered why her article on needlepoint was rejected by *Mademoiselle*. After she read the piece aloud, we checked the *Mademoiselle* entry in the current issue of *Writer's Market*. (It's important to check the most recent edition because editors and publications come and go and requirements change with amazing frequency.) Jean's article dealt with how easy it was to give personalized needlepoint gifts. Why *Mademoiselle* rejected the article became clear to us as we studied the magazine's focus and its readership. (The excerpt below covers only *Mademoiselle's* nonfiction requirements.)

> **MADEMOISELLE,** Conde Nast, 350 Madison Ave., New York NY 10017. (212) 880-8559. Articles Editor: Liz Logan. 95% freelance written. Prefers to work with published/established writers. Columns are written by columnists; "sometimes we give new writers a 'chance' on shorter, less complex assignments." Directed to college-educated, unmarried working women 18-34. Circ. 1.1 million. Reports in 1 month. Buys first North American serial rights. **Pays on acceptance;** rates vary. Publishes ms an average of 1 year after acceptance.
>
> **Nonfiction:** Particular concentration on articles of interest to the intelligent young woman, including personal relationships, health, careers, trends, and current social problems. Send health queries to Jennifer Rapaport, health editor. Send entertainment queries to Debbie Wise, entertainment editor. Query with published clips. Length: 1,500-3,000 words.
>
> **Photos:** Kay Spear, art director. Commissioned work assigned according to needs. Photos of fashion, beauty, travel. Payment ranges from no-charge to an agreed rate of payment per shot, job series, or page rate. Buys all rights. Pays on publication for photos.
>
> **Tips:** "We are looking for timely, well-researched manuscripts." Editor's note: No longer publishes fiction.

Consider some of the information included in the *Mademoiselle* entry:

1. The magazine's readers are working women between the ages of eighteen and thirty-four who probably don't have much time to do needlepoint. It's likely more convenient for them to buy rather than make a needlepoint gift.

2. The editors prefer query letters describing articles to actual completed manuscripts. And 90 percent of the material they use is assigned to writers whose work they already know.

3. *Mademoiselle* publishes material on personal relationships, health, careers, and social problems.

4. Article lengths run 1,500-3,000 words. Jean's article ran about 1,200 words, a bit short for this market.

I asked the other students what Jean might have done to sell the needle-point idea to *Mademoiselle* editors. Terri suggested that the article could be slanted to appeal to working women. Why not send a query letter describing how needlepoint reduces on-the-job stress, she urged.

As we thumbed through *Writer's Market* looking for other possible buyers, Jean thought that *Women's Circle* might be a better target for her article. Below is an excerpt from the entry we analyzed:

> **WOMEN'S CIRCLE,** P.O. Box 299, Lynnfield MA 01940-0299. Editor: Marjorie Pearl. 100% freelance written. Bimonthly magazine for women of all ages. Buys all rights. **Pays on acceptance.** Byline given. Publishes ms an average of 6 months to 1 year after acceptance. Submit seasonal material 8 months in advance. Reports in 3 months. Sample copy $2. Writer's guidelines for #10 SASE.
>
> **Nonfiction:** Especially interested in stories about successful, home-based female entrepreneurs with b&w photos or transparencies. Length: 1,000-2,000 words. Also interesting and unusual money-making ideas. Welcomes good quality crafts and how-to directions in any media—crochet, fabric, etc.

We noted the following information about *Women's Circle:*

1. The readers of the magazine are women of all ages.

2. *Women's Circle* is 100% freelance written and buys "how-to" articles of 1,000-2,000 words on handicrafts, all kinds of needlework, and dolls.

3. The editors want an informational approach in their articles.

4. Black-and-white photos are welcome.

Jean decided that after her husband took a 35mm photo showing her making a needlepoint gift, she would send it—along with her article—to *Women's Circle.*

How A Specialist Looks For Markets

How you go about looking for appropriate markets for your writing may depend on your approach to writing. In other words, are you a specialist or a generalist? Each kind of writer analyzes markets in a different way.

A specialist is a person who has "special" or in-depth knowledge about a particular subject. If you're trained as a scuba diver and have had fifteen years' experience driving a bus, you probably know more about wet suits and maneuvering in city traffic than the average person. It's not necessary for you to do something yourself, however, in order to write about it. As specialist writer Sandra Dark wrote in a previous edition of *Writer's Market*, "It all hinges on the strength of your files and your Rolodex." You can be a specialty writer if you have access to a reservoir of facts, figures, and anecdotes on a subject and know of experts who can provide you with information for a well-documented, lively article.

As a specialist writer, you're often personally interested in your subject and have the ability to share that interest with others. A specialist may write technical articles for *Mechanics Illustrated* about how to change the points and plugs in a car's engine; the same person can write an automobile maintenance article for a non-technical publication such as *Reader's Digest* if he learns to slant his material to a broader group—a general audience interested in less technical, more people-oriented writing. He might, for instance, develop the article around tell-tale sounds that signal trouble for your car engine.

A teacher of handicapped children is a specialist who might draw from her experience and professional reading and write a variety of articles both for specialized and general magazines. As long as she has a specific audience in mind and writes for that audience, she can cover many aspects of her specialty. She can share information—how to facilitate learning for children with hearing problems; how parents can help their children develop confidence in their ability to learn; what exercises are specially designed for children in wheelchairs—both with teachers and counselors reading professional journals, and parents and other lay readers of general interest publications.

A specialist's strength lies in the depth of understanding he has for a subject. In search of a market for his expertise, a specialist may look at various sections of *Writer's Market*—Business and Finance, Home Computers, Men's, Women's, etc. He asks himself: "How can I slant my specialty—making furniture for the workplace—to meet the unique needs of various publications listed in these broad categories?" Except for specialty writers trained in extremely technical or esoteric fields, the demand for specialists is great. Many readers hunger for quality, in-depth information; as long as you know how to target your specialty for a particular audience, you can satisfy their needs.

A Generalist's Search For Markets

Generalists, too, have countless opportunities for getting published—not because of any specialty, necessarily, but because they have a wide range of interests. Their strength lies in their versatility. For a generalist, any subject is fair game—both auto racers and zookeepers can send them into a whirlwind in pursuit of more information. Their insatiable curiosity is satisfied only with answers.

They know the basics of a well-written piece and can apply that know-how to a great many subjects; and, like specialists, they, too, can write about a special subject for various audiences.

A generalist's article antennae are constantly picking up ideas. Take the topic of swimming: a generalist can write a piece on how to swim slanted for a seven-year-old who gets *Boy's Life Reader,* or for an eighty-year-old reader of *Modern Maturity,* terrified of water, but who now wants to conquer his fear and swim with his grandson. While researching the swimming articles, a generalist might become interested in the history of swimming pools and decide to research *that* topic. From there, he may get the idea that an article on the evolution of the swimsuit sounds alluring. His article ideas come from being aware of the world around him. His ears prick up when a neighbor discusses breeding lhasa apsos, and he's the first to stop and introduce himself to the foreign exchange student on the block.

Professional writers like Robert Cormier champion the cause of the generalist. "I don't think a writer should limit himself or herself to a particular specialty, particularly in the beginning," he said in a previous edition of *Writer's Market.* "To write as much as possible, about as big a variety of topics as possible—this is essential." Cormier, whose juvenile fiction "specialty" *(The Chocolate War, I Am the Cheese)* has won him wide acclaim, says that even now, he occasionally takes the route of the generalist and writes articles, book reviews, and columns "just to keep myself fresh and sharp."

In the same edition of *Writer's Market,* Isaac Asimov says he started out to be a science fiction writer, and "I ended up writing on anything under the sun."

How do generalists find markets? Writer Gary Turbak suggests that generalists should read *Writer's Market* "the way you would a novel—page by page. There are markets out there of which you could not possibly have dreamed," he said in an edition of the guide.

For generalists, reading the market entries themselves can spark article ideas. A generalist skimming the entry for *Sea Frontiers* may pause for a moment on the publication's list of nonfiction needs: "Articles covering interesting and little-known facts about the sea, marine life, chemistry, geology, physics...." He wonders: "Might the editors be interested in an article describing the brief life of the two-headed turtle found in South Florida?" The same generalist might be equally enthusiastic about finding out for *Referee* magazine how a five-foot basketball official learned to love the game.

Whether you're a specialist or a generalist, marketing your work is essential if you hope to find readers to share it with. In order to expand your interests and increase the availability of markets to tap, focus on a topic that's particularly fascinating for you. If you're a specialist, it might be your expertise as a gourmet cook, your experience in backpacking, how you started your own business, your hobby of growing orchids, or your fascination in gazing at the stars. If you're a generalist, it might be snake behavior one day, and how to make stained glass gifts the next.

Whatever your bent, go through *Writer's Market* and pick five different types of magazines that might be (even remotely) interested in your topic. How can you package an idea to best suit the variety of readers who can be *your* audience?

Doug, an avid golfer, was a student in one of the Write-Now workshops. He wrote an article on three specific ways golfers can improve their putting. Doug was in a good position to offer advice, since he maintained his own golf score in the 70s, often played in tournaments, and taught golf to various groups. He sent his article to *Sports Parade;* they rejected it.

Study the *Sports Parade* entry and compare it with the *Golf Digest* description that follows. Do you think because *Golf Digest* is a specialty publication for golfers its editors might be interested in Doug's article?

> **SPORTS PARADE,** Meridian International, Inc., P.O. Box 10010, Ogden UT 84409. (801) 394-9446. 65% freelance written. Works with a small number of new/unpublished writers each year. A monthly general interest sports magazine distributed by business and professional firms to employees, customers, clients, etc. Readers are predominantly upscale, mainstream, family oriented. **Pays on acceptance.** Publishes ms an average of 3 months after acceptance. Byline given. Buys first rights, second serial (reprint) rights and nonexclusive reprint rights. Reports in 6 weeks. Sample copy $1 with 9x12 SAE; writers guidelines for #10 SASE.
>
> **Nonfiction:** General interest and interview/profile. "General interest articles covering the entire sports spectrum, personality profiles on top flight professional and amateur sports figures. *Sports Parade* is now combined with *People in Action.* We are looking for articles on well-known athletes in the top 10% of their field. We are still looking at articles and profiles of well-known celebrities. These are cover features; photogenic appeal is important." Buys 20 mss/year. Query. Length: 1,200-1,580 words. Pays 15¢/word.
>
> **Photos:** Send with query or ms. Reviews 35mm or larger transparencies with 5x7 or 8x10 prints. Pays $35 for transparencies; $50 for cover. Captions and model releases required.

Tips: "I will be purchasing more articles based on personalities—today's stars in sports, entertainment, the arts. Celebrities must have positive roles and be making a contribution to society. No nostalgic material."

GOLF DIGEST, Dept. WM, 5520 Park Ave., Trumbull CT 06611. (203) 373-7000. Editor: Jerry Tarde. 10% freelance written. Emphasizes golfing. Monthly magazine. Circ. 1.4 million. **Pays on acceptance.** Publishes ms an average of 6 weeks after acceptance. Buys all rights. Byline given. Submit seasonal/holiday material 4 months in advance. Reports in 6 weeks.

Nonfiction: Lisa Sweet, editorial assistant. How-to, informational, historical, humor, inspirational, interview, nostalgia, opinion, profile, travel, new product, personal experience, photo feature and technical; "all on playing and otherwise enjoying the game of golf." Query. Length: 1,000-2,500 words. Pays $150-1,500 depending on length of edited mss.

Photos: Nick DiDio, art director. Purchased without accompanying ms. Pays $75-150 for 5x7 or 8x10 b&w prints; $100-300/35mm transparency. Model release required.

Poetry: Lois Hains, assistant editor. Light verse. Buys 1-2/issue. Length: 4-8 lines. Pays $25.

Fillers: Lois Hains, assistant editor. Jokes, gags, anecdotes, and cutlines for cartoons. Buys 1-2/issue. Length: 2-6 lines. Pays $10-25.

Golf Digest emphasizes only golf, whereas *Sports Parade* covers all family-oriented sports. *Golf Digest's* readers are devoted golfers like Doug. When they read the magazine, they know they'll read about "playing and . . . enjoying the game of golf." Since Doug is a specialist in the field of golf, he decided to submit his article this time to *Golf Digest*.

Targeting Your Fiction

Nonfiction isn't the only category of writing for which editors have specifications: fiction requirements also vary from one publisher to another. Note the types of fiction, the age and sex of their readers, and the length of the stories used by the two magazines described below in these excerpts from *Writer's Market:*

'TEEN MAGAZINE, 8490 Sunset Blvd., Hollywood CA 90069. (212) 854-2222. Editor: Roxanne Camron. 20-30% freelance written. Prefers to work with published/established writers. Monthly magazine for teenage girls. Circ. 1.1 million. Publishes ms an average of 6 months after acceptance. Buys all rights. Reports in 4 months. Sample copy and writer's guidelines for 9x12 SAE and $2.50.

Fiction: Dealing specifically with teenage girls and contemporary teen issues. More fiction on emerging alternatives for young women. Suspense, humorous, and romance. "Young love is all right, but teens want to read about it in more relevant settings." Length: 2,500-4,000 words. Pays $100. Sometimes pays the expenses of writers on assignment.

Tips: "No fiction with explicit language, casual references to drugs, alcohol, sex, or smoking; no fiction with too depressing outcome."

VENTURE, Christian Service Brigade, P.O. Box 150, Wheaton IL 60189. (708) 665-0630. Editor: Deborah Christensen. 15% freelance written. Works with a small number of new/unpublished writers each year. "Venture is a bimonthly company publication published to support and compliment CBS's Stockade and Battalion programs. We aim to provide wholesome, entertaining reading for boys ages 10-15. Estab. 1959. Circ. 22,000. Pays on publication. Publishes ms an average of 6 months after acceptance, sometimes longer. Byline given. Offers $35 kill fee. Buys first North American serial, one-time and second serial (reprint) rights. Submit seasonal/holiday material 6 months in advance. Previously published submissions OK. Reports in 2 weeks. Sample copy $1.85 with 9x12 SASE and 4 first-class stamps; writer's guidelines for #10 SAE.

Nonfiction: Exposé, general interest, historical/nostalgic, humor, inspirational, interview/profile, personal experience, photo feature, and religious. Buys 10-12 mss/year. Send complete ms. Length: 1,000-1,500 words. Pays $75-150 for assigned articles; pays $40-100 for unsolicited articles. Sometimes pays expenses of writers on assignment. Reprints OK; send photocopy of article or short story or typed ms with rights for sale noted. Pays 5-6¢ per word.

Photos: Send photos with submission. Reviews contact sheets and 5x7 prints. Offers $35-125/photo. Buys one-time rights.

Fiction: Adventure, humorous, mystery, and religious. Buys 10-12 mss/year. Send complete ms. Length: 1,000-1,500 words. Pays $40-125.

Tips: "Talk to young boys. Find out the things that interest them and write about those things. We are looking for material relating to our theme: Building Men to Serve Christ. We prefer shorter (1,000 words) pieces."

Diane, one of the students in the workshop, wondered about the chance of getting her short story published in *'Teen Magazine.* Her main character was a young man of seventeen who had problems identifying with his stepbrothers and sisters. After rescuing one of his stepbrothers from a near-fatal swimming accident, the character experienced a spiritual awakening that helped him cope with his problem.

After looking through *Writer's Market,* Warren (another student) suggested that Diane try *Venture Magazine* instead of *'Teen Magazine.* Since the main character in Diane's story was a teenage boy caught up in a spiritual crisis, *Venture* seemed a more appropriate market for her story. The length of Diane's story—1,200 words—was also more in line with *Venture's* word count requirements. According to *'Teen Magazine's* guidelines, the main character in the fiction they publish could be either male or female—but since most of *'Teen's* readers are girls, it's likely they'd most enjoy reading about a strong female character. The magazine is predominantly staff-written, which also narrows a freelance writer's chances of "breaking in."

Book Markets

If you're looking to publish your novel or nonfiction book, the same suggestion applies: study the book publishers in *Writer's Market, Literary Market Place,* and other sources to discover the kinds of books and subject matter that are their specialty. A James Bond-type thriller wouldn't sell to a university press, which is likely to publish mostly scholarly works. Similarly, a romance novel that might be right for Harlequin Books has no place in the ranks of Davis Publications, Inc. The 1993 *Writer's Market* tells what types of books interest each company.

> HARLEQUIN ENTERPRISES, LTD., Subsidiary of Torstar Corporation, Home Office: 225 Duncan Mill Rd., Don Mills, Ontario M3B 3K9 Canada. (416) 445-5860. President and Chief Executive Officer: Brian E. Hickey. Vice President and Editor-in-Chief: Horst Bausch. Editorial divisions: Harlequin Books (Editorial Director: Karin Stoecker); Silhouette Books (Editorial Director: Isabel Swift; for editorial requirements, see separate listing, under Silhouette Books); and Worldwide Library/Gold Eagle Books (Editorial Director and Assistant to the Editor-in-Chief: Randall Toye; see separate listing under Worldwide Library). Imprints: Harlequin Romance and Harlequin Presents (Paula Eykelhof, Editor); Harlequin Superromance (Marsha Zinberg, Senior Editor); Harlequin Temptation (Brigit Davis-Todd, Senior Editor); Harlequin Regency Romance (Marmie Charndoff, Editor); Harlequin Intrigue and Harlequin American Romance (Debra Matteucci, Senior Editor and Editorial Coordinator); Harlequin Historicals (Tracy Farrell, Senior Editor). Estab. 1949. Submissions for Harlequin Intrigue, Harlequin American Romance, and Harlequin Historicals should be directed to the designated editor and sent to Harlequin Books, 300 E. 42nd St., New York, NY 10017. (212) 682-6080. All other submissions should be directed to the Canadian address. Publishes mass market paperback originals. Averages 780 titles/

year; receives 10,000 submissions annually. 10% of books from first-time authors; 20% of books from unagented writers. Pays royalty. Offers advance. Publishes book an average of 1 year after acceptance. Reports in 2 weeks on queries. *Writer's Market* recommends allowing 2 months for reply. Free writer's guidelines.

Fiction: Adult contemporary and historical romance, including novels of romantic suspense (Intrigue), short contemporary romance (Presents and Romance), long contemporary romance (Superromance), short contemporary sensuals (Temptation), period historical (Regency) and adult historical romance (Historicals). "We welcome submissions to all of our lines. Know our guidelines and be familiar with the style and format of the line you are submitting to. Stories should possess a life and vitality that makes them memorable for the reader."

Tips: "Harlequin's readership comprises a wide variety of ages, backgrounds, income, and education levels. The audience is predominantly female. Because of the high competition in women's fiction, readers are becoming very discriminating. They look for a quality read. Read as many recent romance books as possible in all series to get a feel for the scope, new trends, acceptable levels of sensuality, etc."

DAVIS PUBLICATIONS, INC., 50 Portland St., Worcester MA 01608. (508) 754-7201. FAX: (508) 753-3834. Managing Editor: Wyatt Wade. Acquisitions Editor: Martha Siegel. Estab. 1901. Averages 5-10 titles/year. Pays 10-12% royalty. Publishes book an average of 1 year after acceptance. *Writer's Market* recommends allowing 2 months for reply. Book catalog for 9x12 SAE with 2 first class stamps. Write for copy of guidelines for authors.

Nonfiction: Publishes technique-oriented art, design, and craft books for the educational market. Accepts nonfiction translations. "Keep in mind the intended audience. Our readers are visually oriented. All illustrations should be collated separately from the text, but keyed to the text. Photos should be good quality transparencies and black and white photographs. Well-selected illustrations should explain, amplify, and enhance the text. We average 2-4 photos/page. We like to see technique photos as well as illustrations of finished artwork, by a variety of artists, including students. Recent books have been on papermaking, airbrush painting, jewelry, design, puppets, and watercolor painting." Submit outline, sample chapters, and illustrations. Reviews artwork/photos as part of ms package.

Recent Nonfiction Title: *Computers in the Artroom,* by Deborah Greh.

How Readable Is Your Writing?

Whether you're a specialist or a generalist, a writer of articles, essays, or books, your material must be appropriate for your readers. Besides content, style, and tone, you must consider its readability when targeting it for an audience. How easy is it to understand? Rudolf Flesch spent years refining a technique to test readability. He analyzed sentence length, vocabulary, punctuation, and other factors that determined the comprehensibility of written passages.

In his test, a one hundred-word writing sample from an article or story is analyzed by counting the number of syllables, numbers, punctuation marks, symbols, and other items in the sentences. Each item is assigned one point, and your score suggests the readability of the writing. The score is likely to be a number between ten and fifty. Formal writing—the kind found in academic and scientific journals—would range from ten to twenty points. The twenty-six- to thirty-point range would reflect the writing in publications such as *Time* magazine. Mass-circulation fiction and nonfiction magazines such as *Women's Circle* and *Saturday Evening Post* test at thirty-one-plus.

Though no readability formula gives exact results, such a test can help you determine if your writing is too difficult or too easy for your readers. The Flesch test is useful for specialist writers who want to target their articles for a general market: they can determine if their writing is comprehensible for a lay audience. The generalist, on the other hand, can discover by using the readability formula if his writing is too informal for a specialized, technical audience.

For more information on the readability test and how you might apply it to your writing, consult Rudolf Flesch's book *A New Way to Better English,* listed in the bibliography.

Query Letters

When you've analyzed the marketplace, carefully listed appropriate outlets for your work, and considered the readability factor, you may be tempted to package your manuscript and send it on its way. But take a minute to check *Writer's Market* to see how you should submit your work to a specific market. Most editors prefer query letters to completed articles or stories.

What are the advantages of sending a query instead of an entire manuscript? There are several. First, a query letter is a potential timesaver. If there's little or no interest in your subject or angle as outlined in a query, you haven't spent the time researching and writing a book or article you may not be able to sell; you've merely tested editors' reactions to your idea. Their response may spur you to research the subject further, or cause you to do enough research to convince an editor that you know what you're talking about—he'll want to be sure you're knowledgeable about a topic before giving you the go-ahead to write the piece.

Another advantage is that query letters go directly to an editor and not to a "first reader" assigned to unsolicited manuscripts. Since letters are more concise than a pile of manuscript pages four inches high, you can usually expect a reply from within one to four weeks; a decision on a manuscript can take months.

There's also the matter of postage—which can get *very* expensive when you're sending out a book manuscript or a lengthy article for consideration. Query letters for articles don't usually cost more than two first-class stamps— one for the outside envelope, and one for the self-addressed envelope you include for a reply. A query letter (including a title and description of the work) for a nonfiction book costs more to send, since it includes a detailed outline, a synopsis of the balance of the manuscript, and one or two chapters along with a self-addressed stamped envelope. But it's still less than mailing the complete manuscript.

Fiction writers marketing their books should send two or more sample chapters plus a summary of the rest of the novel. In his book *Freelance Writing— Advice from the Pros,* Curtis Casewit asked Arthur Hailey what he thought of the idea of querying a publisher.

> *The outline will show a publisher if there is a potential novel of interest to that publisher. The sample chapters will demonstrate how well the individual can write. Also, a good editor can suggest a change of direction, adaptation of ideas, etc., and this may save the writer a lot of time and effort compared with going to the end of his book without advice from an outside source. My own practice, even now, is to show the editor with whom I work my outlines as they develop and every half dozen chapters as I write them.*[2]

Whether your query letters are invaluable tools to marketing your work depends on how well you write them. Query letters are your calling cards; they reflect your professionalism or lack of it. It's very important to make that editor's first impression a positive one.

Most editors recommend the following do's and don'ts for query letters.

Do

1. Use only business stationery or plain white bond paper.

2. Always type the letter. Proofread it carefully; correct any errors in spelling and punctuation.

3. Address it to a specific editor. Check the current edition of *Writer's Market* or *Writer's Handbook* (available in most libraries).

4. If you send the query letter before you've finished the manuscript, do enough research so the editor realizes you know the subject well.

5. Get the editor's attention in the opening paragraph of the letter. Make him or her want to read more. The beginning of a query is as important as the opening paragraph of an article or book. "Hook" your reader.

6. State your idea clearly. A general topic such as "work" needs a specific slant to give it a theme, a focus. You might introduce a subject such as the rewards of working after sixty-five, for example.

7. Explain how you're going to develop the subject. Will you use interviews with experts, case histories, research? For fiction, include the genre (romance, mystery, science fiction, etc.), a brief synopsis of the book, an outline, and two chapters.

8. Tell a little about yourself in relation to the subject. If you're writing about the school system and you're a teacher, mention that. Include reference to any pertinent skills or special talents you have that might help you sell your idea.

9. Include a few tear sheets of your work. (Tear sheets are samples of your writing in published form.) If you have no published credits yet, don't mention it.

Don't

1. Don't boast that you're the only one qualified to write the article. Editors know better. Don't challenge them to accept your idea.

2. Don't exceed two single-spaced pages. Brevity is best for a query letter.

3. Don't call the editor a week after sending the letter. Wait four weeks and then drop a note asking if a decision has been made. Always include your phone number and address.

4. Don't send the letter if it has any typographical errors. Retype it.

5. Don't send it to the wrong magazine or publisher. Study the requirements for each one. Know who the reader is and what the editor wants.

6. Don't expect your manuscript to be accepted on the basis of your query letter. The usual policy is that editors will suggest you do the article "on speculation"—then, if they like it, they'll buy it.

7. Don't forget to enclose a self-addressed, stamped envelope (SASE) with your letter to ensure a reply.

8. Don't use a form query letter that includes printed statements for the editor to check off indicating why the manuscript was accepted or rejected: "Send the completed story/article"; "Not right for us"; "Wrong subject." These forms are too impersonal and they take up space you ought to use to discuss your idea.

Below is a query letter I sent to publishers to interest them in my nonfiction book. Accompanying the letter were an outline, a summary of the balance of the book, and two sample chapters. The letter was single-spaced; it fit on one sheet of paper.

(Always type the letter)	(Home Address) (Date)
(Write to a specific editor at a current address)	(Publisher or magazine's name and address)
(Dear Mr., Ms., Dr.)	Dear (Editor's Name)
(Get the editor's attention)	One of the most popular sections of a magazine or newspaper is the question-and-answer page. Facts about athletes, movie stars, dieting and other subjects fascinate and inform readers.
(Tell about yourself in relation to subject and/or research completed)	While teaching adults and teenagers for the last ten years, I conducted discussions, surveys and seminars on what interested them. They wanted to know if biofeedback, meditation, dream interpretation, and other things could enrich their lives and help them overcome problems. I asked doctors, psychologists, and others for the answers. They

agreed that many people who spend money visiting them each year could eliminate their own depression, bad habits, and fears by using dream analysis, meditation and by becoming more aware of how their body functions. Their comments, combined with my research and my background as a therapist, teacher and writer enabled me to write a question-and-answer book entitled *How You Can Get Rid of Your Hang-Ups By Yourself.*

(State the idea) The first section of the book focuses on the mind.
(Tell about subject: how you're going to develop it) Some of the questions from various chapters are: How do you program nightmares out of your dreams? Can suggestion help you to get a better job? How can you stop feeling depressed? How do you meditate? Why do many successful people meditate? Is it possible to teach yourself to be assertive? Part one includes chapters on meditation, dream interpretation, and self-improvement techniques.

(Tell how subject will be developed) Section two deals with the body. It contains lucid, concise answers to questions such as: What foods make you smarter? How can you get extra physical and mental energy? Do face-lifts really work? What drugs are available to keep you young? How do birth control pills work? Are certain types of personalities more susceptible to cancer than others? What is it like to die? How does the body become addicted to drugs? There are chapters on miracle and addictive drugs, dangerous food additives, vitamins, diseases, cosmetic surgery, and the functions of different organs of the body.

The question-and-answer format has proven to be a popular style for books. People are inquisitive but they don't have the time or the inclination to wade through a dry, verbose explanation for their question. A brief easy-to-read answer is what they want. My book deals with high-interest topics and gives the reader the opportunity to try different methods to overcome his/her problems.

(Briefly mention pertinent background) I have been copyediting and writing articles for the Philadelphia newspapers and conducting adult seminars in dream therapy and creative writing. Prior to this, I taught

high school, college, and adult classes in fiction and
nonfiction writing, science, reading, psychology, English
and journalism. These experiences have provided me with
considerable material for my book.

Enclosed are two chapters and an outline of the book.

I am looking forward to hearing from you.

Sincerely,

What type of response can you expect from a query letter? If an editor is
interested, he'll write and tell you to send the manuscript "on speculation."
If he's not interested, he'll say so.

I sent out ten query letters like the one above, all at the same time.
I received nine replies: four publishing houses sent printed rejection slips that
stated they weren't interested in publishing my type of book in the next year;
four editors wrote letters thanking me for sending the letter and related
materials—they commented favorably on the content and writing, but didn't
like the question-and-answer format; a textbook company asked if I'd drop the
question/answer approach and rewrite it for high school students—they thought
the subjects covered would interest them. I decided to consider this offer and
am slanting the material for teenagers. I plan to resubmit it when I've finished
the revisions.

Dealing With Rejection And Criticism

When you send the completed piece "on spec" in response to an editor's request,
there's still no guarantee it will be published. If, on receiving the manuscript, the
editor decides not to use it, he'll probably send you a form rejection letter. Most
writers think this method of communication is impersonal, but editors say it's
the only way they can handle the daily volume of mail.

Though we may understand why standard rejection slips exist, it's still
not easy to find them in the mailbox. Sometimes, it's even harder to deal with
them. What do you do if your manuscript has been rejected?

If an editor has suggested how it can be improved, take the suggestions
into consideration; decide if you want to make the changes. If you decide that
the comments either don't improve your work or don't add to its salability, then

don't make those changes. Use your good judgment. You may also want to seek constructive input from a teacher, writer friend, or someone who'll be objective and candid with you.

Try to look at your writing analytically—not defensively. What *can* you do to make it better? Perhaps just rewriting several sections will improve it. Or maybe the piece is good as is, and you've sent it to the wrong market. Think about other publishers or magazines that might be interested.

When the editor wrote the comment "not slanted for our readers" on the rejection slip for Matt's article on tax deductions, Matt was understandably disappointed. But he still wanted to sell his article. He tried to look at the editor's remark as constructive rather than destructive. To help assimilate the editor's recommendation into his own thinking, Matt did the next Write-Now exercise each day for a week right before his writing sessions.

Practicing the exercise will make you more open to constructive criticism from people whose opinions you respect.

Write-Now Exercise
Being Objective About Criticism

Goal: To be objective about the constructive criticism you receive and help you make the suggested changes in your writing if you think they'll improve your work.

1.
2. Do steps 1-3 of the Write-Now exercise as outlined on pages 206-207.
3.

4. See yourself making improvements in your house or apartment. You feel good about asking an interior decorator whose judgment you trust to suggest some changes. What color should the living room be? What's the best decor for the bedrooms? See yourself thinking about what the decorator says as an objective observer; weigh the decorator's suggestions with your own views.

5. Give yourself this suggestion ten times: "When I get objective, constructive comments about my writing from people I trust, I will consider the changes in order to make my writing better."

Say, "When I open my eyes, I'll feel great."

After completing the exercise, Matt realized he needed to be more aware of the readers he was trying to reach. To do that, he practiced the Write-Now exercise on pages 185-186. He did the exercises for a month and soon began to slant his articles to certain readers—and sell his work.

Looking At Local Markets

What can you do if none of the major national markets has responded positively to your query letters, and you have no constructive criticism to act on? Is your idea unsalable? Not necessarily; maybe you should try some of the local markets you may have overlooked.

In his book *1,000 Tested Money-Making Markets for Writers,* Walter Oleksy gives writers precisely this advice:

> *Local newspapers and Sunday supplements can be some of your best local freelance markets. Payments may range from $10 to $250, but if the money isn't high, the exposure can earn you higher sales. Others see your byline, read your articles, and become acquainted with your name and the type of writing you do. When they need a writer, they may call on you.*[3]

When I did a series of articles on volunteer service organizations in Philadelphia, I studied the Philadelphia newspapers and magazines and decided to query the *Philadelphia Inquirer.* The editor replied that because these service agencies didn't have offices in all the circulation areas outside Philadelphia proper, my articles wouldn't apply to all their readers. It would be too far for many readers to travel to volunteer their services.

With his comment in mind, I sent another query letter to *The News Gleaner* publications, which cover the northeast section of Philadelphia where the agencies I featured had their offices. *The News Gleaner* published the articles.

Studying and analyzing local, regional, and national markets is an effective way to get your work published. For names and addresses of various markets, check the *Editor and Publisher Yearbook, N.W. Ayer & Sons Directory of Newspapers and Periodicals,* or the current *Writer's Market*—all available in most public libraries.

The *Ayer Directory* is especially helpful for uncovering small town daily and weekly newspaper markets you may have overlooked. Perhaps in your hiking adventures out West, you've learned about the famed jackalope, and have subsequently uncovered some "new" theories about the mythical creature that the residents of Douglas, Wyoming might be interested in. The *Ayer Directory* tells you that Douglas, a town of about 6,000, is served by *The Budget,* a weekly newspaper. Why not query the editor about a story?

A very real part of finding an outlet for your writing is knowing where to look. The "right" place is usually the one you've taken time to research. Getting in the habit of systematically searching for markets is worth the effort.

Stacey, a librarian in the Write-Now workshop, shared her thoughts on the subject of looking for the right market.

> *Once I realized the importance of finding the right market for my articles, I began to sell on a regular basis. Marketing shouldn't be a hit-or-miss thing. It's something that requires time. It's like looking for a house. If you know basically what you want and where you want to live, you go to that part of town and start looking for a place to buy. The same with writing: if you know who your readers are and what they're interested in reading about, you find the magazine that meets your writing needs and their reading needs.*

The Element Of Patience

Even with the most sophisticated marketing strategy, part of getting published is being in the right place at the right time. Just because a piece of writing is good, doesn't mean some editor is ready to snatch it up. What about the classics? What about those works that are obviously beautifully crafted? Even for them, there are no guarantees.

According to Somerset Maugham, "What makes a classic is not that it is praised by critics, expounded by professors and studied in schools, but that large numbers of readers, generation after generation, have found pleasure and spiritual profit in reading it."

Thus, the question still exists: How does a piece of writing that might be a classic become one if it never gets published? The strange irony is that many of the titles we now consider classics were rejected many times before they were finally published.

F. Scott Fitzgerald's short stories were rejected one hundred twenty-two times before they went to press. Robert Frost wrote for twenty years before his first book of poems, *A Boy's Will,* was published. At the age of twenty, Taylor Caldwell decided to be a novelist; it took her eighteen years to get a book published. In the interim she wrote six other novels. After *Dynasty of Death* was published and became a bestseller, the publisher bought her six other novels as well! Norah Lofts wrote her first book in 1930 and spent five years marketing it;

I Met a Gypsy was published in 1935. But before that, it had been returned/
rejected so many times that her family affectionately named it "Norah's Hom-
ing Pigeon."[4]

Ernest Hemingway faced similar frustrations. Both his parents and his
editors failed to recognize his talent and for years rejected his writing. His now-
famous short story, "The Undefeated," was submitted to every major magazine,
only to be rejected. As a favor, Hemingway's friends published it in their literary
quarterly, *This Quarter*.

Believe In Yourself

Why do people keep writing after years of rejection? How do they preserve their
creative spirit when constant rejection threatens to stifle it? How do they keep
rejection from being a major distraction to their writing (as discussed in
Chapter 5)?

Hemingway's definition of courage—grace under pressure—helps answer
these questions. Writers who don't let rejection block their desire to write have
the courage of their convictions. They see themselves as writers and believe they
have something worthwhile to say. They're convinced that other people will
one day believe it, too. Faith in themselves and in their work enables them to
persevere.

Writers in the Write-Now workshops have talked candidly about how
they feel when their work isn't accepted. Many take it very personally. But
negative attitudes contribute nothing to getting published. To help reverse any
counterproductive attitudes they may be harboring about their writing, my
students practice the following Write-Now exercise.

Try it every day (or at bedtime) for a month. You'll become more
persistent; your belief in yourself as a writer will grow stronger.

Write-Now Exercise
Persistence, Belief in Self as a Writer and a Seller

Goal: To believe in your abilities as a writer and to be persistent about
improving your work and your marketing ability.

1.
2. Do steps 1-3 of the Write-Now exercise as outlined on pages 206-
   207.
3.

4. Picture yourself walking through a bookstore. You see someone picking up a copy of your book or a magazine containing your story or article. He looks it over and decides to buy it. You feel the pride and pleasure of an established author.

5. Say to yourself ten times: "I am a writer with something worthwhile to say. I am becoming better at my craft and better at selecting the right market for my work. I'll continue to be persistent and to believe in myself and my writing."

If you're doing the exercise during the day, say, "When I open my eyes, I'll feel great."

If you do the exercise at bedtime, drop off to sleep.

Feeling the pride and pleasure of having your work published and knowing that people are reading your writing is a treasured experience. A first sale is especially rewarding. In an article that appeared in *Writer's Digest* magazine in 1981, some of today's most popular writers shared their feelings on the occasion of their first sale.

Isaac Asimov's "Marooned Off Vesta" brought him $64 and made him feel "triumphant." There's a market for all his work today, but in 1938 he had trouble selling it. His advice for writers: develop a thick skin and persevere.

Danielle Steel made her first sale in 1971—a poem to *Cosmopolitan*. Payment was "not much, $50 or $75," she said. But the sale brought her "sheer delight and the self-confidence that I could sell."

Erma Bombeck's exposure to the publishing world came when she worked as a copy girl for the *Dayton Journal Herald*. "I ran errands; I didn't write," she said, "but when I interviewed Shirley Temple as one sixteen-year-old to another, they published it on a feature page. Since I was on the staff, I got the award for the feature of the week: $10 and a spot on the bulletin board." What was her response to her first sale? "I knew I would own the paper in two weeks."

That sale inspired her to write and continue writing. It's that same inspiration that has brought her success.

> *If you are not awed by the craft of putting a white sheet of paper into a typewriter and filling it with words that can extract humor, pain, knowledge and every emotion in the galaxy from people, then sell your I.B.M. The magic is gone.*[5]

For Matt, the magic of writing returned. By practicing the Write-Now exercises and writing daily, he boosted his confidence and his persistence—and became a successful writer. By learning to selectively choose just the right "shop" for his work, he solved the mystery associated with marketing his writing. His writing life now is not only a destination—getting published—but also a journey leading to new levels of personal growth and creative awareness.

I hope that you, like Matt and other writers I've met along my own creative journey, will, as Thoreau said, "advance confidently in the direction of [your] dreams and endeavor to live the [writing] life which you have imagined and meet with success unexpected in common hours."

Notes/Chapter Eight

1. Anne Mollegan Smith, "Why Do Editors Use Form Rejection Slips?" *The Writer,* Vol. 89 (January, 1976), pp. 5-6.

2. Curtis Casewit, *Freelance Writing—Advice from the Pros* (New York: Macmillan Publishing Co., 1974), p. 182.

3. Walter Oleksy, *1,000 Tested Money-Making Markets for Writers* (New York: Harper & Row, 1973), p. 23. (Current publisher, Parker Publishing Co.: West Nyack, N.Y.)

4. Ralph Daigh, *Maybe You Should Write a Book* (Englewood Cliffs, N.J.: Prentice-Hall, 1977), p. 111, 131.

5. "My First Sale," *Writer's Digest,* Vol. 61 (December, 1981), pp 21-28.

CHAPTER NINE

Everything You Still Wanted to Ask About the Write-Now Method

I keep six honest serving men
They taught me all I knew;
Their names are what and why and when
And how and where and who.

Rudyard Kipling

I N WRITING THIS BOOK, I've frequently called on my experiences with students in the Write-Now workshops to explain why and how the Write-Now method can help you become the writer you want to be. It seems fitting then—before sending you on your way to apply the Write-Now method to your own writing—that I share with you some of the questions my writing students have asked me over the years. Indeed, questions are evidence of thought. And answers provide direction.

Here are questions about writing and questions about the Write-Now method: questions about the writing craft, the writing business, and writing as a fulfilling activity. In the workshops, I've found that the same concerns and questions come up again and again. Perhaps you're asking them right now.

I hope this chapter gives you the answers, and in the process, provides you with greater insight into the Write-Now method and how it can become a part of your life.

How-To's Of The Write-Now Method

Q. Why is it important to do the progressive relaxation exercises?

A. Because they reduce physical and mental stress. Their aim is to put you in the relaxed or alpha state in which your subconscious mind soaks up the suggestions you give it.

Besides the improvement in your writing skills, there's an added benefit. The relaxation steps will help you get a good night's sleep because your body will be completely relaxed. If you do the exercises during the day, you'll feel more energetic afterward.

Q. How do I know if I'm doing the relaxation exercises right? I don't feel completely relaxed after the exercises.

A. After finishing an exercise, ask yourself the following questions: Did I feel physically relaxed after Steps 1 and 3, or was I still tense? Was it hard to relax my feet, legs, hips, back, neck, shoulders, stomach, chest, arms, hands, and facial muscles? Did I inhale deeply through my nose and take the air down to the diaphragm?

If you answered "no" to these questions, try this: Concentrate completely on each muscle group as you repeat the exercise. You visualize yourself relaxing in a lounge chair beside the tranquil pond (Step 2). See your heels push down firmly on the chair. Curl your toes as though you were trying to wrap them around a pencil. Next, point your toes to stretch your leg muscles. Don't strain your muscles as you tighten your hips and try to make them look smaller. Do the same thing with your stomach muscles—tighten and relax them. Visualize your back, neck, and head pushing against the chair as though you were trying to leave your imprint on it. As you press your arms down on the armrest, pretend you have a small rubber ball in each hand. Squeeze it and relax your fingers.

Picturing each muscle group as you flex and relax the muscles will reduce tension, and you'll feel completely relaxed after the exercise.

Q. How do mental pictures help you reach your writing goal?

A. Imaging, or the forming of mental pictures, is based on the tendency in human nature to become what we imagine ourselves to be. An image formed and accepted by the conscious mind will eventually be accepted by the subconscious. So dynamic is the effect of mental pictures that regularly visualizing a goal can make it a reality.

See yourself stretched out on your sofa. The only thing you can think about is how scrumptious a hot fudge sundae would taste. You see the scoops of vanilla and chocolate ice cream hidden under thick, creamy fudge syrup. You can almost taste the mountains of whipped cream dotted with walnuts and topped with a maraschino cherry.

If you concentrated on this picture for awhile and no conflicting thoughts negated it, you'd most likely go into the kitchen and make the exact sundae you imagined. That's how a mental picture works. It implants the desire. Your brain tells your body to do what's necessary to satisfy that desire—in this case, make the sundae.

A stronger conflicting mental picture—seeing yourself standing in front of your Weight Watchers' group, red-faced because you have to confess that sundae and tell the others you've gained five pounds this week—will cancel the first picture.

When you do the Write-Now exercises, you picture in Step 4 your writing goal. You see vividly how you want to be as a writer. Regularly picturing yourself as having already attained your objective, and coupling that with a suggestion telling you that you've reached it, will make your objective a reality.

Q. It's hard for me to think in pictures. I seem to have trouble concentrating on the relaxing scene in Step 2 of the Write-Now exercises. How can I improve my ability to visualize?

A. If someone asked you to describe your "dream" house, you could in all probability visualize each room clearly. You could describe the decor in detail. When you think about a favorite food, a special person, or an unusual event, you form a corresponding mental image of each one and concentrate on it. With practice, you can develop these same skills in your writing in order to do the Write-Now exercises.

Think about a place where you can go for a day or more just to get away from it all. Is it in the mountains? Near a lake? Along the ocean? Try to see the place as though you were looking at a picture of it. What do you do there to unwind? Swim? Play tennis? Eat and drink 'til your stomach's content?

See yourself doing the activity. Now hold this picture in your mind's eye for at least three or four minutes. Do this each day for two weeks before doing the Write-Now exercises. You might want to substitute your peaceful spot in Step 2 for the pond scene. If you're able to hold the favorite place in your mind for several minutes, Step 2 in the exercise will be easy for you to visualize.

Q. I feel as though I'm resisting a certain suggestion. Is that possible?

A. It is. Consider the man who tries unsuccessfully to lose weight. After a few weeks of dieting, he hasn't lost an ounce. His real problem may be an emotional one: though his wife constantly teases him about being over-weight, he's getting some attention from her. Maybe he feels that's better than no attention at all—i.e., if he loses weight, will his wife pay *any* attention to him? A counselor may be able to help him identify his real problem and help him deal with it.

The same kind of thing could be happening with a particular exercise you're practicing. Let's say you're doing the Write-Now exercise on rejection (Chapter 5, pages 115-116). If you feel resistance to the suggestion in the exercise and it's blocking your progress, it might be that you have feelings of rejection about other things in your life. It's a good idea to discuss your feelings with a counselor and get some advice/insight on how to deal with those emotions.

Q. How do I know how many times I should repeat a Write-Now suggestion? How important are the number of repetitions?

A. Repeating a suggestion is very important because that's how you condition your subconscious mind. When you give yourself a suggestion while you're totally relaxed, your inner mind will accept it as fact. To see how successful this technique is, just think about how advertisers use an oft-repeated commercial message to get you to buy a product.

The more often you repeat a suggestion, the stronger it will be in your mind—a minimum of ten times is appropriate for the exercises.

Q. What should I do if I don't get results from a Write-Now exercise?

A. The first thing to do is make sure you've picked the right exercise to correct your writing problem. If you've selected the wrong one, the result will be similar to what happens if you take a Tums to relieve your backache.

I recall one writer telling me how frustrated she was during her writing sessions. Kim had done the Write-Now exercise (Chapter 4, page 79) in order to "see" herself writing between 7:00 and 8:00 in the evening. After a week, she still hadn't made headway on her short story. I asked her if interruptions or noise bothered her while she tried to write. She said that she had to get up a few times each session to check on the children who were playing in the basement or answer the phone. Kim also said that she hadn't done a "typical day" schedule to identify any of her uninterrupted leisure time (Chapter 4, pages 73-75). After we outlined her "typical day" together, Kim decided that from 2:00 to 3:00 in the afternoon—just before the kids came home from school—was really the best time for her to write.

She did the Write-Now exercise (Chapter 4, page 79) and pictured herself writing at her new time, 2:00 to 3:00 in the afternoon. A week later, she had finished her story. She couldn't believe how much easier it was to write just by switching the time for her writing session.

If you've done a particular exercise every day or night for a month and haven't seen results, don't give up. Instead, reword the suggestion you give yourself in the exercise. Just be sure to keep the point or focus of the suggestion intact. Change the mental picture you use to fit your *exact* need. If you write at your desk after work, picture yourself writing there.

Remember, too, that a deep-rooted habit takes awhile to rout. More practice might be just the "tool" you need. If you've never been able to sit still for five minutes, then trying to write for thirty may be difficult. Self-discipline is an essential ingredient in a successful writing formula. The Write-Now exercises help you develop it.

The Writing Craft

Q. Where do you get ideas for stories, articles, books, or poems?

A. Ideas can come from anywhere—newspapers, movies, families, magazines, friends, jobs, and daily experiences. These stimuli can ignite an idea for a how-to book on scuba diving or an article on sky diving, a biography of your great-grandfather, magazine articles on health, home management, child care, or popcorn poppers.

The key is to be tuned in to the right frequency for those ideas to come in loud and clear. Active readers and active viewers train their eyes and ears always to be on the alert for ideas for writing projects.

Q. I get so many ideas for writing, but I can't seem to get anything down on paper. Any suggestions?

A. When you experience this blitz of ideas, feelings, and emotions, write them down immediately. The terrific idea for a children's book that came to you yesterday in the dentist's office is too often a hazy afterthought today—unless you write it down. Get in the habit of carrying a small (5x7-inch) notebook in your pocket or purse. Jot down thoughtful phrases, impressions, or words that strike you.

Developing them comes later. In the meantime, your subconscious can go to work. When you saw the little boy wince with fear when the door to the dentist's inner office opened, you were reminded of your first introduction to the six-month checkup. If you haven't taken a minute to record the "I'm-trying-to-be-brave" expression on that seven-year-old's face, its significance may be lost to you forever.

If you've recorded it—not in any formal way, just enough to recall it—you can later transfer it to your writing notebook, and develop or add to it. The act of writing it down not only helps you remember it, but puts that thought into your subconscious. The observation you captured may later lead you to explore and write about other childhood fears.

Try keeping a journal, too. Write in it every day. You'll see how your fertile imagination plucks from it just the right idea to produce a poem, complete an article, or develop an essay topic.

Q. How can you visualize characters so that they seem real to you?

A. Close your eyes. Now mentally picture a woman you know very well. It might be your wife, mother, sister, best friend, or neighbor. What color are her eyes and hair? How tall is she? What kind of personality does she have? See her doing something just for fun. Why do you like/dislike her? Is she married? Does she work for a living? Hold the image of the woman in your mind for at least two minutes.

Was it hard to "see" the person? Were you able to visualize her having fun—playing the piano, baking cookies, playing racquetball? If you couldn't picture her, try answering the above questions again.

The way you visualize this woman that you know is the same way you'll see the basketball player, pregnant teenager, cab driver, or drug addict who might be a character in your story. By doing the character biography exercise on pages 127-128, you'll discover how you can "see" your fictional character as clearly as you saw the real person.

Q. Why is it important to keep a writing notebook?

A. Keeping a notebook provides you one special place—a filing cabinet of sorts—for your ideas. It's easy to jot things down on scraps of paper only to forget which coat pocket they're in or on which cash register tape they're scribbled. A writing notebook keeps you organized.

I use one large, loose-leaf notebook for both my fiction and nonfiction writing. It's divided into sections very similar to those Phyllis Whitney uses in her notebook (described in Chapter 4, pages 84-86). My journal is included in the back. At the end of each year, I remove my journal pages and file them for use or reference in future story or article projects. I have a separate (6x9-inch) stenographer's notebook in which I record my dreams. I have a small (5x7-inch) notebook in my pocketbook so it's readily available for recording random thoughts and ideas for future writing projects or ones already in progress.

The Marketing End Of Things

Q. What's the best source to use for marketing my articles and stories?

A. I've found that a current edition of *Writer's Market* gives the most up-to-date listings of potential markets. Most listings give specific requirements for submitting manuscripts to all types of publications and book publishers. See Chapter 8 for more information on *Writer's Market* and how you can use it to successfully market your writing.

Q. Do most magazines accept articles or stories from beginning writers?

A. As long as your article or story is well written, submitted in a professional manner, and appropriate for a particular magazine, it will be judged on its own merit. If a particular editor wants to publish only writers with a track record, your material might be rejected no matter how good it is.

Check the current edition of *Writer's Market* before submitting your material to any magazine. Many magazines indicate it in their listings if published credits are necessary for acceptance. Read the *Writer's Market* entries carefully; pay close attention to specific advice and tips editors share with writers interested in breaking in to their magazines.

Q. How do you snap back after getting rejection slips and start writing again?

A. Everyone feels disappointed when his or her work isn't accepted. It's a natural feeling. Only when the disappointment deepens into depression and lasts for weeks or months will it impair your writing. This sometimes happens when writers assume that because their material was rejected, they have no talent. If you personally identify with rejection—"My article wasn't good enough to be accepted, so I'm not a good writer"—you're drawing an erroneous conclusion. Your article may not be what a particular editor wants; perhaps it needs revision. But your experience with one article is not a definitive statement about your abilities as a writer.

If you tend to get depressed after your work is rejected, do the exercise in Chapter 5, pages 115-116. You'll begin to feel more objective about yourself as a writer.

The Writing Life And Everyday Reality

Q. I can't seem to get away from noise and distractions when I'm writing. How can I get them under control so I can be more productive?

A. Nearly every writer I've ever talked to would like to be able to turn down the noise to a soft hum as soon as they start to write. Fortunately, we can control the noise to a certain extent so it doesn't interfere with our writing sessions.

We can block out offensive sounds (a loud radio, a blaring television set across the hall) with a less offensive one such as a large fan or an air conditioner. The Write-Now exercise in Chapter 5, page 107, explains how to do this.

Of course, those times when noise and distractions are the greatest should be nonwriting times. When children come home from school, when dinner is being prepared, when there's lots of family activity in the early evening—these aren't the most opportune times for describing your heroine or fine-tuning the elements of your article.

Pick your writing time wisely, and you'll have better control over the noise and distractions in your environment.

Q. I'm exhausted at night and don't have the energy to write in the evening. I work in a busy office with little or no privacy during the day. Where do I get the energy to write at all?

A. Many writers find themselves in the same predicament. What has worked best for my students is doing the Write-Now exercise that boosts their energy levels and reduces fatigue (like Joan's exercise in Chapter 1). Many of them do the exercise about an hour after dinner and begin writing after they've completed it.

Q. Why is it hard for me to justify the time I spend writing? I get paid for things I do that require time and effort. But so far, I haven't made much money from my writing.

A. The rewards of writing aren't always financial. Sometimes they're better than that. Touching a sensitive chord in your nature that results in a poem or story lifts your spirit in a way that money cannot. One writer put it this way: "Even if I never earn another dime for my poems, I'd still write them. I've never bought anything that gives me the same 'high' I get after finishing a poem."

We all do things that require both time and effort but yield no pay— being a Boy Scout leader, spearheading a fundraising drive. Must we justify that time? Why should we have to justify our time spent writing if it gives us pleasure?

Q. I feel guilty going to my room for an hour each night to write. I feel I'm taking time away from my family. Yet I want to write. How can I deal with my guilt?

A. With two children in my life, I understand this guilt. I've often felt the same way. I remedied my situation by looking closely at my typical day's schedule (Chapter 4). I realized that I set up my writing session when the boys were still awake and very active. The minute I began writing, there seemed to be a run on cookie requests. Since my uninterrupted leisure time was between 10:00 and 11:00 at night and between 7:00 and 8:00 in the morning, I switched to writing in the early morning when my children were asleep and my husband was at work.

To overcome any guilt you feel, also consider this point: Do you feel guilty when you tell your children not to disturb you when you're watching your favorite TV show, or soaking in the bathtub, or talking to an old friend on the phone? These are things you do for yourself; you're entitled to do them. Why shouldn't writing for thirty to sixty minutes a day be something you do for yourself?

Set a policy that at a certain time every day you will not be available to pump air into your son's bicycle tire, locate the screwdriver that disappeared from the garage, or type your daughter's term paper that was due last week. Take as much control of your writing as you do of other areas of your life, and you won't feel guilty about writing.

Working Toward Your Writing Goals

Q. Why do you believe so strongly in the philosophy that "Whatever the mind can conceive and believe, it will achieve?"

A. Because I've seen proof that this philosophy works—not just in my own life, but in the lives of people I know. Your thoughts literally control your actions. Think about how your mind can trigger feelings of fear, anxiety, happiness, and pride.

Do you remember when you fell in love, had your first child, or bought your first car? Don't those thoughts make you happy? If you wanted to be cheerful but began dwelling on your divorce, your sick cat, or your car that was totaled in an accident last week, you'd be depressed.

To maintain a belief in yourself and to reach your writing goals, conditioning your mind with positive writing suggestions is imperative. If you see yourself as a creative person with something worthwhile to say, you'll have faith in your talents. And you will be an effective writer.

Q. I want to be a writer, but I just can't seem to get my act together. How can I discipline myself to write?

A. The simple fact is that in order to be a writer, *you must write*. It's easy to dream up reasons not to write—you're afraid your article won't be up to par; you don't think you'll be able to come up with an idea; you remember all the chores you could be finishing instead of "stealing" time to write, etc.

Get in the habit of writing. Write every day—for at least an hour, if possible. If you're not sure when to schedule your writing sessions, examine your weekly schedule and plan accordingly. Use any uninterrupted leisure time for writing. Do the exercise on page 79 where you see yourself at your desk at a specific hour. This will help you stick with your schedule.

Start each writing session with a warm-up exercise (see pages 87-88). Journal writing is an excellent way to loosen your mental muscles to make your writing hour more productive.

Have your writing materials and desk organized before you sit down to write so your thoughts won't be interrupted with having to jump up to sharpen a pencil or insert a new typewriter ribbon.

If you can get your act together for things you like to do—fish, read, watch a football game, sail—you can get it together for writing. It takes planning, practice, and perseverance.

Q. How does stress keep you from doing your best writing?

A. Stress prevents you from doing your best in any situation. Job stress that causes you to be tense at home will affect the quality of your home life. If you're worried about a deadline or a rejected story, your writing will reflect that anxiety—and it won't be your best effort.

Stress resulting from procrastination, disorganization, and noise can even cause writer's block. Not being able to come up with an idea for a story, or a poem you want to write for a friend's birthday, or a slant for an article due in forty-eight hours produces stress. Left unchecked, it can decrease your chances of success.

The Write-Now exercises in this book are targeted to writers' stress areas. If you practice them in conjunction with your writing, you'll lower your stress and enjoy more peace of mind as you write.

Q. How can I become more aware of my writing problem?

A. Most writing problems are easily identifiable. Occasionally, however, there are some that can't be pinned down. A brainstorming session can help.

Put the word "writing" at the top of your paper. For ten minutes, list quickly what you like about writing, and then what you hate about it. The good feeling you get after writing a poem, short story, or article might be a plus. Sticking with a writing schedule, getting rejection slips, doing research might be minuses.

When the time is up, go over your list. Circle those items that seem to give you the most trouble. Quite often, your writing problem will stand out clearly. By doing this exercise while you're relaxed, your subconscious mind will make you aware of a problem you didn't think you had. The next step is to do the Write-Now exercises that can eliminate it.

Q. How do I know if my writing goals are realistic?

A. Trying to overcome too many writing obstacles simultaneously is an unrealistic goal. Take one specific problem, select the Write-Now exercise designed to overcome it, and practice it daily or at bedtime for the suggested amount of time. If you don't see a change, do the exercise for another week. Once you've reached that goal, tackle the next writing problem with the appropriate exercise.

Writers sometimes set unrealistic goals by planning to write more than they could possibly accomplish during their writing sessions. You can't hope to write the Great American Novel if you write only for one hour a day. That would be like trying to run five miles the first day of your running program. You have to build up your endurance before you're ready for that challenge. Setting realistic goals will help you stick with them.

Q. Once I've reached my writing goal after doing the Write-Now exercise, will I be free of that particular writing problem forever? Do I still have to do the exercise?

A. It's not necessary to continue doing the exercise once you've achieved your objective. However, we human beings sometimes slip back into our old patterns. You've heard of the person who stops smoking for six months and one day decides to have just one cigarette after dinner to calm his nerves. One cigarette often leads to three or four. By the end of the week, he could be back to two packs a day.

Writers can return to old habits. Two rejection slips in one day might trigger an onset of the depression you thought you had conquered. If that happens, go back to the Write-Now exercise that earlier helped you overcome the anxiety caused by depression (the exercise on pages 115-116, Chapter 5). Give yourself a booster shot via a suggestion to help you replace your negative attitude with a positive one about your work.

You can always go back to an appropriate Write-Now exercise to once again rid yourself of a particular writing problem.

Q. Does practicing the Write-Now exercises guarantee that I'll get my writing published?

A. There are few guarantees in the writing business. No method, book, or teacher can guarantee that if you try their plan or adopt their philosophy, you'll see your work in print.

What the Write-Now exercises help you do is decrease the stress that complicates your writing life and stifles creative expression. They teach you how to constructively deal with procrastination, rejection, and fatigue. They show you how to discipline yourself and practice the skills necessary to write engaging fiction and interesting nonfiction. If you learn to do these things, your chances of getting published will increase.

The renowned historian Arnold Toynbee once conducted an extensive study on famous people who refused to allow failure to discourage them from reaching the heights of fortune and fame. As a result of that study, he concluded, "Failure can be overcome by two things: First, a goal which takes the imagination by storm, and second, a definite and intelligible plan for carrying that goal into action."

If your writing goal is clear in your mind, the Write-Now method can be the plan that helps you reach it. Toward that end, I offer my sincerest wish that your writing experience will bring you not only satisfaction and fulfillment, but great personal joy.

BIBLIOGRAPHY

Psychology, Stress, Relaxation

Benson, Herbert. *The Relaxation Response.* New York: Avon Books, 1975. Progressive relaxation, the relaxation response, Transcendental Meditation, and other methods of relaxation are examined.

Bristol, Claude. *The Magic of Believing.* Englewood Cliffs, N.J.: Prentice-Hall, 1948. Successful people use the subconscious mind to attain their objectives. The power of suggestion is covered along with how suggestions affect thinking.

Brown, Barbara B. *Stress and the Art of Biofeedback.* New York: Bantam, 1978. This is a study of how the body reacts to stress. Biofeedback techniques can help people control the mind and body.

Burns, David D. *Feeling Good, The New Mood Therapy.* New York: New American Library, 1980. Burns discusses how the way we think determines our moods. Depression, loss of self-worth, and other emotional problems are discussed. Writers who have had their work rejected can benefit from Burns's advice.

Green, Elmer and Alyce. *Beyond Biofeedback.* New York: Dell Publishing Co., 1977. Research pertaining to brain wave activity and how it relates to creativity is one of the topics discussed in detail.

Hill, Napoleon. *Grow Rich with Peace of Mind.* New York: Fawcett World Library, 1968. Offers helpful advice on how to take control of your thoughts to achieve your potential. Many case histories of people who have gained inner peace and purpose by following this advice.

James, William. *Psychology.* Cleveland: The World Publishing Co., 1948. Ways to deprogram negative thoughts through visualization and suggestions. James believed that if you acted as though you had attained your goal, you would attain it.

Nicklaus, Jack. *Golf My Way.* New York: Simon and Schuster, 1974. The professional golfer describes the visualization technique that he uses to improve his game.

Norvell, Anthony. *How to Control Your Destiny.* Hollywood: Wilshire Book Co., 1975. Discussion pertains to mental pictures and suggestions and how important they are in reaching your goals.

Ostrander, Sheila, and Lynne Schroeder. *Superlearning.* New York: Dell Publishing, 1979. Research and studies illustrating how stress is related to illness and how it can be controlled. Also covered are increasing learning power, improving memory, and expanding mental capabilities.

Wilson, Donald L. *Total Mind Power.* New York: Berkley Publishing, 1978. A technique that helps you use your mind to the maximum.

The Creative Process

Baker, Samm S. *Your Key to Creative Thinking.* New York: Bantam Books, Inc., 1964. Suggestions and exercises to stimulate creative thought.

Bertagnolli, Olivia, and Jeff Rackman, eds. *Creativity and the Writing Process.* New York: John Wiley & Sons, 1982. Essays by authors, poets, and psychologists describing their creative experiences.

Beveridge, William I. *The Art of Scientific Investigation.* New York: Norton, 1957. How insight occurs during the gestation period of the creative process; includes details on creativity and how it develops.

DiCyan, Erwin. *Creativity: Road to Discovery.* New York: Harcourt Brace Jovanovich, 1978. Many examples of people who have used their subconscious minds to generate ideas and to enhance their creativity.

Ghiselin, Brewster, ed. *The Creative Process.* New York: New American Library, 1952. Thirty-eight people discuss creativity and share their insights into the creative process. Albert Einstein, Henry James, and Carl Jung are included.

May, Rollo. *The Courage to Create.* New York: W.W. Norton and Co., 1975. Stresses the role the subconscious mind plays in creativity.

Norvell, Anthony. *The Million Dollar Secret Hidden in Your Mind.* New York: Barnes & Noble Books, 1973. How the subconscious mind works. Examples of how to use your subconscious to improve various aspects of your life.

Osborn, Alex. *Applied Imagination.* New York: Charles Scribner's Sons, 1963. Here are ways to use creative ability to improve your jobs, relationships, and the quality of your thinking.

Wallas, Graham. *The Art of Thought.* New York: Harcourt and Brace, 1926. Explanation of the four stages of the creative process.

Dream Research

Corriere, Richard, and Joseph Hart. *The Dream Makers: Discovering Your Breakthrough Dreams.* New York: Funk & Wagnalls, 1977. An explanation of how breakthrough dreams provide information that can be valuable to the dreamer's understanding of unexplained phenomena in his/her waking life.

Garfield, Patricia. *Creative Dreaming.* New York: Ballantine Books, 1974. A leading dream researcher discusses the fascination that ancient civilizations had with the dream state; also covered is the relevance that understanding dreams has for modern man.

Hall, Calvin. *The Individual and His Dreams.* New York: New American Library, 1972. The importance of dreams and recording them is stressed.

Hawthorne, Nathaniel. *Hawthorne's Conception of the Creative Process.* Cambridge, MA: Harvard University Press, 1965. Hawthorne used his dreams to enhance his creativity and his ability to write fiction.

Stevenson, Robert Louis. "A Chapter on Dreams," *Memories and Portraits, Random Memories of Myself.* New York: Scribner, 1925. This is the author's account of how he developed the plot for his book *The Strange Adventures of Dr. Jekyll and Mr. Hyde.*

Fiction Writing

Benchley, Peter. *Jaws.* New York: Bantam Books, 1974. This is a good example of a structured plot.

Burnett, Hallie and Whit. *Fiction Writer's Handbook.* New York: Harper & Row Publishers, 1975. This book offers excellent advice on plot and character development and a variety of other topics for fiction writers.

Crane, Stephen. *Red Badge of Courage.* New York: Dodd, Mead & Co., 1951. This novel illustrates how successfully you can picture scenes, e.g., battlegrounds during the Civil War, and describe them without actually being there—good examples of scene descriptions throughout.

Dickens, Charles. *David Copperfield.* New York: Dodd, Mead and Co., 1948. This novel contains fine examples of well-developed characters—suitable for study.

Durham, Marilyn. *The Man Who Loved Cat Dancing.* New York: Dell Publishing Co., 1972. Well-drawn characters for fiction writers to analyze.

Flaubert, Gustave. *Madame Bovary.* New York: The Modern Library, 1957. An excellent study in characterization.

Forster, E.M. *Aspects of the Novel.* New York: Harcourt, Brace and World, 1927. The author reveals his professional insights on novel writing.

Hemingway, Ernest. *A Moveable Feast.* New York: Charles Scribner's Sons, 1964. This is a fascinating book that describes Hemingway's life in Paris in the 1920s. Both fiction and nonfiction writers will benefit by studying the descriptive passages.

Hoffman, Frederick J. *William Faulkner.* Boston: Twayne Publishing, 1966. A biography of Faulkner; it analyzes the plots and characters of *Sanctuary, The Sound and the Fury,* and other major works.

Klein, Marcus. *The American Novel Since World War II.* New York: Fawcett Publications, 1969. The author discusses major changes in plots and themes in novels written since World War ll.

Kuehl, John, ed. *Creative Writing* & *Rewriting. Contemporary American Novelist at Work.* New York: Appleton-Century-Crofts, 1967. The rough drafts and final copies of such authors as Eudora Welty, F. Scott Fitzgerald, and others are included. They provide insight and instruction for fiction writers.

Levin, Gerald. *Prose Models: An Inductive Approach to Writing.* New York: Harcourt, Brace and World, 1964. Here are prose models for fiction writers to analyze and get a better understanding of characterization, setting, and plot.

McCullough, Colleen. *The Thorn Birds.* New York: Harper and Row, Publishers, 1977. The novel contains excellent examples of style for writers to study. Characters and scenes are vivid and realistic.

McKenzie, Belle, and Helen Olson. *Experiences in Writing.* New York: Macmillan Co., 1962. Prose models by contemporary authors are presented for critical analyses of style.

Meredith, Robert C., and John D. Fitzgerald. *Structuring Your Novel: From Basic Idea to Finished Product.* New York: Barnes & Noble Books, 1972. All aspects of novel writing are discussed. The character and plot development sections are excellent.

Mitchell, Margaret. *Gone with the Wind.* New York: Macmillan Co., 1936. This is a novel filled with fine examples of style. Dialogue, description, and character development are plentiful and suited for analysis by fiction writers.

Orvis, Mary B. *The Art of Writing Fiction.* New York: Prentice-Hall, 1948. Thorough discussion of plot, characterization, settings and themes.

Whitney, Phyllis A. *Writing Juvenile Stories and Novels.* Boston: The Writer, 1976. Helpful advice to fiction writers; describes how she used her subconscious mind to help her write more than sixty books.

Nonfiction Writing

Casewit, Curtis. *Freelance Writing—Advice From the Pros.* New York: Macmillan Publishing Co., Inc., 1974. Tips on nonfiction and fiction techniques. Arthur Hailey, Irving Wallace, and others share their insights about writing.

Evans, Glen, ed. *The Complete Guide to Writing Nonfiction.* Cincinnati: Writer's Digest Books, 1983. Successful writers talk about how they research, write, and market their work. A treasure chest!

Gunther, Max. *Writing and Selling a Nonfiction Book.* Boston: The Writer, 1973. How to develop and sell an idea for a nonfiction book.

Gunther, Max. *Writing the Modern Magazine Article.* Boston: The Writer, 1982. How to write an informative article. Topics covered include: research methods, outlining, editing, and revising.

Newman, Edwin. *Strictly Speaking.* New York: Warner Books, 1975. Fascinating, humorous, and informative book about our changing language.

Oleksy, Walter G. *1,000 Tested Money-Making Markets for Writers.* New York: Harper & Row, 1973. Everything from specialized to general-interest markets for writers.

Business Writing

Brown, Leland. *Effective Business Report Writing,* third ed. Englewood Cliffs, N.J.: Prentice-Hall, Inc., 1973. This volume shows you how to organize and write a report; offers helpful tips on making the job easier.

Hodges, John C., and Mary Whitten. *Harbrace College Handbook.* New York: Harcourt Brace Jovanovich, Inc., 1977. Punctuation, grammar, and usage questions are answered.

Mullins, Carolyn J. *Complete Writing Guide to Preparing Reports, Proposals, Memos, etc.* Englewood Cliffs, N.J.: Prentice-Hall, Inc., 1980. This text offers explanations on how to communicate ideas clearly in your business writing.

Paxton, William C. *The Business Writing Handbook.* New York: Bantam Books, Inc., 1981. This guide shows you how to write effective business letters and other on-the-job assignments.

Perrin, Porter G. *Writer's Guide and Index to English.* Chicago: Scott Foresman and Co., 1950. The mechanics of English are explained here.

Books On The Craft Of Writing

Burack, A.S., ed. *The Writer's Handbook.* Boston: The Writer, Inc., 1970. Professionals advise writers on how to improve their craft.

Coffman, Ramon P., and Nathan Goodman. *Famous Authors for Young People.* New York: Dodd, Mead & Co., 1943. Nineteen biographies of writers and poets reveal why they wrote and how they overcame writing obstacles.

Cowley, Malcolm, ed. *Writers at Work.* New York: The Viking Press, 1958. Interviews revealing the writing habits of contemporary authors.

Daigh, Ralph. *Maybe You Should Write a Book.* Englewood Cliffs, N.J.: Prentice-Hall, 1977. Twenty bestselling authors offer advice and suggestions for writers. Included are James Michener and Taylor Caldwell.

Emerson, Ralph Waldo. *Essays First and Second Series.* Edited by Ernest Rhys. New York: E.P. Dutton & Co., 1906. Emerson's essays on self-reliance, compensation and art are inspirational. Required reading for all writers.

Engle, Paul, ed. *On Creative Writing.* New York: E.P. Dutton and Co., 1966. How self-knowledge, memories, imagination and discipline emerge in creative expression. Engle cites Chekhov, Flaubert, Faulkner, Henry James, and others.

Freedman, Russell. *Thomas Alva Edison.* New York: American R.D.M. Corporation, 1966. Reveals how Edison used his subconscious to help him find solutions to problems relating to his inventions.

Gelfano, Ravina, and Letha Patterson. *They Wouldn't Quit.* Minneapolis: Learner Publications, 1962. A collection of case histories of handicapped people and how they handled their handicaps in order to reach their goals.

Halcrim, Robert C. *The Edison Record.* Fort Myers, FL: Historical Society of Fort Myers, 1972. Edison's qualities of persistence and inquisitiveness are inspirational for writers. This biography offers many examples of how Edison wouldn't give up until he reached his objectives.

Herbert, Brian. *Classic Comebacks.* Los Angeles: Price Stern Sloan Inc., 1981. Witty anecdotes; these may suggest ways you can liven up a nonfiction piece, set a tone, or help develop a theme in an article.

Joy, C.R., and M. Arnold. *The Africa of Albert Schweitzer.* New York: Harper, 1948. A well-illustrated narration about Dr. Schweitzer's work, his philosophy, and his humanitarianism.

Leavitt, Hart D., and David Sohn. *Stop, Look and Write!* New York: Bantam Books, 1964. This book contains pictures to stimulate writing.

Montague, Joseph F. *The Why of Albert Schweitzer.* New York: Hawthorn Books, 1965. Insights into Dr. Schweitzer's life offer a deeper understanding of why and how he dedicated his life to the service of others.

Rainer, Tristine. *The New Diary.* Los Angeles: J.P. Tarcher, 1978. The importance of keeping a diary or journal is stressed. Writing in a journal helps writers come up with story ideas.

Shepard, Odell, ed. *The Heart of Thoreau's Journal.* New York: Dover Publications, 1961. Included are excerpts from Thoreau's journals and writings.

Steinbeck, John. *Journal of a Novel, The East of Eden Letters.* New York: The Viking Press, 1969. This is a series of letters Steinbeck wrote to his editor. In them, he talks of how he handled distractions, fatigue, and writer's block.

Sutherland, James, ed. *The Oxford Book of Literary Anecdotes.* New York: Simon and Schuster, 1975. A storehouse of fascinating anecdotes to add color to nonfiction writing.

Sweetkind, Morris. *Teaching Poetry in the High School.* New York: Macmillan Co., 1964. A collection of poems, interpretations, and descriptions.

Todd, Alden. *Finding Facts Fast.* Berkeley, CA: Ten Speed Press, 1979. Takes the mystery out of research by offering you different approaches to the process of finding information you need.

Reference Books And Resources For Writers

Books in Print. New Providence, NJ: R.R. Bowker Co., Annual. This yearly set of books (available in libraries) tells you what's in print and from more than 15,000 book publishers. Arranged by author, title, and subject, this multi-volume set is an excellent way to find books for your research project or to find out what's already available on your topic.

Flesch, Rudolf. *A New Way to Better English.* New York: Doubleday and Co., 1958. The Flesch readability test is explained here. The test can help you determine whether your writing is too complicated or too easy for a specific market.

Horowitz, Lois. *Knowing Where to Look: The Ultimate Guide to Research.* Cincinnati: Writer's Digest Books, 1984. This complete research handbook shows you how and where to get information; the book is written by a librarian who has found answers to thousands of writers' research questions.

Kissling, Mark, ed. 1993 *Writer's Market.* Cincinnati: Writer's Digest Books, 1993. Annual writer's "bible" of markets and marketing information.

Literary Market Place. New York: R.R. Bowker. Annual. Resource book for locating markets for all types of manuscripts.

Norback, Craig and Peter. *The Must Words.* New York: McGraw-Hill Book Co., 1979. Words with which all writers should familiarize themselves.

Pei, Mario. *What's in a Word?* New York: Hawthorn Books, 1968. A study of semantics; includes interesting examples of how words evolve and change.

Polking, Kirk, ed. *Writer's Encyclopedia.* Cincinnati: Writer's Digest Books, 1983. This resource defines and explains many literary terms and writing and publishing procedures, and includes information that gives you an overview of the writing world.

Polking, Kirk, and Rose Adkins, eds. *Beginning Writer's Answer Book.* Cincinnati: Writer's Digest Books, 1984. This newly revised edition answers nearly nine hundred questions writers have asked about how to get started in writing.

Prochnow, Herbert V. *The Toastmaster's Treasure Chest.* New York: Harper and Row, 1979. An excellent resource book for nonfiction writers; it contains anecdotes that can add interest to books and articles.

Shakespeare, William. *The Complete Works of William Shakespeare.* Edited by George L. Kittredge. New York: Ginn and Co., 1936. Shakespeare's works provide excellent examples of metaphors, characterizations, plots, etc. for analysis and study. This is a marvelous resource book for all writers.

Strunk, William Jr., and E.B. White. *The Elements of Style.* New York: MacMillan, 1972. Classic resource giving the basics of writing and grammar.

Other useful books from Celestial Arts:

YOU ARE YOUR CHILD'S FIRST TEACHER by Rahima Baldwin

An exciting new vision of parenting in which parents have an active educational role from the moment of birth. Drawing on child development research, Baldwin details how to nurture your child's mind, body, emotions, and imagination.

$12.95 paper or $19.95 cloth, 380 pages

THE COMMON BOOK OF CONSCIOUSNESS Revised Edition
by Diana Saltoon

A beloved sourcebook, newly revised and updated for the 90s. This guide to leading a whole and centered life shows how to use meditation, exercise, and nutrition to gain a higher consciousness and a full, balanced daily life.

$11.95 paper, 160 pages

QUANTUM SOUP by Chungliang Al Huang

Praised by Joseph Campbell as "a gourmet preparation to tickle the sophisticated palate and provoke happy, healthful belly laughs,"...this is a series of philosophical essays and anecdotes which link Eastern wisdom and Western thought in a lively, thought-provoking collage.

$17.95 paper, 144 pages

THE ART OF RITUAL by Sydney Barbara Metrick and Renee Beck

A guide to creating and performing personalized rituals for growth and change. The authors discuss the importance of ritual in traditional cultures, and show how to integrate it into modern life, celebrating birth, achievements, special friendships, and the like.

$11.95 paper, 152 pages

THE PMS SELF-HELP BOOK by Susan Lark, M.D.

A wonderful hands-on workbook that helps women identify the causes of common PMS symptoms (anxiety, pain, weight gain, cravings, etc.) and diminish or eliminate them through diet, exercise, acupressure, and other drug-free methods.

$14.95 paper, 240 pages

THE MENOPAUSE SELF-HELP BOOK by Susan Lark, M.D.

A woman's guide to feeling wonderful for the second half of her life. Explains how and why a woman's body and moods change with menopause, and offers a practical, natural master plan for preventing or relieving negative symptoms.

$14.95 paper, 240 pages

CHOOSE TO BE HEALTHY by Susan Smith Jones, Ph.D.

The choices we make in life can greatly increase our health and happiness—this book details how to analyze one's choices about food, exercise, thought, work, and play, and then use this information to create a better, healthier life.

$9.95 paper, 252 pages

CHOOSE TO LIVE PEACEFULLY by Susan Smith Jones, Ph.D.

By nurturing our inner selves and living in personal peace, we can help to bring about global change. In this book, Susan Smith Jones explores the many components of a peaceful, satisfying life including exercise, nutrition, solitude, meditation, ritual, and environmental awareness—and shows how they can be linked to world peace.

$11.95 paper, 320 pages

IT'S NOT WHAT YOU EAT BUT WHAT EATS YOU by Jack Schwartz

"After seeing what Jack Schwartz can do to/with his body, you've got to be interested in what's going on in his mind."—Richard Bolles, author of *What Color Is Your Parachute*

"What most delights and amazes me in the life, the wisdom, and the teachings of my friend (Jack Schwartz) is the way in which his words so often illuminate for me the sayings of the greatest masters."—Joseph Campbell

An exploration of the intense mind/body connection between nutrition and vitality.

$8.95 paper, 224 pages

STAYING HEALTHY WITH THE SEASONS by Elson Haas M.D.

One of the most popular of the new health books, this is a blend of Eastern and Western medicines, nutrition, herbology, exercise, and preventive health care.

$11.95 paper, 252 pages

STAYING HEALTHY WITH NUTRITION by Elson Haas M.D.

The long-awaited examination of how what we eat determines our health and well-being. Truly a complete reference work, it details every aspect of nutrition, from drinking water to medicinal foods to the latest biochemical research.

$24.95 paper, 1,168 pages

Available from your local bookstore, or order direct from the publisher. Please include $2.50 shipping & handling for the first book, and 50 cents for each additional book. California residents include local sales tax. Write for our free complete catalog of over 400 books, posters, and tapes.

Celestial Arts   Box 7123   Berkeley, Ca 94707

For VISA or MASTERCARD call (800)841-BOOK.